MILANO EXPO SPACE

米兰世博空间

金盘地产传媒有限公司 策划
唐艺设计资讯集团有限公司 编著

中国林业出版社
China Forestry Publishing House

图书在版编目（CIP）数据

米兰世博空间 / 广州市唐艺文化传播有限公司编著 .
-- 北京 : 中国林业出版社 , 2015.8

ISBN 978-7-5038-8108-4

Ⅰ . ①创… Ⅱ . ①广… Ⅲ . ①博览会 - 概况 - 米兰 -
2015 Ⅳ . ① G245

中国版本图书馆 CIP 数据核字 (2015) 第 193548 号

米兰世博空间

编　　著	广州市唐艺文化传播有限公司
责任编辑	纪　亮　王思源
策划编辑	高雪梅
文字编辑	高雪梅
英文编辑	冯婷婷
装帧设计	刘小川
出版发行	中国林业出版社
出版社地址	北京西城区德内大街刘海胡同 7 号，邮编：100009
出版社网址	http://lycb.forestry.gov.cn/
经　　销	深圳汇亿丰印刷科技有限公司
印　　刷	深圳
开　　本	235 mm × 325 mm
印　　张	26.25
版　　次	2016 年 6 月第 1 版
印　　次	2016 年 6 月第 1 次印刷
标准书号	ISBN 978-7-5038-8108-4
定　　价	499.00 元（USD 88）

图书如有印装质量问题，可随时向印刷厂调换（电话：0755-26645100）。

MILANO SPACE

一切源于世博会

世博会有一句为世界广泛认同的口号：一切源于世博会。这句口号的含义是指世博会改写了人类的历史，世博会用它的理念和展示的科技成果，提出了世界发展的方向。世博会与奥林匹克运动会、世界杯一起并称为全球三大顶级盛会。不过与奥运会、世界杯不同的是，举办世界博览会的目的在于教育大众，通过展示人类所掌握的满足文明需要的手段，来展现人类在某一个或多个领域经过奋斗所取得的进步，或展望未来的前景。世博会的全称是世界博览会，它是由一个国家的政府主办、多个国家或国际组织参加的国际性大型博览会，称得上是世界上最高级别的展览活动。每一届世博会都有鲜明的主题，融合世界各国带来的新技术、新理念、新文化于一地，让全世界千百万的民众前来开阔眼界，进行学习与交流。世博会是一场汇聚着人类物质文明与精神文明成果的全球盛会，它的每一次举办，都会对社会的进步、科技的创新、城市的发展、理念的更新产生广泛又积极的影响，带来强大的动力；也会给我们留下大量的物质与精神财富。面对150多年的世博发展历史，我们不由得为它所取得的丰硕成果感到震撼。

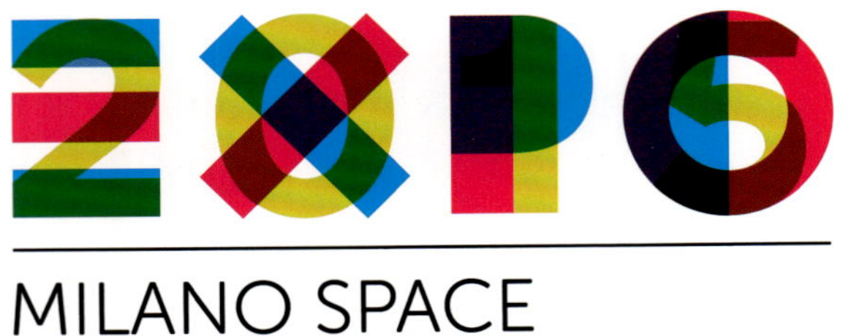

给养地球 生命能源

FEEDING THE PLANT
ENERGY FOR LIFE

2015年米兰世博会将紧密围绕展会主题“滋养地球，生命能源”，在世博场馆内外举办的各种活动也将突显这一主题。在各国家展馆、主题展区、公共会议以及世博会的各项倡议活动中，人们将重点讨论食品安全、环境保护、应对营养不良问题以及食品教育。
世博会的场址将科技创新与周边的农场融为一体，其设计突显了意大利数千年的历史风韵。它的结构受到了古罗马兵营的启发，这种十字形的罗马军营结构在意大利和其他欧洲城市都很常见。所有建筑沿一条主轴（Decumanus）展开，中间横穿一条较短的小道（Cardo），形成一条水平轴和一条垂直轴，参展者可以沿着这两条轴线布置他们的主题展区。各国的展馆将沿主轴布置，而意大利的展馆则沿着小道布置，并按照不同的区域以及各自所属的城市和省份划分展区。
便利的交通以及开放式的综合体设计将为与会人员展现最纯粹的意大利风土人情。一些最重要的建筑将分布于主轴和小道的两端（该场址设想的方位基点），包括接待区、集合点以及为世博会游客提供的娱乐场所，例如：地中海山景公园(Mediterranean Hill)，一座全景式的主题花园；世博中心(Expo Centre)，中心内设有会议室、礼堂和表演区；露天剧场（Open Air Theatre），供演出、各类仪式和露天音乐会使用，可容纳1.1万名观众；湖心剧场（Lake Arena），人们可在剧场内漂浮的平台和舞台上举行音乐会或进行其他表演和展出。
2015年米兰世博会的参展方包括国家、国际组织、公司、协会和民间团体。本届米兰世博会的参展国已突破130个，包括国际组织在内，官方参展成员数量目前已达到130个以上。
参展方需要通过展览项目说明他们自己对米兰世博会的诠释，项目内容可以包括建筑结构、演出、实验设施和其他参展形式。60多个国家将建造自己的展馆，而其他国家则将在“集群区”进行展出，这也是2015年米兰世博会设计的一种新型参展形式。
此次世博展包含了九大集群区，分布于9个以不同农副产品为主题的建筑体内，集群区的各国需要进行具有代表性的主题展览。集群模式加强了主办方和参展国以及参展各国之间的合作，鼓励他们体现各自不同的文化传统，对米兰世博会主题进行不同的诠释，一起为农业、营养和福利领域所共同面临的挑战提供解决方案，并加以比较。

The Expo Milano 2015 proposed the theme of “Feeding the Planet, Energy for Life” which can be witnessed in all sorts of events in Expo exhibition areas. In this Expo, food security, environment protection, malnutrition and food education issues will be deeply discussed in country pavilions, thematic exhibitions, public conventions and all kinds of advocacy campaigns.
The site of Expo takes technology innovation and peripheral farms in one combined. The design implicits thousands years of historic flavor in Italy. The general structure is inspired by castrum which is familiar in cities in Italy and other European countries. All the volumes are alongside Decumanus with a Cardo perpendicular with it, and thematic exhibitions are displayed aside. On either side of the Decumano and Cardo are the national pavilions of the participant countries and Italian pavilions repectively.
Convinient transportation and open complexes embrace visitors with Italian customs. Public buildings are arranged on the ends of Decumanus and Cardo for reception, gathering and entertainment. Among them, Mediterranean Hill is a panoramic thematic garden; Expo Centre consists of meeting area, auditorium and open plaza; Open Air Theatre is dedicated to outdoor events with accommodation of 11,000 audiences; Lake Arena will be the venue for water games, concerts and other performances.
The Expo Milano 2015 attracts participants of countries, international organizatios, corporates and civil societies. The country participants arrive up to 130, and more than 130 international and official institutions also take part in this world-level gathering.
Every participant has its own interpretation for the Milano Expo through their architectural design, performances, experimental facilities and innovative exhibition forms. Over 60 countries build independent pavilions, and other countries will display their products and concepts in clusters with various themes, which is a creative exhibition arrangement in this Expo.
The Expo set nine clusters with their own themes relating agricultural and sideline products, so the countries and organizations in these clusters will hold typical thematic exhibitions. The cluster exhibition mold strengthens the cooperation between curators and participants, meanwhile provokes the mutural improvement among participant countries. Various cultural customs will bring Milano Expo particular annotations, which is conducive to together confront challenges from the aspects of agriculture, nutrition and welfare.

MILANO SPACE

Official Map

Welcome to Milan
Welcome to the Universal Expo

1st May - 31st October 2015
Feeding the Planet - Energy for Life

Opening Hours
Mon-Sun 10-23
Evening entrance 19-23

For further information
www.expo2015.org
Infoline: 020 2015

@AskExpo

App Store · Google play

en

What to expect at Expo

Welcome to the biggest event ever organized on food and nutrition. The theme *Feeding the Planet, Energy for Life* is addressed by all the participating countries, International Organizations and by Civil Societies and Companies, in the Thematic Areas or those dedicated to the Events.

The concept follows five thematic routes: *The history of humankind, the history of food; Feast and famine: a contemporary paradox; The future of food; Sustainable food = an equitable world; Taste is knowledge.* For details, consult the information screens or the official app.

Countries
Pavilions and exhibition spaces of the participating countries of Expo
The Italian Pavilion is in the Cardo and includes Palazzo Italia and the spaces of the various regions

Clusters
Different countries share a particular genius loci or food chain

Civil Society
Organizations and associations reflect on the future of food and nutrition

Companies
The pavilions and stands of private companies

Thematic Areas
Pavilions and narrative paths on the Expo theme with exhibitions and insights

Events Areas
Common areas host events, sh[…] and cultural initiatives

Rice 37 H10
Bangladesh, Cambodia, Myanmar, Lao People's Democratic Republic, Sierra Leone; Basmati Pavilion

Cocoa and Chocolate 45 H12
Cameroon, Côte d'Ivoire, Cuba, Gabon, Ghana, Sao Tomé & Principe

Coffee 58 H14
Burundi, El Salvador, Ethiopia, Guatemala, Kenya, Dominican Republic, Rwanda, East Timor, Uganda, Yemen

Fruits and Legumes 61 G15
Benin, Gambia, Guinea, Equatorial Guinea, Kyrgyzstan, Democratic Republic of Congo, Sri Lanka, Uzbekistan, Zambia

Spices 64 G16
Afghanistan, Brunei Darussalam, United Republic of Tanzania, Vanuatu - Pacific Islands Forum (Marshall Islands, Solomon Islands, Kiribati, Nauru, Niue, Papua New Guinea, Samoa, Tonga, Tuvalu)

Bio-Mediterraneum 97 D21
Albania, Algeria, Egypt, Greece, Lebanon, Malta, Montenegro, San Marino, Serbia, Tunisia; World Expo Museum

Islands, Sea and Food 108 D22
Caricom (Barbados, Belize, Dominica, Grenada, Guyana, St. Vincent and Grenadine, Saint Lucia, Suriname), Comoros, Guinea Bissau, Madagascar, Maldives, North Korea

Cereals and Tubers 120 H22
Bolivia, Congo, Haiti, Mozambique, Togo, Venezuela, Zimbabwe

Arid Zones 121 D23
Djibuti, Eritrea, Jordan, Liberia, Mali, Mauritania, Palestine, Senegal, Somalia

STOP 1 · STOP 2 · STOP 3 · STOP 9 · STOP 10
1 Expo Centre · Media Centre · 0 Pavilion Zero · ONU
Triulza West Entrance · Fiorenza West Entrance
38 Cascina Triulza · 51 Children Park
DECUMANO
2 · 3 · 4 · 5 · 6 Casa Algida · 7 Czech Republic · 8 Kip · 9 UN Garden · 10 Caritas · 11 Veneranda Fabb. del Duomo · 12 Irlanda · 13 · 14 · 15 · 16 · 17 · 18 Bahrain · 19 Angola · 20 Nepal · 21 Sudan · 22 · 23 · 24 · 25 · 26 Brazil · 27 Save The Children · 28 Enel · 29 South Korea · 30 · 31 Belgium · 32 · 33 Vietnam · 34 · 35 · 36 Technogym · 37 Rice · 39 Moldova · 40 Perugina · 41 Lithuania · 42 Bielorussia · 43 Malaysia · 44 · 45 Cocoa and Chocolate · 46 Lindt · 47 Distretti Cioccolato · 48 · 49 Thailand · 50 Uruguay · 52 · 53 · 54 · 55 Corriere della Sera · 56 China · 57 Colombia · 58 Coffee · 59 · 60 Argentina · 62 Eataly

At the Info Point (H17) tickets can be purchased for shows at the Open Air Theatre.

Railway Station Rho-Fiera Expo 2015
Metro Station M1 Rho-Fiera
Parking Fieramilano
Trains Suburban Line High Speed
Metro from Cadorna

A feast of cultures, populations, tastes

Throughout the Expo site, visitors can taste the different specialities. You can have a drink, try for the first time a dish never heard of, eat standing or sitting comfortably, whether it is the dish of a renowned chef or a skewer: you will enjoy a real world tour between Cardo and Decumano.

** For the list of Service Areas see back*

World Cuisine

In addition to the offer of the pavilions of participating countries, where you can enjoy their traditional specialities, the following are also available:

BBQ Hooligans	141 I 24
China Seeds Kitchen	113 E 22
La Piada & Le Bolle	15 J 7
Los Granos de mi Tierra	141 I 24
	54 G 14
Street Burger	54 G 14
USA - Food Truck Nation	122 E 23
Zen Express	17 G 14
	54 G 14

The cuisine of Italy and its regions

Agripizza - Agrigelato	*North East Cardo*
Alto Adige	*North West Cardo*
Ape Pizza	22 H 8
Aromatica	75 H 17
Casa Ferrarini	77 D 18
Coldiretti	*South East Cardo*
Dispensa Emilia	35 E 10
Eataly	62 H 15
Ecco Pizza e Pasta	*North West Cardo*
Granarolo	*South East Cardo*
Kip - International School	8 H 7
Popi	17 F 8
Regione Sicilia	97 D 21
Varvello Experience	120 H 22
Wine Pavilion	*North East Cardo*
Zini Gourmet	52 F 14

Chef Experience

Davide Oldani	16 J 7
Identità Expo	44 G 12
Peck a Palazzo Italia	*Palazzo Italia*
Slow Food	152 H 26
Unico Milano The Rolling Star	52 F 14

Breaks for families

Cascina Triulza	38 F 11
Chioschi Ristoro Coop	93 I 19
Let's Toast	Areas F2, G1, H1, H2*
McDonald's	146 H 25
Tracce	Areas A, G1, G2, H1*
Via Vai	Areas B2, F2, G1, H2*

Light and healthy

Acqua S. Pellegrino	*South East Card[o]*
Cucina e Pizza Biologica	109 D 2[…]
Gluten Free Fest	25 G […]
	140 I 2[…]
Juice Bar	23 J […]
	148 I 2[…]
Toast & Zuppe	52 F 1[…]

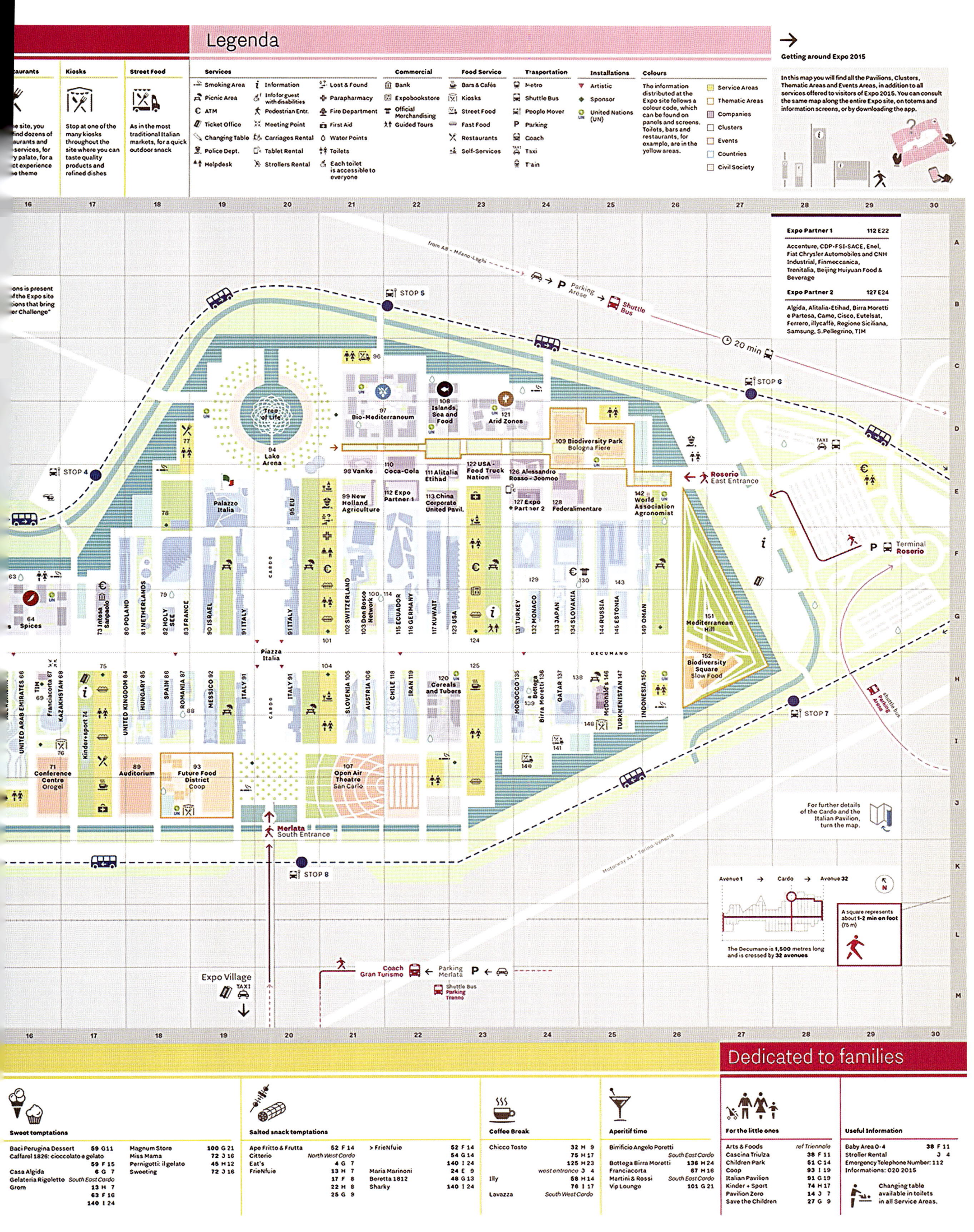

Legenda
Getting around Expo 2015
In this map you will find all the Pavilions, Clusters, Thematic Areas and Events Areas, in addition to all services offered to visitors of Expo 2015. You can consult the same map along the entire Expo site, on totems and information screens, or by downloading the app.
Kiosks
Stop at one of the many kiosks throughout the site where you can taste quality products and refined dishes
Street Food
As in the most traditional Italian markets, for a quick outdoor snack
Services
Smoking Area
Picnic Area
ATM
Ticket Office
Changing Table
Police Dept.
Helpdesk
Information
Info for guest with disabilities
Pedestrian Entr.
Meeting Point
Carriages Rental
Tablet Rental
Strollers Rental
Lost & Found
Parapharmacy
Fire Department
First Aid
Water Points
Toilets
Each toilet is accessible to everyone
Commercial
Bank
Expobookstore
Official Merchandising
Guided Tours
Food Service
Bars & Cafés
Kiosks
Street Food
Fast Food
Restaurants
Self-Services
Trasportation
Metro
Shuttle Bus
People Mover
Parking
Coach
Taxi
Train
Installations
Artistic
Sponsor
United Nations (UN)
Colours
The information distributed at the Expo site follows a colour code, which can be found on panels and screens. Toilets, bars and restaurants, for example, are in the yellow areas.
Service Areas
Thematic Areas
Companies
Clusters
Events
Countries
Civil Society
Expo Partner 1 112 E22
Accenture, CDP-FSI-SACE, Enel, Fiat Chrysler Automobiles and CNH Industrial, Finmeccanica, Trenitalia, Beijing Huiyuan Food & Beverage
Expo Partner 2 127 E24
Algida, Alitalia-Etihad, Birra Moretti e Partesa, Came, Cisco, Eutelsat, Ferrero, illycaffè, Regione Siciliana, Samsung, S.Pellegrino, TIM
from A8 - Milano-Laghi
Parking Arese
Shuttle Bus
20 min
STOP 4
STOP 5
STOP 6
STOP 7
STOP 8
94 Lake Arena
Tree of Life
97 Bio-Mediterraneum
108 Islands, Sea and Food
121 Arid Zones
109 Biodiversity Park Bologna Fiere
98 Vanke
110 Coca-Cola
111 Alitalia Etihad
122 USA - Food Truck Nation
126 Alessandro Rosso - Joomoo
Roserio East Entrance
Palazzo Italia
99 New Holland Agriculture
112 Expo Partner 1
113 China Corporate United Pavil.
127 Expo Partner 2
128 Federalimentare
142 World Association Agronomist
Terminal Roserio
64 Spices
73 Intesa Sanpaolo
80 POLAND
81 NETHERLANDS
82 HOLY SEE
83 FRANCE
90 ISRAEL
91 ITALY
95 EU
102 SWITZERLAND
103 Don Bosco Network
115 ECUADOR
116 GERMANY
117 KUWAIT
123 USA
131 TURKEY
132 MONACO
133 JAPAN
134 SLOVAKIA
144 RUSSIA
145 ESTONIA
149 OMAN
151 Mediterranean Hill
152 Biodiversity Square Slow Food
CARDO
DECUMANO
Piazza Italia
UNITED ARAB EMIRATES 66
TIM
Franciacorta 67
KAZAKHSTAN 68
Kinder+sport 74
UNITED KINGDOM 84
HUNGARY 85
SPAIN 86
ROMANIA 87
MESSICO 92
ITALY 91
SLOVENIA 105
AUSTRIA 106
CHILE 118
IRAN 119
120 Cereals and Tubers
MOROCCO 135
Bottega Birra Moretti 136
QATAR 137
McDonald's 146
TURKMENISTAN 147
INDONESIA 150
71 Conference Centre Orogel
89 Auditorium
93 Future Food District Coop
107 Open Air Theatre San Carlo
Merlata South Entrance
Shuttle bus Parking Arese
For further details of the Cardo and the Italian Pavilion, turn the map.
Motorway A4 - Torino-Venezia
Avenue 1 → Cardo → Avenue 32
The Decumano is 1,500 metres long and is crossed by 32 avenues
A square represents about 1-2 min on foot (75 m)
Expo Village
TAXI
Coach Gran Turismo
Parking Merlata
Shuttle Bus Parking Trenno
Dedicated to families
Sweet temptations
Baci Perugina Dessert 59 G11
Caffarel 1826: cioccolato e gelato 59 F 15
Casa Algida 6 G 7
Gelateria Rigoletto South East Cardo
Grom 13 H 7
63 F 16
140 I 24
Magnum Store 100 G 21
Miss Mama 72 J 16
Pernigotti: il gelato 45 H 12
Sweeting 72 J 16
Salted snack temptations
Ape Fritto & Frutta 52 F 14
Citterio North West Cardo
Eat's 4 G 7
FrieNfuie 13 H 7
17 F 8
22 H 8
25 G 9
> FrieNfuie 52 F 14
54 G 14
140 I 24
24 E 9
Maria Marinoni 48 G 13
Beretta 1812 140 I 24
Sharky
Coffee Break
Chicco Tosto 32 H 9
75 H 17
125 H 23
west entrance 3 4
Illy 58 H 14
76 I 17
Lavazza South West Cardo
Aperitif time
Birrificio Angelo Poretti South East Cardo
Bottega Birra Moretti 136 H 24
Franciacorta 67 H 16
Martini & Rossi South East Cardo
Vip Lounge 101 G 21
For the little ones
Arts & Foods ref Triennale
Cascina Triulza 38 F 11
Children Park 51 C 14
Coop 93 I 19
Italian Pavilion 91 G 19
Kinder + Sport 74 H 17
Pavilion Zero 14 J 7
Save the Children 27 G 9
Useful Information
Baby Area 0-4 38 F 11
Stroller Rental J 4
Emergency Telephone Number: 112
Informations: 020 2015
Changing table available in toilets in all Service Areas.

国家馆

COUNTRIES' PAVILIONS

欧洲 Europe

012 意大利馆 ITALY PAVILION
意大利苗圃
The Nursery of Italy

028 英国馆 UNITED KINGDOM PAVILION
源于英国 全球共享
Grown in Britain: Shared Globally

038 法国馆 FRENCE PAVILION
多产市场
Different Ways of Producing and Providing Food

050 德国馆 GERMANY PAVILION
灵感的田野
Fields of Ideas

066 俄罗斯馆 RUSSIAN FEDERATION PAVILION
增长的领域
Growing for the World. Cultivating for the Future

072 西班牙馆 SPAIN PAVILION
培育未来
Cultivating the Future

076 荷兰馆 NETHERLANDS PAVILION
分享，成长，生活
Share, Grow, Live

082 瑞士馆 SWITZERLAND PAVILION
瑞士联邦
Confooderatio Helvetica

084 比利时馆 BELGIUM PAVILION
永续未来的比利时宴乐
Belgium's conviviality has a sustainable future

092 梵蒂冈馆 HOLY SEE PAVILION
上帝的餐桌供全人类享用
Not only Bread Alone. At the Lord's Table with all Mankind

094 波兰馆 POLAND PAVILION
百宝箱
A Treasure Box

096 奥地利馆 AUSTRIA PAVILION
呼吸・奥地利
Breathe. Austria

100 捷克馆 CZECH REPUBLIC PAVILION
生命实验室
Laboratory of Life

108 匈牙利馆 HUNGARY PAVILION
取自最纯净的资源
From The Purest Sources

112 罗马尼亚馆 ROMANIA PAVILION
与自然共存
Living with Nature

114 爱尔兰馆 IRELAND PAVILION
绿色爱尔兰 与自然协作
Origin Green Ireland: Working with Nature

116 白俄罗斯馆 BELARUS PAVILION
生命之轮
The Wheel of Life

118 爱沙尼亚馆 ESTONIA PAVILION
艺术展廊
Gallery of

126 斯洛伐克馆 SLOVAKIA PAVILION
袖珍世界
The World in Your Pocket

134 斯洛文尼亚馆 SLOVENIA PAVILION
感受斯洛文尼亚：绿色. 积极. 健康
I Feel Slovenia. Green. Active. Healthy

140 立陶宛馆 LITHUANIA PAVILION
传统与现代结合只为和谐未来
A Fusion of Traditions and Innovations for a Balanced Future

146 摩尔多瓦馆 Moldova Pavilion
来自阳光和土地的食物
Shine the Light–Energy of Sun, Energy of Earth, Food for People

美洲 America

148 美国馆 UNITED STATES OF AMERICA PAVILION
美国食物2.0：联合起来滋养地球
American Food 2.0: United to Feed the Planet

156 巴西馆 BRAZIL PAVILION
粮食危机的解决方案
Feeding the World with Solutions

162 阿根廷馆 ARGENTINA PAVILION
养育你的阿根廷
Argentina Feeds You

166 墨西哥馆 MEXICO PAVILION
新世界的种子
Mexico, the Seed for the New World: Food, Diversity and Heritage

176 智利馆 CHILE PAVILION
富饶的国度
A Country Rich in Variety

182 乌拉圭馆 URUGUAY PAVILION
乌拉圭的生活
Life Grows in Uruguay

188 厄瓜多尔馆 ECUADOR PAVILION
演变之地
The Land of Evolution

190 哥伦比亚馆 COLOMBIA PAVILION
自然的可持续发展
Naturally Sustainable

亚洲 Asia

196 中国馆 CHINA PAVILION
希望的田野
Land of Hope, Food for Life

206 日本馆 JAPAN PAVILION
和谐多样性
Harmonious Diversity

218 韩国馆 REPUBLIC OF KOREA PAVILION
人如其食
You are what you eat

228 泰国馆 THAILAND PAVILION
滋养地球，欢乐世界
Nourishing and Delighting the World

234 越南馆 VEITNAM PAVILION
水和莲
Water and Lotus

236 马来西亚馆 MALAYSIA PAVILION
可持续性发展的食品生态系统
Towards a Sustainable Food Ecosystem

242 印度尼西亚馆 INDONESIA PAVILION
传统与富于现代性的智慧
Tradition and Local Wisdom with a Touch of Modernity

244 尼泊尔馆 NEPAL PAVILION
食品安全与可持续发展
Food Security and Sustainable for Development

248 阿塞拜疆馆 AZERBAIJAN PAVILION
为了下一代，保护有机食物和生物多样性
Protection of Organic Food and Biodiversity for Future Generations

260 土库曼斯坦馆 TURKMENISTAN PAVILION
水即生命
Water is Life

262 哈萨克斯坦馆 KAZAKHSTAN PAVILION
希望之地
The Land of Opportunities

国家馆
COUNTRIES' PAVILIONS

中东 Middle East

266 阿联酋馆 UNITED ARAB EMIRATES PAVILION
精神食粮–塑造并分享未来
Food for Thought–Shaping and Sharing the Future

276 伊朗馆 ISLAMIC REPUBLIC OF IRAN PAVILION
神赐的餐桌
Global Sofreh, Iranian Culture

280 科威特馆 KUWAIT PAVILION
自然的挑战
Challenge of Nature

286 阿曼馆 OMAN PAVILION
收获文化遗产
Heritage in Harvest

292 以色列馆 ISRAEL PAVILION
未来田地
Fields of Tomorrow

298 土耳其馆 TURKEY PAVILION
挖掘历史，发掘未来
Digging into History for Future Food

304 卡塔尔馆 QATAR PAVILION
推行可持续发展用创新保证食品安全
Sowing Sustainability.Innovative Solutions for Food Security

非洲 Africa

310 安哥拉馆 ANGOLA PAVILION
饮食和文化：教育与创新
Food and Culture: Educate to Innovate

314 摩洛哥馆 MOROCCO PAVILION
摩洛哥，一趟味道之旅
Morocco, a Journey of Flavours

企业馆
COPORATE PAVILIONS

322 可口可乐馆 COCA-COLA PAVILION
软饮之王
The King of Soft Drink

326 中国企业联合馆 CHINA CORPORATE UNITED PAVILION
中国种子
Seeds of China

330 万科馆 VANKE PAVILION
食堂
Shitang

334 纽荷兰馆 NEW HOLLAND AGRICULTURE'S PAVILION
尊重土地，发展未来
Respect the land and grow the future

338 费力罗馆 FERRERO PAVILION
孩子是我们的未来
The Future Belongs to the Children of Today

346 意大利航空公司馆 ALITALIA AIRWAYS PAVILION
连接世界
Connecting the World

348 意大利国家电力公司馆 ENEL PAVILION
开发智能能源
Cultivating Smart Energy

民间组织馆
CIVIL SOCIETY PAVILIONS

354 圣 · 鲍思高馆 DON BOSCO PAVILION
教育年轻一代，为生命提供能源
Educating the Young, Energy for Life

356 Triulza协会馆 FOUDAZIONE TRIULZA PAVILION
发掘能源，改变世界
EXPIOding Energies to Change The World

358 零展馆 PAVILION ZERO
故事的起源
The Beginning of All Stories

364 KIP 国际馆 KIP PAVILION
美丽土地，永恒世界
Attractive Territories for a Sustainable World

公共与集群区

PUBLIC AREA AND CLUSTERS

370 世博中心 **The Expo Center**

374 慢食运动区 **Slow Food's space**

378 未来食物区 **The Future Food District**

380 大米集群区 **THE RICE CLUSTER**
富足和安全
Abundance

382 可可和巧克力集群区 **THE COCOA AND CHOCOLATE CLUSTER**
神赐之食
The Food of the Gods

384 咖啡集群区 **THE COFFEE CLUSTER**
思想的能量
The Energy of Ideas

388 水果和豆类集群区 **THE FRUITS AND LEGUMES CLUSTER**
精神和物质，神话和生存
Spirit and Substance, Myth and Subsistence

390 谷物和块茎集群区 **THE CEREALS AND TUBERS CLUSTER**
新旧作物
Old and New Crops

392 生态地中海集群区 **THE BIO-MEDITERRANEAN CLUSTER**
健康，美丽与和谐
Health, Beauty and Harmony

396 干旱作物集群区 **THE ARID ZONES CLUSTER**
旱地的食物和农业
The Food and Agriculture of the Arid Zones

400 海产品集群区 **THE ISLAND, SEA AND FOOD CLUSTER**
世上无孤岛
No Man is an Island

401 香料集群区 **THE SPICES CLUSTER**
香料世界
The World of Spices

公共设施及景观

PUBLIC FACILITIES AND LANDSCAPES

COUNTRIES' PAVILIONS
国家馆

来自全球的各参展国是构成2015年米兰世博会的核心。世博展把各参展国安排在展区主干道两侧呈一字排开，这样每个国家馆都临街而立，只是展馆面积从500平方米到5000平方米不等。这样的展馆布局突破了以往根据参展国所在地理位置布局的模式，使得每个国家都是主角，并拥有平等的地位。这也呼应了在全球食物可持续发展问题上每个国家都肩负着同样的责任并能贡献出同等价值的理念。

应米兰世博会主办方的要求，每一个参与米兰世博会的参展国都提炼出自己的参展主题，并发文阐明了参展动机，参展目标，以及参观者可以通过观摩获得哪些跟本次世博展的核心主题“滋养地球，生命能源”相关的知识和信息。

本次世博展在独立国家馆选址上采用先到先得的规则，即率先到达世博会场的可以挑选自己认为最为理想的地段和面积来建馆，这样就打破了按地理位置来布局国家馆的传统。除了在展馆位置和面积上面的竞争，在展馆设计和建造上，各国也拿出看家本领来打造最具特色，最能代表本国文化内涵和技术实力的展馆。各国展馆除了采用先进的环保技术和可回收利用的建材，在造型设计上更是百花齐放，给观众带来一场视觉设计盛宴，也为意大利米兰这座国际大都市增添了一抹靓丽的风采。

Countries have constituted the heart of the Expo Milano 2015. Therefore the Expo provided a decision to locate the pavilions of the participant countries along a single concourse, the Decumanus, with the same frontage for all but differing in area from 500 to 5 000 m^2. This decision marks a departure from the proactice always previously adopted of organizing the pavilions on the basis of geographic grouping. Each country thus has a primary role and equal dignity, just as the requirements and responses in the global challenge of sustainable food all have equal value.

Each of the participant countries in Expo Milano 2015 was invited to produce a Theme Statement, a document setting forth the motivation and objectives of its participation and the ways in which it seeks to involve visitors with the presentation of its approach to the major Expo theme Feeding the Planet, Energy for Life.

The choicest locations and largest areas went to the first to arrive. As stated above, allocation was not on a geographical basis but instead aimed at meeting the demands of the countries that were the first to believe in Expo Milano 2015. The great race between countries to secure the choicest locations and largest areas was accompanied by competition to build the most beautiful pavilion, capable of representing the strong and intensely human Expo theme and of paying homage – not least through the use of sustainable techniques and the recycling of structures – to the beauty of Italy and Milan, the cosmopolitan capital of world design.

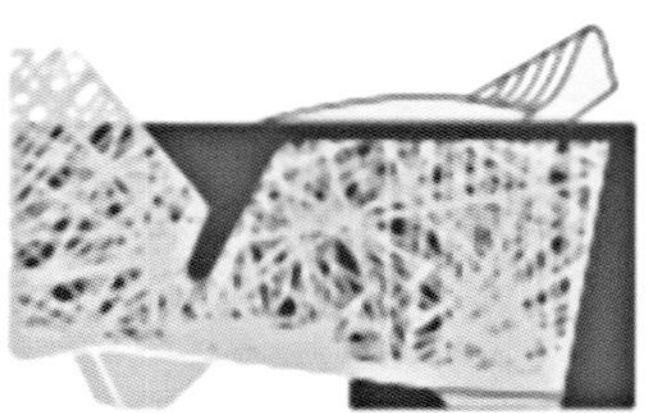

ITALY PAVILION
意大利馆

The Nursery of Italy
意大利苗圃

客户: Expo 2015 SpA / 建筑设计: Nemesi & Partners srl
建筑团队: Alessandro Miele (Coordinator), Alessandro Belilli, Claudio Cortese, Daniele Durante, Enrico Falchetti, Alessandro Franceschini, Davide Giambelli, Alessandra Giannone, Paolo Greco, Mariarosaria Meloni, Fabio Rebollini, Giuseppe Zaccaria, Kai Felix Dorl, Matteo Pavese, Paolo Maselli
工程技术: Proger SpA / 结构与系统: Bms Progetti Srl / 可持续能源: Eng. Livio de Santoli
模型制造: Officina06, Gianluca Brancaleone / 面积：约13 000平方米

Client: Expo 2015 SpA / Architectural Project: Nemesi & Partners srl
Architectural Team: Alessandro Miele (Coordinator), Alessandro Belilli, Claudio Cortese, Daniele Durante, Enrico Falchetti, Alessandro Franceschini, Davide Giambelli, Alessandra Giannone, Paolo Greco, Mariarosaria Meloni, Fabio Rebollini, Giuseppe Zaccaria, Kai Felix Dorl, Matteo Pavese, Paolo Maselli
Engineering: Proger SpA / Structures and Systems: Bms Progetti Srl / Sustainable Energy: Eng. Livio de Santoli
Model Maker: Officina06, Gianluca Brancaleone / Area: approximately 13,000m²

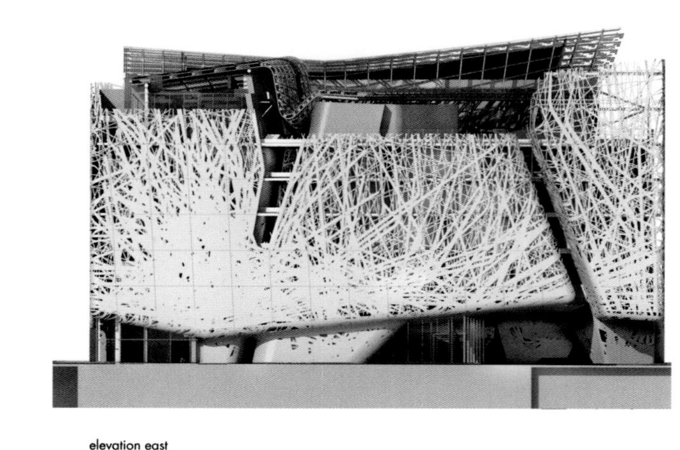
elevation east

elevation north
北立面

elevation south

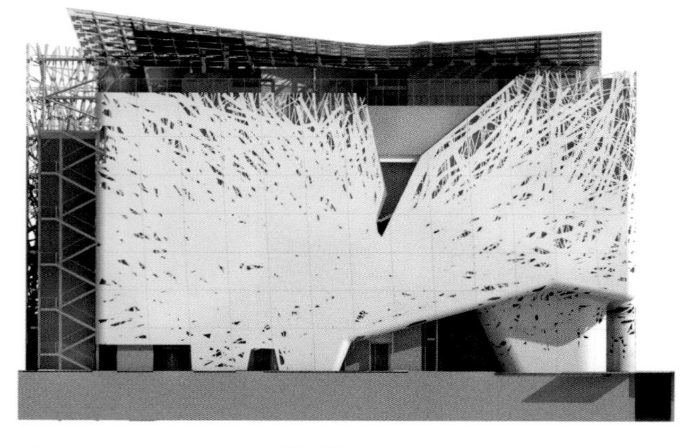
elevation west
西立面

作为少数几个将于世博会结束后保留在原地的展馆，意大利馆受到自然建筑概念的启发，其外表皮覆盖着错综复杂的树枝状结构，产生了光与影的交替变化，创造了虚与实的空间效果。

建筑整体结构由四个由桥连接的区域构成：展示区（西区）、礼堂活动区（南区）、行政办公区（北区）、会议区（东区）。这四个区域构成的建筑体量代表“树干”，而地面上大体量的支撑结构代表“树根”。由内部广场向外望去，树枝交错在透明表皮上，敞开且向上延伸，不经意间“树叶”呼之欲出。

外表皮的树枝状结构交叠而不重复，形状各不同，创造了一个独一无二的几何纹理。整个外表皮面积为9 000平方米，由900块“i.active Biodynamic”水泥嵌板构成，并由Styl-Comp技术制造而成。

由于其表面采用光电玻璃和具有光催化作用的新型水泥覆层（由意大利水泥集团获得专利的的活性物质TX Active构成），意大利馆实现了可持续化设计。在阳光直射下，材料中的活跃分子“俘获”空气中的污物并将它们转化为惰性盐，有助于净化大气中的烟雾。

As one of the few expo structures that will remain on the site after the fair is over, Italy Pavilion is inspired by a natural architecture in which the branched structure of the outer casing, thanks to intertwined lines, generates alternations of light and shadow, empty and full spaces.

The architecture is structured around four blocks interconnected by bridge elements. Like urban theatre wings, the four blocks house respectively: the Exhibition Area (Western Block), the Auditorium-Events Area (Southern Block), the Administrative Offices Area (Northern Block) and the Conference-Meeting Rooms Area (Eastern Block). The four architectural volumes represent large “trees”, with massive supports on the ground simulating large “roots”. As seen from the inner square, the same volumes, by opening and stretching upwards, are released as “foliage” through transparent glazed surfaces, evoking the random interweaving of “branches”.

For the branched structure of the outer facade, the designers developed a system of overlapping layers that produce, in their different combinations, differently shaped panels giving rise to a unique and original geometric texture. The entire outer surface of 9,000 m² will consist of 900 panels made of i.active BIODYNAMIC cement by Italcementi made with Styl-Comp technology.

Palazzo Italia was designed in a sustainable manner also thanks to the contribution of the covering photovoltaic glass and the photocatalytic properties of the new cement for the outer casing, obtained through the active substance TX Active patented by Italcementi. In direct sunlight, the active principle contained in the material “captures” certain pollutants present in the air and converts them into inert salts, helping to purify the atmosphere from smog.

VINO
A TASTE OF
ITALY
"Felicità sia agli homini che nascono dove si trovano i vin buoni"
Much happiness will come to those who are born where good wines are found.
幸福不过生来就有好酒相伴
IL PIACER DEL VINO È MISTO DI CORPORALE E DI SPIRITUALE.
THE PLEASURE OF WINE IS A MIXTURE OF BODY AND SOUL.
葡萄酒带来的快意是肉体与精神上的。
"Un buon vino è come un buon film" F. FELLINI
Good wine is like a good film.
一瓶好酒就如一部好电影
L'ACQUA DIVIDE GLI UOMINI; IL VINO LI UNISCE.
WATER DIVIDES MEN; WINE UNITES THEM.
水将人分隔开,而葡萄酒将人聚拢。
IL VINO È IL CANTO DELLA TERRA VERSO IL CIELO.
WINE IS EARTH'S SONG TO THE SKY.
葡萄酒是大地对天空吟唱的歌
vino is marriage · vino 是

TINTILIA DEL MOLISE
MOLISE
BIFERNO
MONTECARLO
PENTRO
MORELLINO DI SCANSANO
SOVANA
VAL D'ARNO DI SOPRA
SUVERETO
TERRE DI PISA
ELBA ALEATICO PASSITO
BOLGHERI SASSICAIA
SAN TORPÈ
ANSONICA COSTA DELL'ARGENTARIO
TERRE DI CASOLE
CORTONA
MONTEREGIO DI MASSA MARITTIMA
CAPALBIO
BIANCO DI PITIGLIANO
VAL DI CORNIA ROSSO
COLLI DI LUNI
BOLGHERI
VALDINIEVOLE
CANDIA DEI COLLI APUANI
ELBA
COLLINE LUCCHESI
MONTECUCCO SANGIOVESE
MONTESCUDAIO
MONTECUCCO
TERRATICO DI BIBBONA
PARRINA
VALDICHIANA TOSCANA
MAREMMA TOSCANA
VAL DI CORNIA
CARMIGNANO
CHIANTI
VERNACCIA DI SAN GIMIGNANO
VIN SANTO DEL CHIANTI CLASSICO
CHIANTI CLASSICO
VIN SANTO DEL CHIANTI
NOTO
MONREALE
SANTA MARGHERITA DI BELICE
ELORO
FARO
MAMERTINO
VITTORIA
DELIA NIVOLELLI
SCIACCA
ERICE
CONTEA DI SCLAFANI
SICILIA
RIESI
VERNACCIA DI SERRAPETRONA
VERDICCHIO DEI CASTELLI DI JESI
SAN GINESIO
COLLI PESARESI
TERRE DI OFFIDA
ESINO

MONTEFALCO
SAGRANTINO
COLLI PERUGINI
TRASIMENO
LAGO DI CALDARO

Francesca Petrini

ISOLE
PONTINE (LT)

UNITED KINGDOM PAVILION
英国馆

Grown in Britain; Shared Globally
源于英国 全球共享

艺术和创意指导：Wolfgang Buttress / 结构工程：Simmonds Studio / 建筑、景观和环境工程：BDP
建造工程: Stage One / 建造与项目管理: Rise / 物理学家和蜜蜂专家：Dr Martin Bencsik, Nottingham Trent University

Artist and Creative Lead: Wolfgang Buttress / Structural Engineers: Simmonds Studio
Architecture, Landscape Architecture and Environmental Engineering: BDP / Construction Engineers: Stage One
Construction and Project Management: Rise / Physicist and Bee Expert: Dr Martin Bencsik, Nottingham Trent University

为了响应世博会的主题，英国馆强调了蜜蜂的重要角色以及新的研究和技术是如何帮助人们面临食物安全和生物多样性的挑战。

英国馆设计方案的概念通过蜂群和人类共有的复杂性，探讨了蜂群的生活，获得了一种新的理解和洞察力。展馆的设计汲取了蜂群的生态，将其重新诠释成一种体验：参观者在一个果园漫步，然后发现一片野花草地，继而进入由嗡嗡声和发光信号模拟的蜂窝内部。展馆包括四个主要区域：果园、草地、蜂窝、建筑设计方案。

果园中种满了苹果树和梨树，以队列布局。队列间的座位区为参观者提供了小憩的空间。周围的石笼墙填充了废砖、破砖以及二次回收的砖块，创造了一种带有围墙的英国乡村花园的印象。

草地的入口由柯尔顿不锈钢构成的泥土通道打开，共40米长。整个草地季节性变化明显，在世博会6个月期间会不停地成长。植物的高度与参观者的视线持平，目的在于给参观者一个和蜜蜂同样的视角，邀请参观者从另外一个角度去看这个世界。多样的路线设计参考了蜜蜂舞蹈的定向运动，为参观者参观下一站蜂窝的旅途作铺垫。

蜂窝位于3米高的柱子之上，是一个由铝制成的尺寸为14米x14米x14米的立方体晶格结构。晶格由间距为500毫米的横向面板构成，面板间有织带点缀。晶格结构中心经过调整构成了一个直径为12米的球形空体。有两块较低的横向面板未被调整，用以支撑20毫米厚的钢化夹层玻璃板。

“建筑设计方案”使这座建筑充分利用空间，成为英国馆的功能区。与VIP区相连的礼堂为会议和一次性活动提供了绝佳的空间。在其他时候，这个空间也服务于公众，可以作为一个视频播放、投影和展示的空间。

In response to the Expo theme, the UK pavilion highlights the role of the honeybee and ways in which new research and technology are helping to address challenges, including food security and biodiversity.

The concept for this proposal plays on these parallels, exploring the life of a bee colony, to cultivate understanding and insight. The pavilion design takes the ecology of a bee colony and reinterprets it as an experience: visitors meander through an orchard, discover a wildflower meadow and enter a "virtual hive".The pavilion consists of four main areas for visitor experience: The Orchard, The Meadow, The Hive, The Architectural Programme.

An orchard of apple and pear trees creates a queuing system. Small seating areas within the rows provide a place to rest. The surrounding gabion walls are filled with rejected/broken/reused bricks to evoke the feeling of a walled English country garden.

Entrance to the "meadow experience" is gained via an earthy corridor of corten steel, open to the sky. The 40-metre long meadow is seasonal, forever changing and growing over the six month Expo period. Plants are raised to eye-level giving a bees'-eye view and inviting visitors to empathise and see the world from a new perspective. Multiple paths and routes reference the orienteering "bee dance", inviting the visitor to explore and participate in the curation of their own journey towards the hive beyond.

The hive is a 14mx14mx14m cuboid 3D lattice structure made from aluminium, seated on three-metre -tall columns. The lattice consists of horizontal planes spaced at approximately 500 mm with webbing members between these planes. The aluminium provides a filigree yet robust and corrosion resistant structure. The lattice structure has been trimmed away at its centre leaving a 12-metre diameter spherical void inside. Two lower horizontal planes remain untrimmed part way up to support a floor of toughened laminated glass panels approximately 20mm thick.

The architectural programme, this building has been created to provide the functional aspect of the pavilion making effective use of the space provided. A flexible auditorium space connecting to a VIP area provides a perfect space for conferences and one-off events. At other times, this space can form part of the public experience, as a video/projection and exhibition room.

PN CITY
34

FRENCE PAVILION
法国馆

Different Ways of Producing and Providing Food
多产市场

建筑师: XTU | Anouk Legendre + Nicola Desmaziere / 项目负责人: Mathias Lukacs / 合作建筑师: Atelien Architecture
多媒体: Innovision / 灯光设计: LICHT KUNST LICHT / 园林设计: BASE / 声学专家: Viasonora
建筑面积: 3 532 平方米（净面积）/ 3 286 平方米（可用面积）/ 基地面积: 3 500 平方米

Architects: XTU | Anouk Legendre + Nicola Desmaziere / Project leader: Mathias Lukacs / Partner Architects: Atelien Architecture / Multimedia: Innovision
Lighting Designer: LICHT KUNST LICHT / Landscape Gardener: BASE / Acoustic Specialist: Viasonora
Building Surface Area: 3,532 m² shon / 3,286 m² usable / Site's Area: 3,500 m²

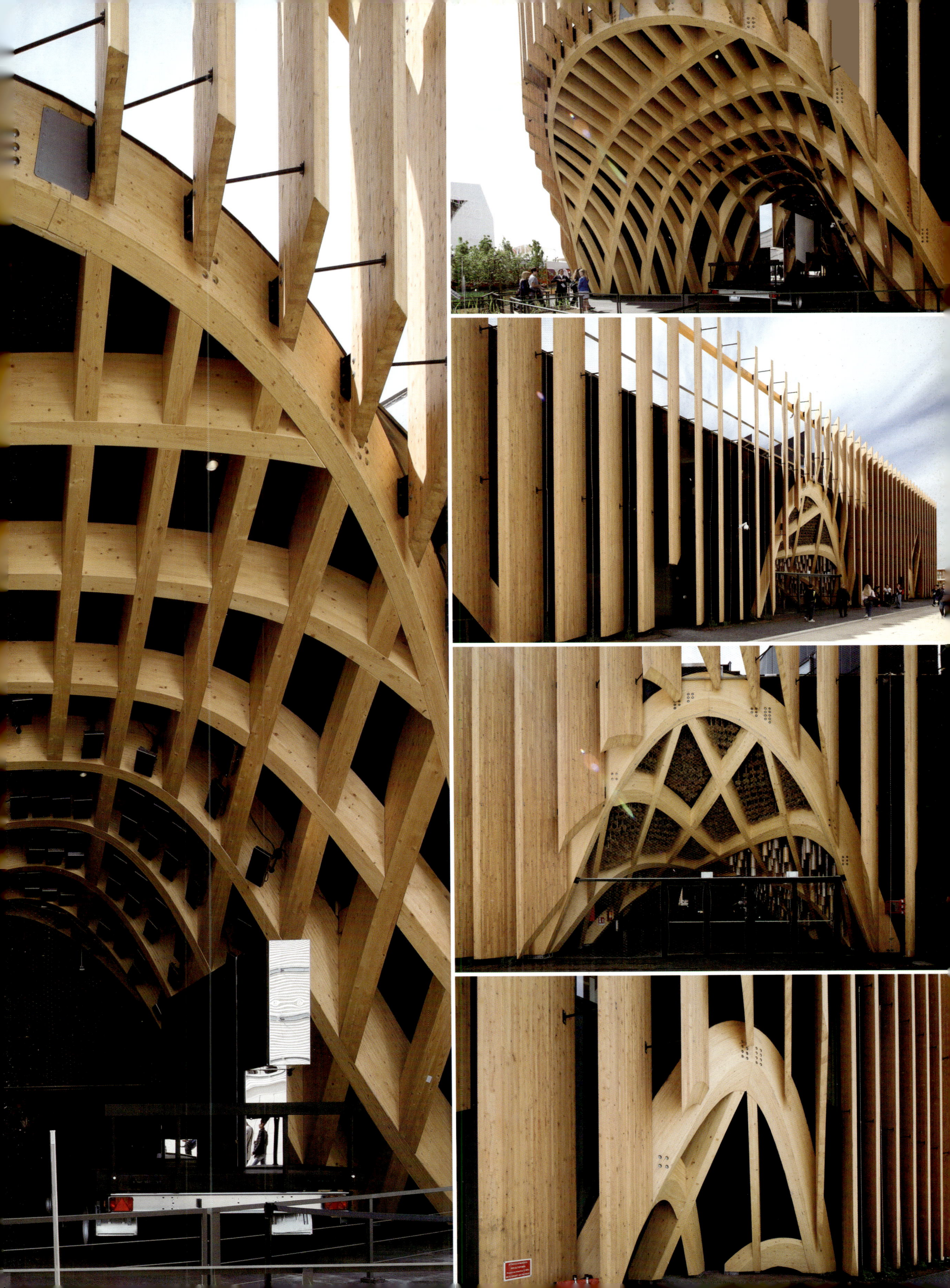

由法国XTU建筑事务所构思的法国馆获胜方案，彰显了法国“丰富的遗产”。这个网格状的“多产市场”，是一个更具凝聚力而可持续的市场，既可种植、收获粮食，还可以现场销售与消费。

市场的拱形大厅内，木格的结构种满了药材和蔬菜。外墙面上种有啤酒花，在阳台上种植芳香植物，餐厅里提供即食蔬菜。水培生产技术描绘了法国在世界领先领域的创新角色。在建筑底层，游客将穿过法国粮食生产主题的展览厅，然后通过楼梯到达楼上的露台餐厅，享用展馆的新鲜农产品。

法国馆通体采用木材（木结构、木楼梯和木立面）建造，通过其最具“创新性”的形式表现了法国在木构架上的专业：自由结构。配件隐形、复杂的几何形状数字化剪裁，所有技术均由服务于建筑质量的公司操控。

Conceived by Paris studio XTU Architects, the competition-winning French pavilion design focuses on Different Ways of Producing and Providing Food. It is a prolific market in grid form, and it is also a cohesive and sustainable market allowing for plantation, harvest, sales and consumption in one spot.

In the arched hall of the market, herbs and vegetables are planted in the structure of wooden grids. On the facades, we grow hops, on the terrace aromatic herbs, and in the restaurant, vegetables to be eaten on the spot. Hydroponic production that depicts the French innovation in partnership with the world leader of the sector! On the ground level, visitors will pass through a French food production thematic exhibition hall to the top terrace restaurant by staires to enjoy fresh food produced in the pavilion.

The project, all wood (structures, floors and facades), expresses the French expertise in timber frame, in its most “innovative” form: free forms. Assemblies are invisible, complex geometry is made of digital cutting, all technologies that the company controls, serving the architectural quality.

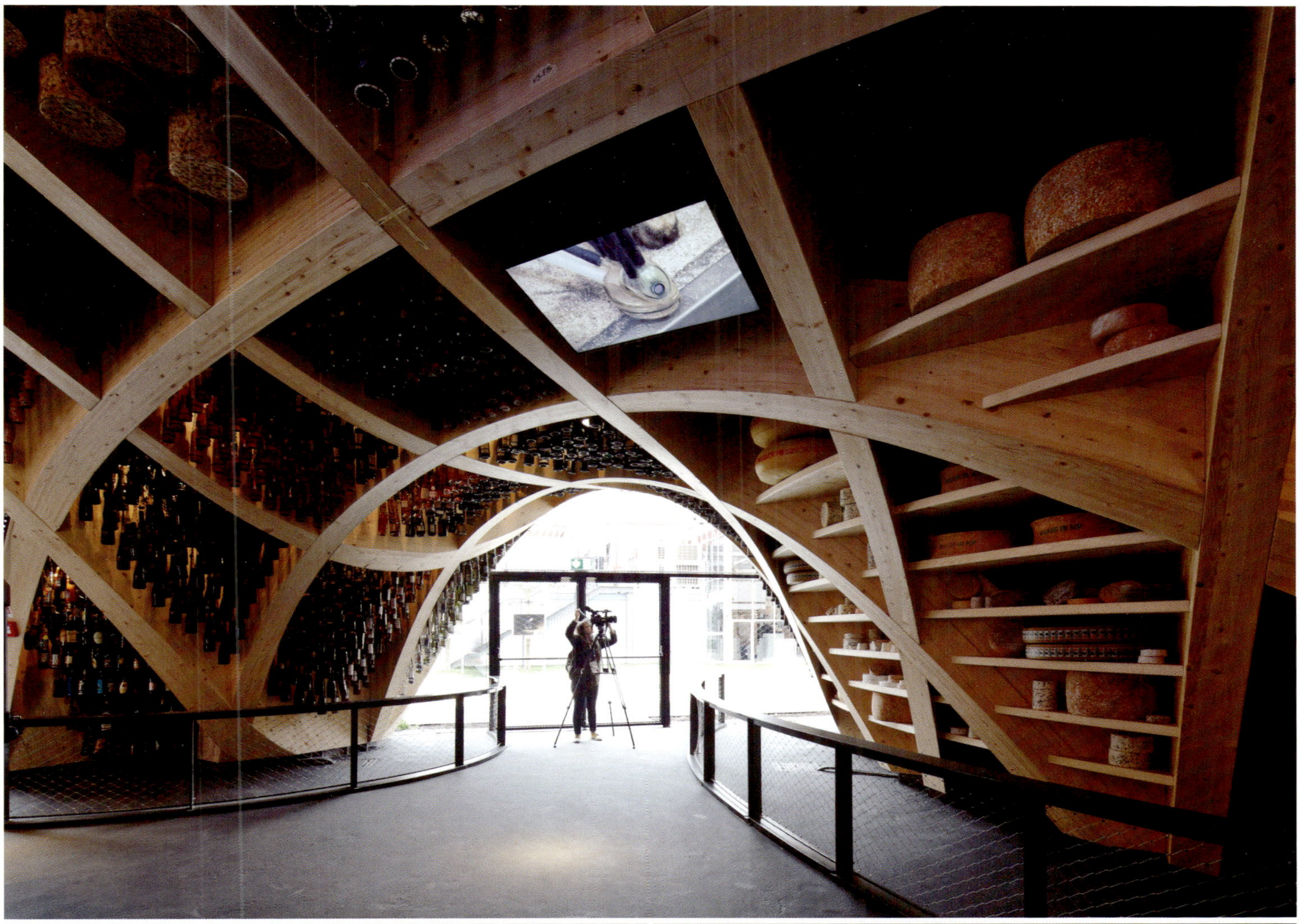

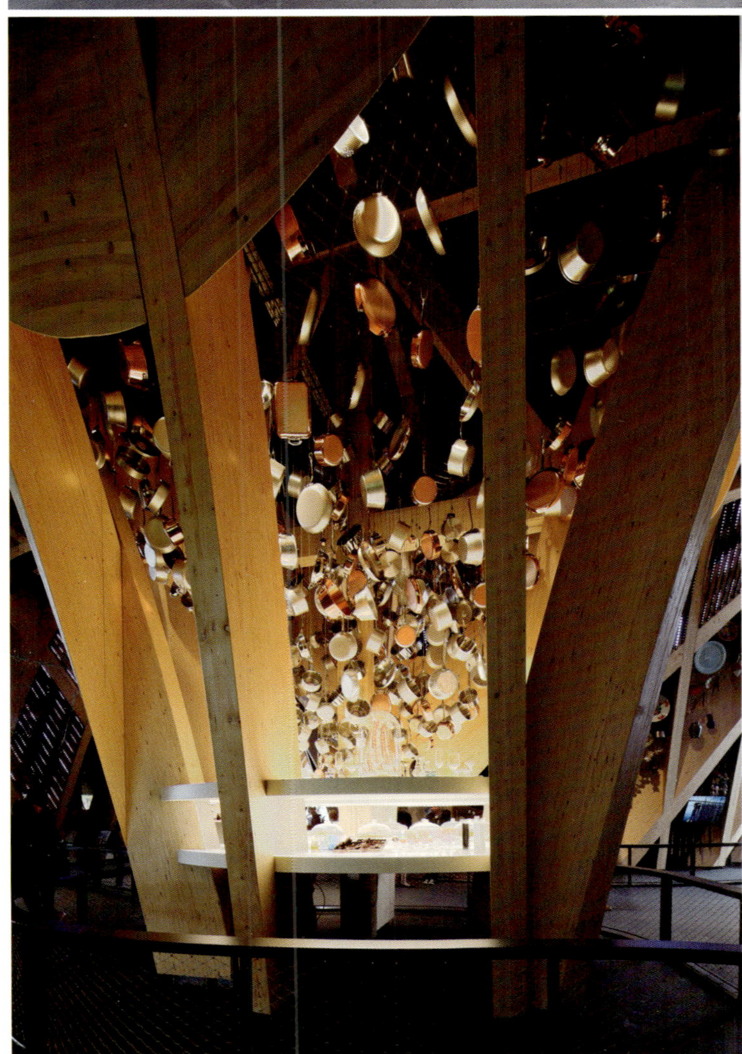

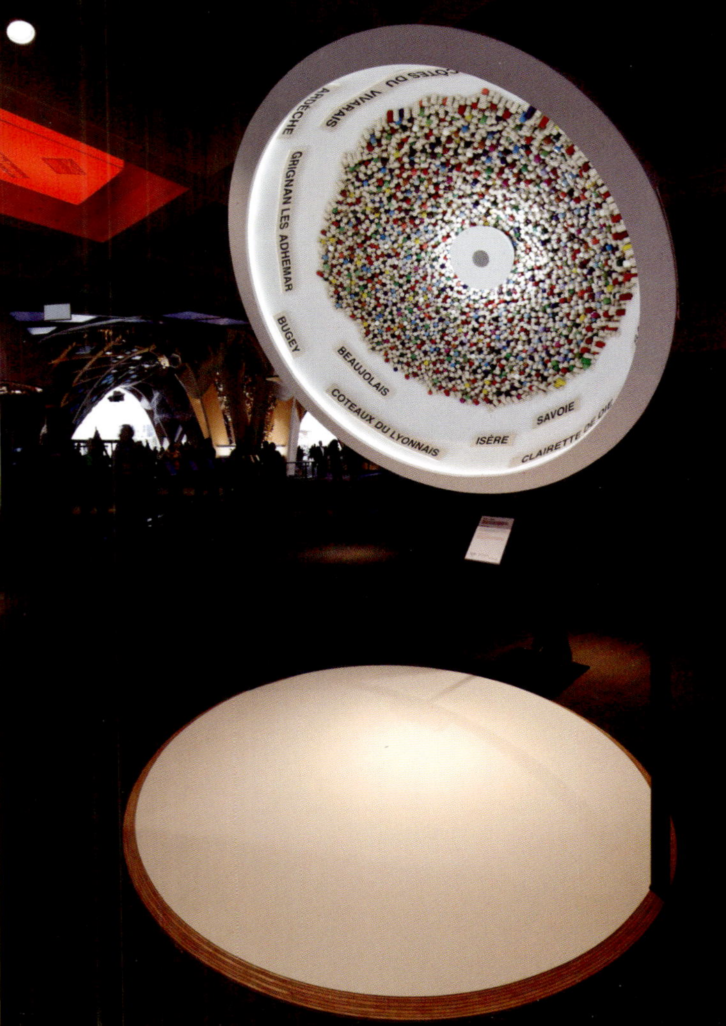

DU VIVARAIS
ARDÈCHE
GRIGNAN LES ADHEMAR
BUGEY
BEAUJOLAIS
COTEAUX DU LYONNAIS
ISÈRE
SAVOIE
CLAIRETTE DE DIE

OPINEL

2014, Monsieur Stéphane Le Foll
de l'agriculture, de l'agroalimentaire
porte-parole du Gouvernement
à Milan la construction
France pour
2015

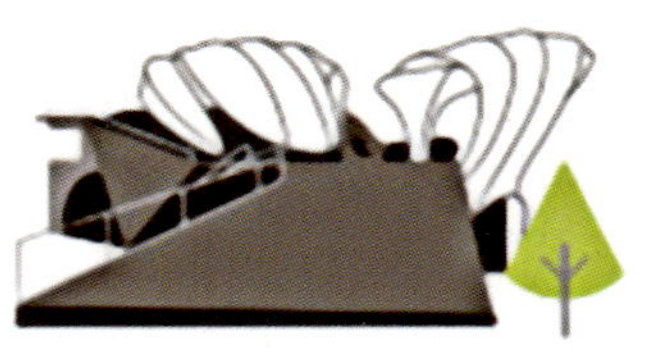

GERMANY PAVILION
德国馆

Fields of Ideas
灵感的田野

设计、规划、实施：Deutscher Pavilion Expo Milano consortium / 空间概念、建筑、总体规划：Schmidhuber, Munich
内容概念、展示、媒体：Milla & Partner, Stuttgart / 工程管理与建造：N ü ssli (Deutschland) GmbH, Roth / 面积：4 913平方米

Design, Planning, Realization: Deutscher Pavilion Expo Milano consortium / Spatial Concept, Architecture, General Planning: Schmidhuber, Munich
Content Concept, Exhibition, Media: Milla & Partner, Stuttgart / Project Management and Construction: Nüssli (Deutschland) GmbH, Roth / Area: 4,913m²

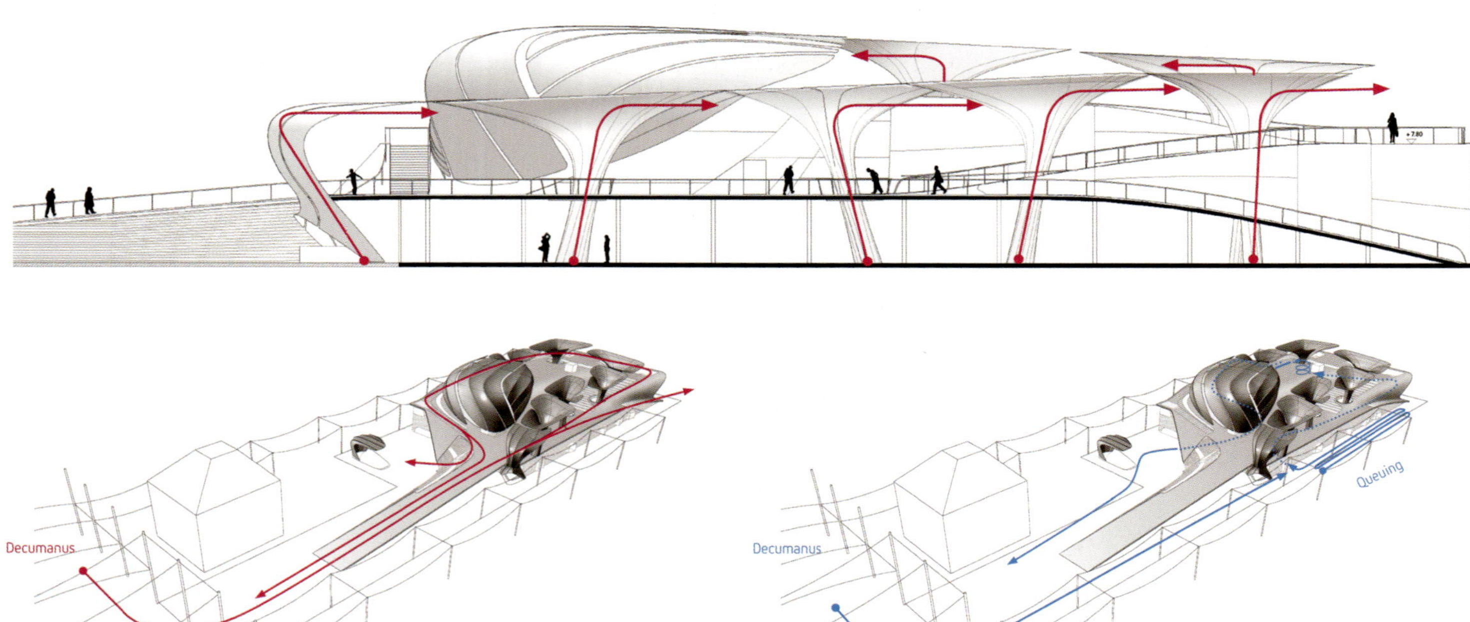

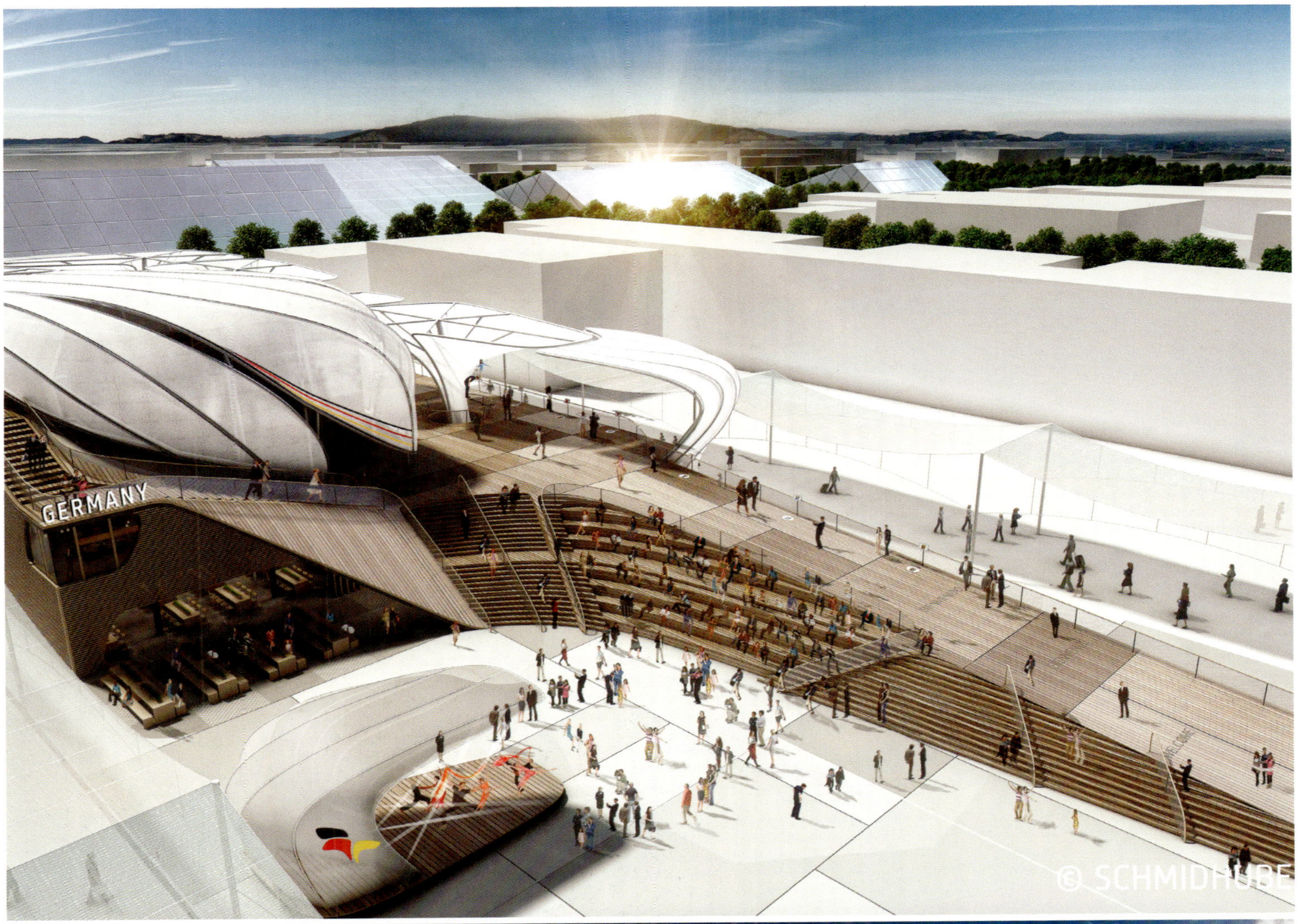
GERMANY
© SCHMIDHUBE

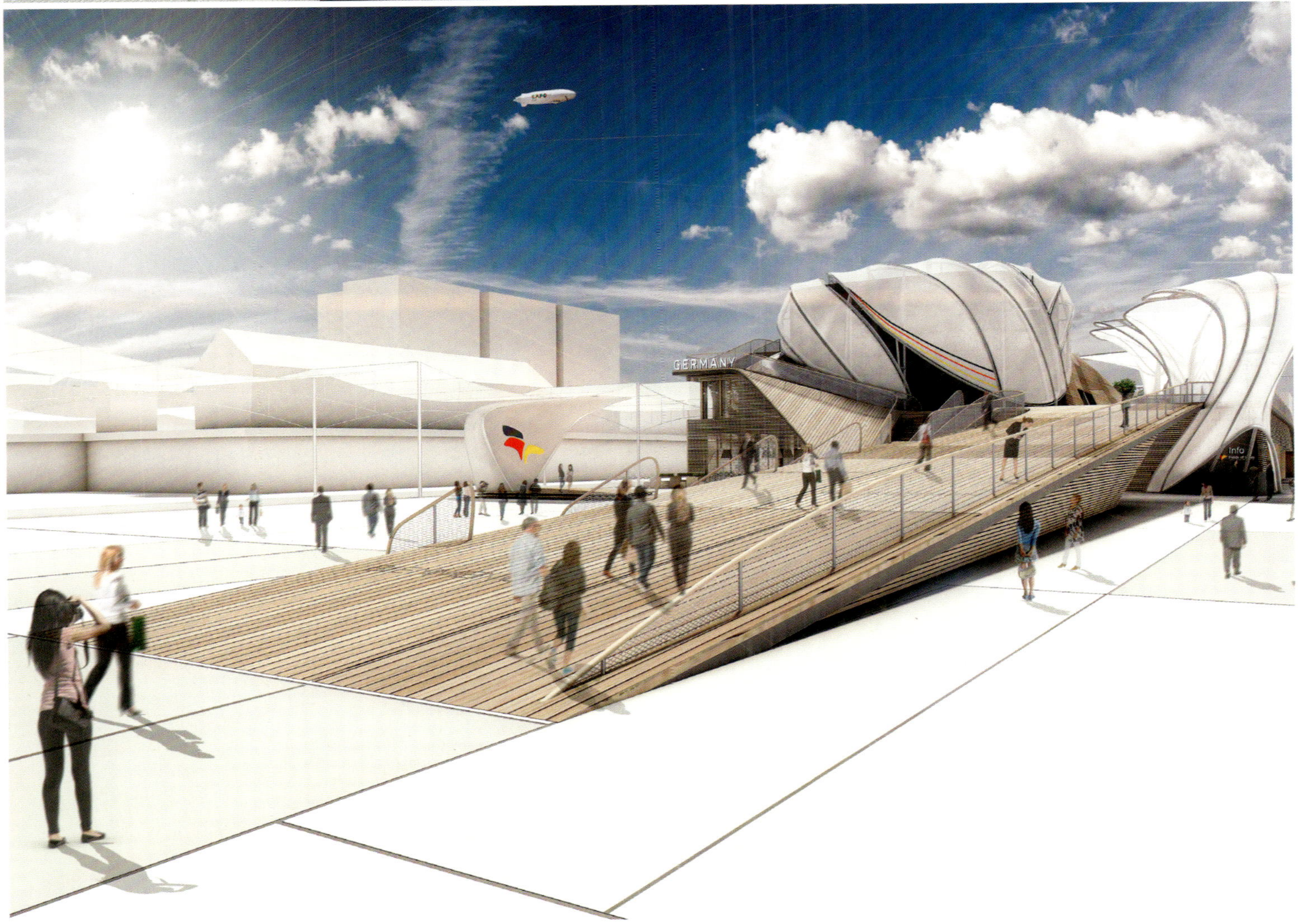
GERMANY
Info

德国馆将会是世博会最大的展馆，其主题是“灵感的田野”，将会向参观者们展示德国的新面貌以及在保护环境上的大量举措和努力，如政府政策、前沿研究、创意公司和民间团体的巨大贡献。

德国馆以一种醒目的、惊人的方式将德国的田野和草地诠释成建筑；这座建筑由微倾斜的景观平台、易接近的表面和内部主题展示空间构成。在可辨度极高的田野景观之中，典型化的“植物”似“灵感的种子”从内部展示空间冲出，构成了一个大型的、具有保护作用的华盖。这些“植物”连接了内部和外部空间，使建筑和展示空间相吻合。在田野上空漂浮着叶子，这种有机的流畅设计创造了一种让人印象特别深刻的映像。

德国馆将现代设计语言融入传统的材料，在资源和空间最大化利用的基础上采用气候概念，并实施科技和智能建造。在展馆规划和建造初期，“灵感的田野”这一主题对世博会提出的问题作出的答案不仅具有可持续性而且具有创意。

形式上，建筑类似一个“移换的景观”，逐渐向上倾斜以致10米高。在材料选择上，德国馆采用当地多种木头，特色鲜明。田野和草地延伸向木制甲板。木头不仅能营造热情欢迎的氛围，而且力证了可再生资源的谨慎利用。立面是一个水平层状结构，依倾斜的景观和开口而建，看似水平的大地地层。立面简单却智能，层状结构促成了它的通透性和自然通风，实现了高效的室内气候概念，并采用能效技术为所有的展示空间提供了舒适的温度。

Germany will build the biggest pavilions at the upcoming Universal Exposition. With the theme “Fields of Ideas”, Germany Pavilion will present visitors with a new image of the country and its massive efforts towards environmental protection through government policies, cutting-edge research, innovative companies and the extraordinary contribution of civil society.

The German Pavilion translates the German field and meadow landscape into its architecture in a striking and surprising way: a building consisting of a gently sloping landscape level with a freely accessible surface and a thematic exhibition inside. In this landscape, with clearly discernible fields, stylised plants grow as "idea seedlings" up from the exhibition to the exterior surface, creating a large, protective canopy. These are the connecting elements, dovetailing the exterior and interior, the architecture and the exhibition itself. The organically flowing design language – floating leaves hovering over the landscape – creates a distinctive and unforgettable image.

A modern design language flowing into traditional materials, a climate concept based on the economic use of resources and space, lean technologies and intelligent construction all converge in the German pavilion. As early as in the pavilion’s planning and construction phase, “Fields of Ideas” provides sustainable, creative answers to the questions showcased at EXPO.

Formally, the architecture is reminiscent of a “supplanted landscape” set in the pavilion’s premises which gradually slopes upward to a height of 10 m. The use of different native woods, with varied grains and tones, creates a highly distinctive design. The fields and meadows evolve into a walk-through wooden deck. Wood is not only warm and inviting, it also attests to the deliberate use of renewable resources with a balanced CO^2 audit. The facade design consists of a horizontal lamellar structure. It follows the sloping landscape and facade openings, reminding viewers of horizontal earth strata. The facade is as simple as it is “intelligent”. Its permeability and natural ventilation – achieved through a lamellar structure – are part of a simple yet very effective interior climate concept, which, in combination with energy-efficient technologies, ensures comfortable temperatures in all exhibition areas.

GERMANY

GERMANY

RTENVIELFALT
BIODIVERS
ODIVERSITY
BIODIVERSITE

PRESERVARE LA FERTILITÀ DEL TERRENO
MAINTAINING SOIL FERTILITY
B

SFRUTTARE LE

GEMEINSAM ETWAS BEWEGEN
INSIEME PER FARE LA DIFFERENZA
MAKING A DIFFERENCE TOGETHER
FAIRE BOUGER LES CHOSES ENSEMBLE
BODEN
ERRENO
SOIL
TERRE
CLIMATE
CLIMAT

TIERE ARTGERECHT HALTEN
TELA DEL BENESSERE DEGLI ANIMALI
ANIMAL-SPECIFIC HUSBANDRY
BIEN TRAITER LES ANIMAUX
THE EXPERIMENTAL COWSHED
Put the sensors on the cow to find out how she is.

BODEN
TERRENO
SOIL
TERRE

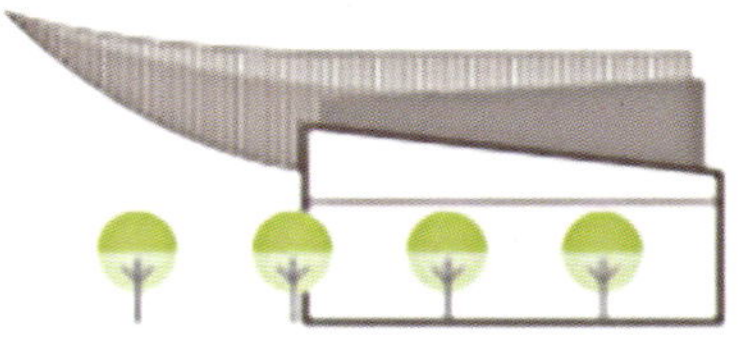

RUSSIAN FEDERATION PAVILION

俄罗斯馆

Growing for the World. Cultivating for the Future

增长的领域

建筑师：Sergei Tchoban, Alexei Ilyin, Marina Kuznetskaya / 项目面积：超过4 000 平方米

Architects: Sergei Tchoban, Alexei Ilyin, Marina Kuznetskaya / Project Area: over 4,000 m²

RUSSIA
RUSSIA
RUSSIA
RUSSIA

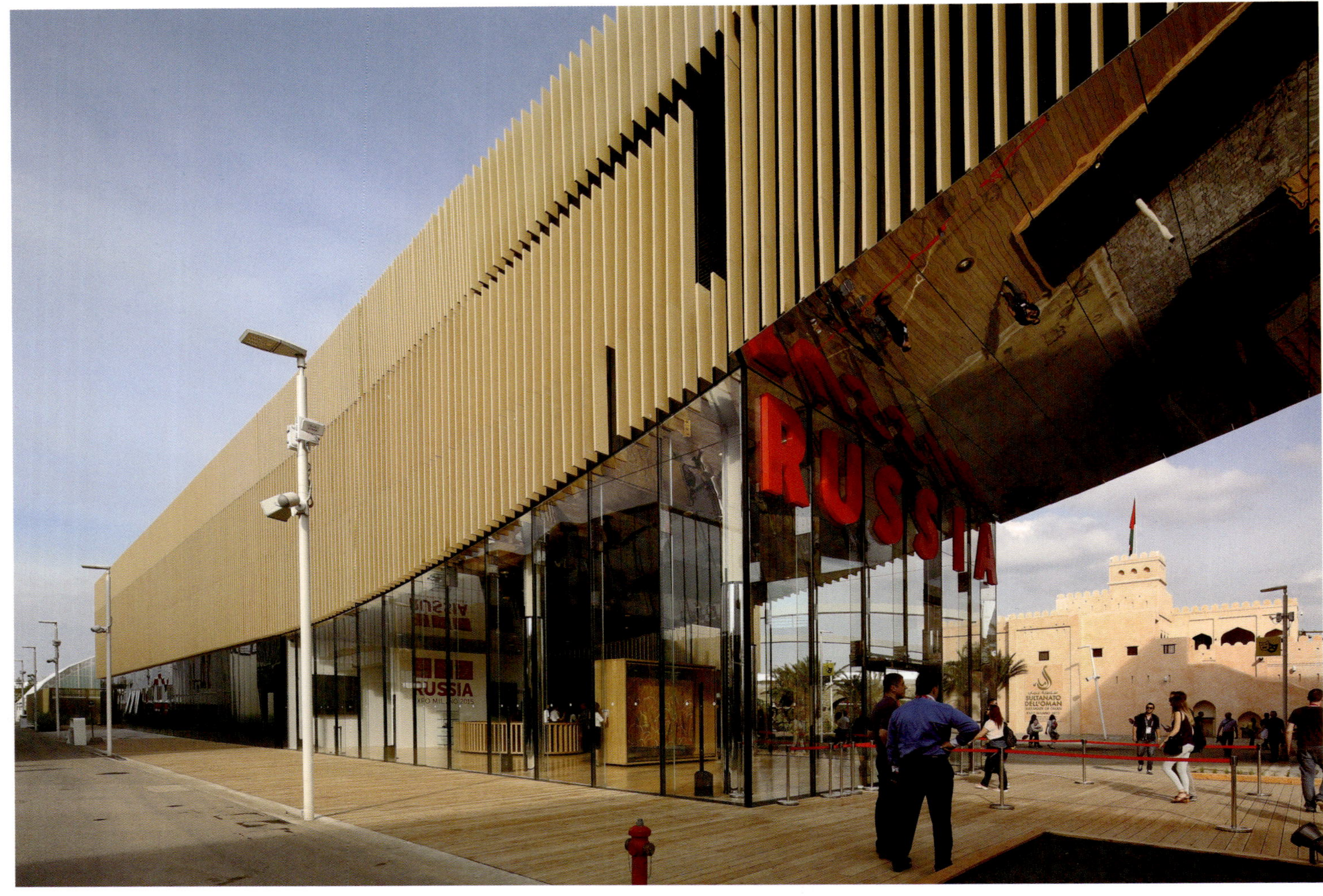

俄罗斯馆展示了一座现代设计的顶级多功能建筑，它的建造工艺也是让人过目不忘的一个典范。它采用典雅的木立面，半透明的室内地铺和清雅的绿色屋顶。木制的立面有两个好处：防晒和遮荫；平整的屋顶能带领参观者步入场馆的主入口，入口处有30米长的天篷作为遮盖。俄罗斯展馆将给参观者创造一个和谐又亲和的空间体验。

俄罗斯馆占地面积超4 000平方米，结合先进的工程技术和绿色技术，俄罗斯馆展现了它的活力和昂扬的精神面貌。场馆运用可持续的环保材料建造了一个简单而令人难忘的建筑结构及立面设计，同时注入俄罗斯特色元素。丰富的山体造型形成自然景观，在有机木板的围合下像一艘航船的船头，这样的造型不禁让人联想到诺亚方舟。

俄罗斯展馆内部被分作多个开放式空间，它的观景平台像设置在传统的经典意大利庭院里。建筑的上部像古老的巴比伦空中花园；场馆结构的最高点是一个覆满植物沿缓坡蜿蜒的屋顶平台，它预示着俄罗斯广袤无垠的国土。这个覆盖了30米长的顶篷的屋顶平台随缓坡慢慢攀升，很好地与周围的自然环境融合，在这宽敞的平台上可以举办各种活动，也可以一览整个世博会的全景。

Russia's Pavilion proposes a supremely multi-functional building of contemporary design and an example of striking and memorable craftsmanship. Its elegant wooden façade, the semi-transparent ground floor interior and its green rooftop, together create a harmonious suite of spaces that are easily accessible to visitors. The wooden facade has a dual functionality: to protect the building from the sun and to create shelter outside. The flat roof of the pavilion, which is accessible to all visitors, gently rises towards the main entrance, where the main access to the pavilion is covered by a 30m long canopy.

Built on an area that extends over 4,000 m², the Pavilion is a dynamic and expansive structure with an ambitious form that surges skywards, combining unique engineering solutions and green technologies. Its simple, yet memorable façade is made from sustainable, ecologically-sound materials that offer protection from the elements. Its voluminous hill becomes an element of the natural landscape, surrounded by organic wooden hoops that form the elegant 'nose' of a sailing boat – a metaphor of Noah's Ark.

Inside, the Pavilion is divided into a series of open spaces and viewing platforms in the tradition of classical Italian gardens. In the upper part of the building are hanging gardens reminiscent of Babylon, whilst the highest point of the Pavilion structure is the sloping serpentine of the vegetation-clad rooftop, symbolizing the boundless fields of Russia. This unique architectural and decorative element gently rises upwards, offering a 30 meter-long canopy that merges the building harmoniously into the natural surroundings, a space for special events and a superb vista across the Exhibition Site.

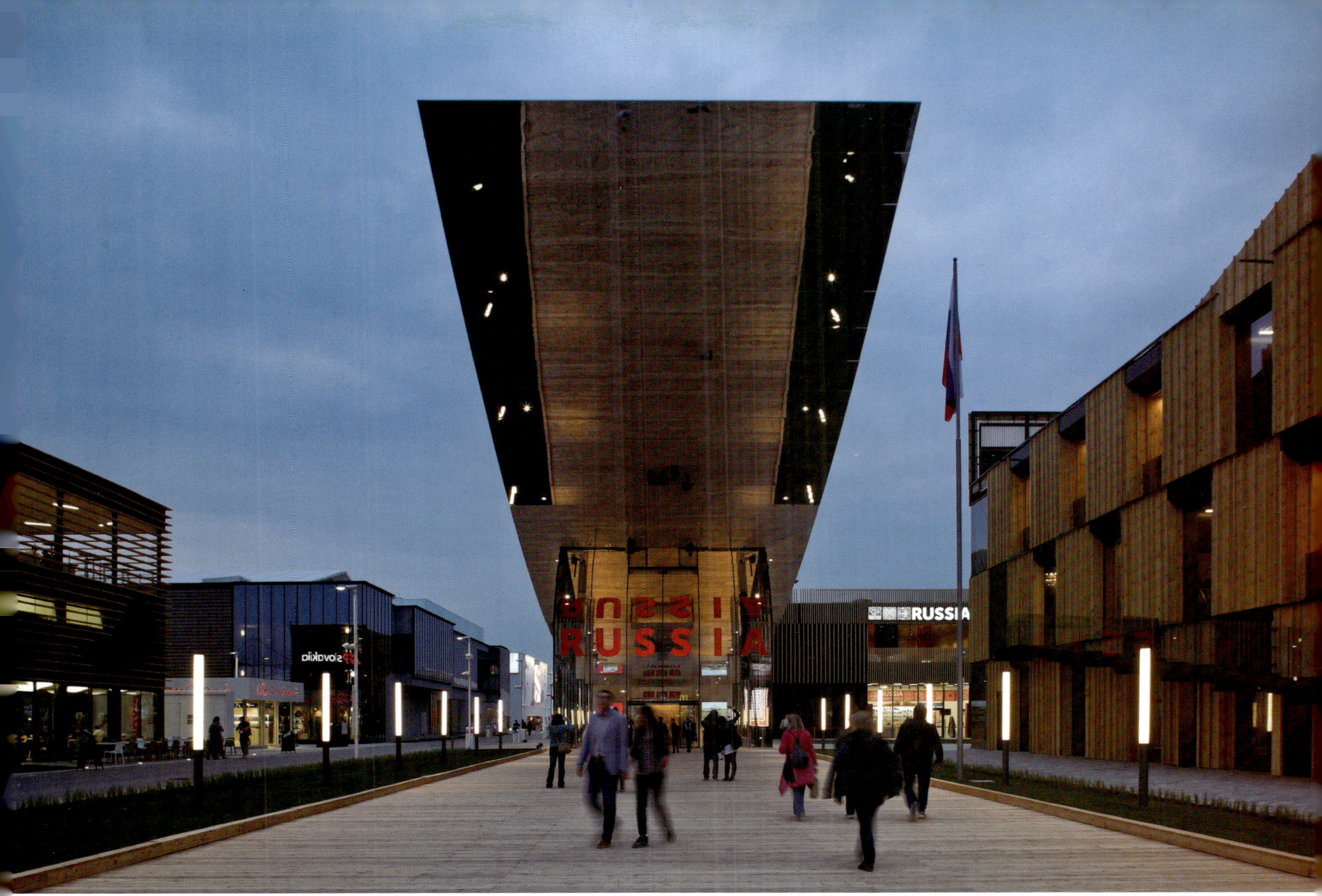
RUSSIA
RUSSIA
slovakia

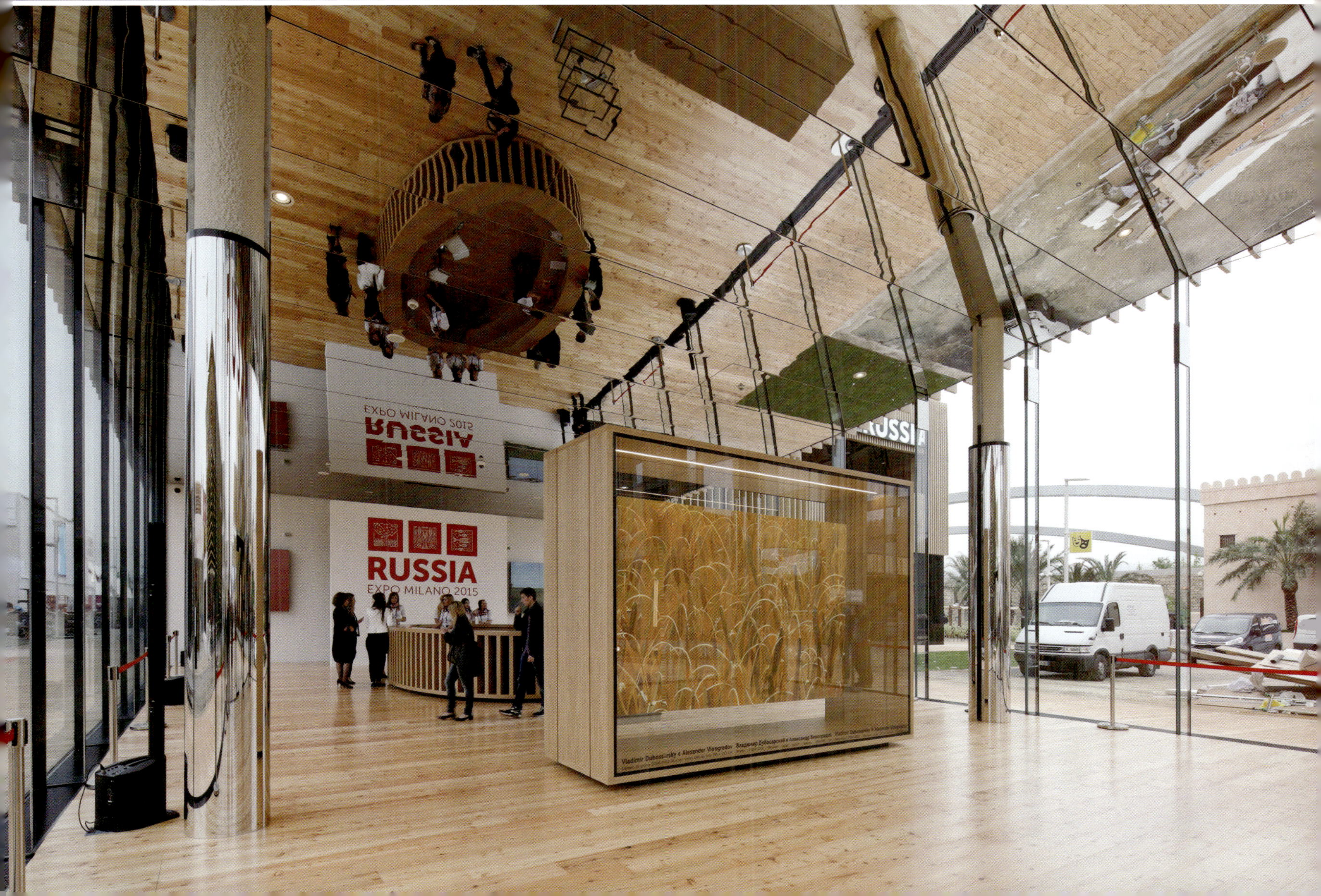
EXPO MILANO 2015
RUSSIA
EXPO MILANO 2015
RUSSIA

Vladimir Dubossarsky e Alexander Vinogradov
Владимир Дубосарский и Александр Виноградов
Vladimir Dubossarsky & Alexander Vinogradov

RADISHES
ИКРА
MEAD
KVASS
ZUCCA
SMOKED MEATS
CAVIAR
WHITEFISH

SPAIN PAVILION
西班牙馆

Cultivating the Future
培育未来

设计团队：b720 Arquitectos(Ferm í n V á zquez, Peco Mulet, Albert Freixes, Eduardo Varas, Caterina Dominioni, Alberto Garcia, Alejandro Garcia, Valerio Decrecchio, Gemma Ojea, Pablo Garrido, Iv á n Arellano, Javier Artieda, Julita Jaskulska, Ourania Pappa, Annie Michaelides)
当地建筑师: Arquipielago, B2fR Architetti / 结构工程: Miguel Nevado / 服务工程: K2 Consulting sl
照明设计: Artec 3 / 景观: Manel Colominas / 面积: 2 341平方米

Design Team: b720 Arquitectos(Fermín Vázquez, Peco Mulet, Albert Freixes, Eduardo Varas, Caterina Dominioni, Alberto Garcia, Alejandro García, Valerio Decrecchio, Gemma Ojea, Pablo Garrido, Iván Arellano, Javier Artieda, Julita Jaskulska, Ourania Pappa, Annie Michaelides)
Local Architects: Arquipielago, B2fR Architetti / Structure Engineering: Miguel Nevado / Services Engineering: K2 Consulting sl
Lighting Design: Artec 3 / Landscape: Manel Colominas / Area: 2,341 m²

ESPAÑA
EL LENGUAJE DEL SABOR

西班牙的美食融合了传统和创新，在国际上拥有极高的声誉。在2015年米兰世博这样一个国际舞台上，西班牙馆依然主打传统和创新的二元性，创造了两个独立的区域，并运用不同的构造加以区分。

传统棚屋中，木制结构框架和售票房的饰面参考了传统的食物文化：葡萄酒瓶的软木塞、木制葡萄酒桶、细茎针草。创新棚屋中，结构框架明亮且由抛光的不锈钢覆盖着。展示区和其他区域的售票房同样采用明亮和反光材料，而颜色上则参考了西班牙橄榄油和酒的颜色。

整个空间魅力无限，而且具有较强的通透性，能够方便参观者自由进入各个空间，不用排队等候。展馆内有一个栽满了橙子树的庭院——庭院是西班牙建筑文化的身份象征。这个庭院与无土栽培草莓天蓬下的光影空间相辅相成。

西班牙展馆通过采用可回收和天然的材料以及预制和现场组装来保证时间、成本和质量，进而打造一个环保的展馆。整个展馆由复合木材门廊构成，并由不均匀的CL木制棱柱体加固。在门廊之间，轻型的聚碳酸酯板充当天蓬，以保护天蓬下面的空间。为了促进自然通风，屋顶上安装了百叶窗，以疏散高温。门廊的深度和间距经过计算，为半敞开区域提供了一个合适的遮阳角度，相对于传统的全封闭空间，大大地减少了能源消耗。所有的建造过程都是基于组装，容易安装、拆卸和可回收的前提。

The Spanish gastronomy reputation, based on the balanced combination of tradition and innovation, makes it a global reference on international markets. This fact has a relevant role on the generation of the pavilion, creating two separated areas — and applying different tectonics to them — according to this duality.

In the shed shaped side representing tradition, timber structural frames and the finishes of the boxes refer to traditional food culture: the cork of wine bottles, the wooden wine barrels where the wine ages; and the esparto grass fabric used for pressing the oil. In the shed shaped side representing innovation, structural frames are bright, polished stainless steel covered, and the material of the boxes that locate the exhibition and other areas are equally bright and reflective, colored as some of the most recognizably Spanish products such as olive oil and wine.

The whole space is attractive and permeable to allow all public to cross and participate of the space without queuing the exhibition. There is a "patio de naranjos" (orange trees courtyard), identity element of the Spanish architectural culture. This patio, as a representation of one of the key quality products Spain exports, will coexist with the shadow spaces underneath a strawberries hydroponic canopy, under which will be found restaurant and auditoria terraces.

Spanish Pavilion is also an environmental friendly pavilion, made from both recycled and natural materials, pre-industrialized and assembled on site to guarantee time, cost and quality. The pavilion is basically constructed by a 1.50 m series of laminated timber porticos, fastened by a sequence of uneven prismatic volumes made from CL timber. In between these porticos, light polycarbonate panels acting as canopies that protect from climate the outdoors areas underneath them. To promote natural ventilation, fixed roof shutters are located to evacuate heat at high levels, in a similar mechanism to those used in greenhouses. The depth and distance between porticos are calculated to provide a comfortable degree of shadow to the semi-external areas below, resulting in a major reduction of energy consumption in comparison to traditionally enclosed areas. All the construction process is based in dry assembling, easy to mount, dismount and recycle.

NETHERLANDS PAVILION
荷兰馆

Share, Grow, Live
分享，成长，生活

建筑设计：Totems / 项目面积：2 369平方米

Architectural Design: Totems / Project Area: 2,369 m²

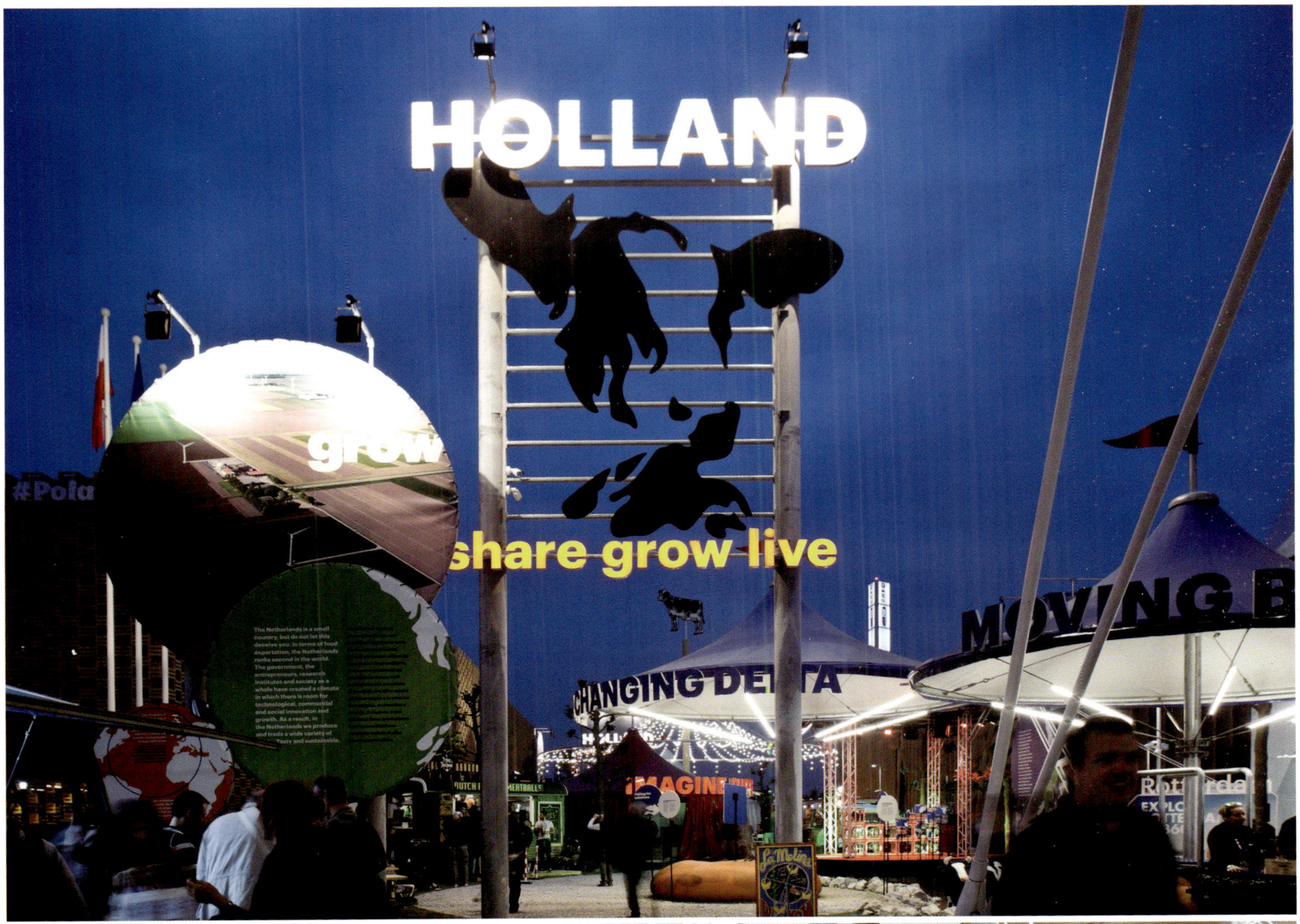

DELTA
rotterdam
EXPLORE ROTTERDAM IN 360°

DUTCH FRIES & MEATBALLS

DUTCH FRIES & MEATBALLS
BITTERBALLEN

此次2015米兰世博会荷兰设计了以大气的游乐场为形式的展馆来参展，展馆名为欢庆荷兰。荷兰馆不但会呈现思想的交锋而且还有味蕾的盛宴，所以荷兰馆是参观者游览世博会歇脚逗留的绝佳之处。

围绕食物，水资源和能源问题，荷兰在近百年来一直在倾力寻找解决方案。此次参展，荷兰人带来了他们独特的解决思路：分享，成长，生活。这些理念将通过中心展示和流动展览的形式以具体的故事来呈现，如未来的水果和蔬菜，生产食物的新方式，食物与技术的关系，食物艺术和人造食物。

The Netherlands brings to Expo Milano 2015 an atmospheric, fun fair-like pavilion named Dutch Festival, with plenty of things going on: thoughts will provoked, taste buds will be activated and tired feet will be given a break.

For centuries the Dutch have come up with solutions for issues around food, water and energy and they do this in their own particular way: Share, Grow, Live. This story is told at the pavilion through a central exhibition and temporary shows about, among other things, the future of fruits and vegetables, new ways of producing food and the relationship between food and technology. Food art and artificial food are't forgotten either.

IMAGINE

SEEK

SHOP
delta

entrance

circular
behaviour
culture
BAR

grow
The Netherlands is a small country, but do not let this deceive you. In terms of food exportation, the Netherlands ranks second in the world. The government, the entrepreneurs, research institutes and society as a whole have created a climate in which there is room for technological, commercial and social innovation and growth. As a result, in the Netherlands we produce and trade a wide variety of foods. Tasty and sustainable.
I Paesi Bassi sono un paese piccolo, ma non lasciatevi ingannare: sono il secondo esportatore di beni alimentari al mondo. I governi e l'imprenditoria, la ricerca e la società nel suo insieme hanno tutti contribuito alla creazione di un clima che offre spazio all'innovazione e la crescita tecnologica, economica e sociale. Il risultato è che nei Paesi Bassi produciamo e commercializziamo un'ampia varietà di cibo buono e sostenibile.

SHARE GROW LIVE
HOLLAND
share grow live

Sharing
solutions
for growth

SWITZERLAND PAVILION
瑞士馆

Confooderatio Helvetica
瑞士联邦

建筑设计：Netwerch AG
项目面积：4 433 平方米

Architectural Design: Netwerch AG
Project Area: 4,433 m²

瑞士馆设计强调了全球食物资源的稀缺性。这个临时展馆由五幢独立建筑组成，每栋建筑都装满了瑞士当地产品并可供游客带走。然而，这里的食品虽然可以任取，但不会持续添加。也就是说，每名游客的拿取量都决定着后来的游客是否还能拿到，或能够拿到多少。这就意味着索取太多的游客会剥夺了他人获取食物的平等权利。通过这样的方式，游客可以借此反思自己的消费行为。

展馆建筑面积为4 443平方米，运用了工业元素和瑞士传统的木质平台和人字形屋顶元素。游客通过一个坡道进入中央抬升的平台，这里是接待区，为参观者提供咨询、售票等服务。项目还设置了音乐会舞台、商店、餐饮设施和VIP休息区等。

Switzerland, the first country to confirm its involvement in Expo Milano 2015, has presented its pavilion for the international event, a design that highlights the limited nature of worldwide food resources. The temporary structure comprises five individual towers that are each filled with local food produce that visitors can take away. However, the reserves are finite meaning that guests who take an excessive amount deprive others of the same right to food. As the units are emptied the platform upon which the structure stands is lowered, presenting the public with a visual representation of their consumption habits.

The 4,443 m² pavilion brings together industrial elements and vernacular swiss tradition with wooden terraces and gabled roofs that allude to mountain villages. Visitors approach via a ramp that leads to the centrally raised plinth, where a reception area provides visitor information and ticket sales. A stage for concerts, a shop, dining facilities and VIP lounge area are also incorporated within the scheme.

Ce n'è
per
tutti?

BELGIUM PAVILION
比利时馆

Belgium's conviviality has a sustainable future
永续未来的比利时宴乐

建筑设计：P. Genard & Asociados, Marc Belderbos
项目面积：2 717 平方米

Architectural Design: P.Genard & Asociados, Marc Belderbos
Project Area: 2,717 m²

BELGIUM

BENVENUTO
BIENVENUE
WELKOM
WILLKOMMEN
WELCOME

BELGIAN FRIES
BELGIUM

比利时馆的整个设计强调环境的可持续发展，技术的创新和民族的认同。从建筑总体到布景细节以及食物的呈现，场馆在设计上将这些元素统一连贯地表达出来。比利时馆大量使用可循环利用材料，三个展厅中的两个阳光玻璃“温室”和一个黑暗“地窖”，由一个玻璃双螺旋形式楼梯串联。参观者可循序了解比利时的生态农场，以及目前尚处于实验室阶段的未来农业技术。
谈到比利时文化，不得不提她古老的饮食传统。高品质的比利时巧克力，炸薯条，还有传统的比利时啤酒将供游客们逐一品尝，由未来农业技术生产出来的创新食品也会与比利时的传统食物一起呈现在游客面前。通过了解这些食物以及它们的生产，参观者也就同时了解了比利时在生态保护，城市发展以及食物创新技术方面取得的成就。

Belgium Pavilion highlights Belgium's environmental sustainability, technological innovation and national identity. The aim is to express the theme of Expo Milano 2015 at every level: from the architecture to the details of its scenography, and the range of food on offer, to give an integrated, coherent response to the vital issues under investigation. Belgium Pavilion employs enomous eco-recyclable materials.
A double helix glass stair connects two glass “greenhouses”and a dark “cellarage”in three halls respectively. Along the stairway, visitors will progressively look around Belgian Eco-farm and futuristic agricultural technology under experiments.

The culture of Belgium and its regions, plus its age-old culinary traditions, have not been forgotten. A diverse range of high-quality products such as Belgian chocolate and Belgian fries, as well as traditional Belgian beers will be proposed in a warm, friendly setting. The most innovative products from alternative technologies sit alongside these traditional products. Visitors will therefore learn about the key themes of the Expo, such as ecology and intensive urban development, but will also be attracted by Belgium's welcoming culture and its innovative expertise in food production.

critical
situation
tropical rainforest
and woodland
45

URBAN
AGRICULTURE
FOOD CULTURE
& GASTRONOMY
FOOD SAFETY
MANAGEMENT
year
2015

The
Belgian
BEER BAR

Food.be
Small country. Great food.

We
Own
Nearly
1250

URBAN
FOOD CULTURE & GASTRONOMY
year
20

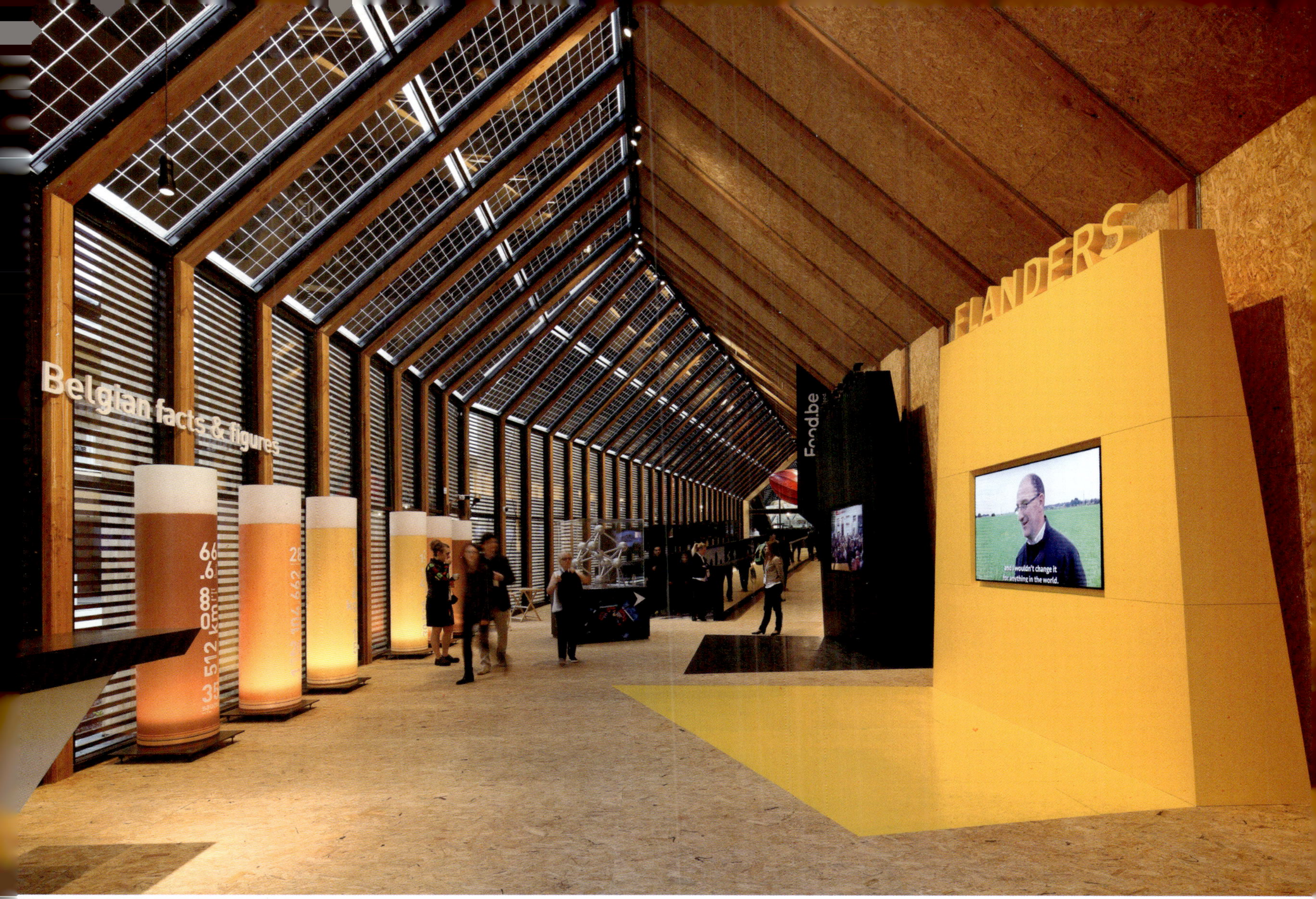

Belgian facts & figures
Food.be
FLANDERS 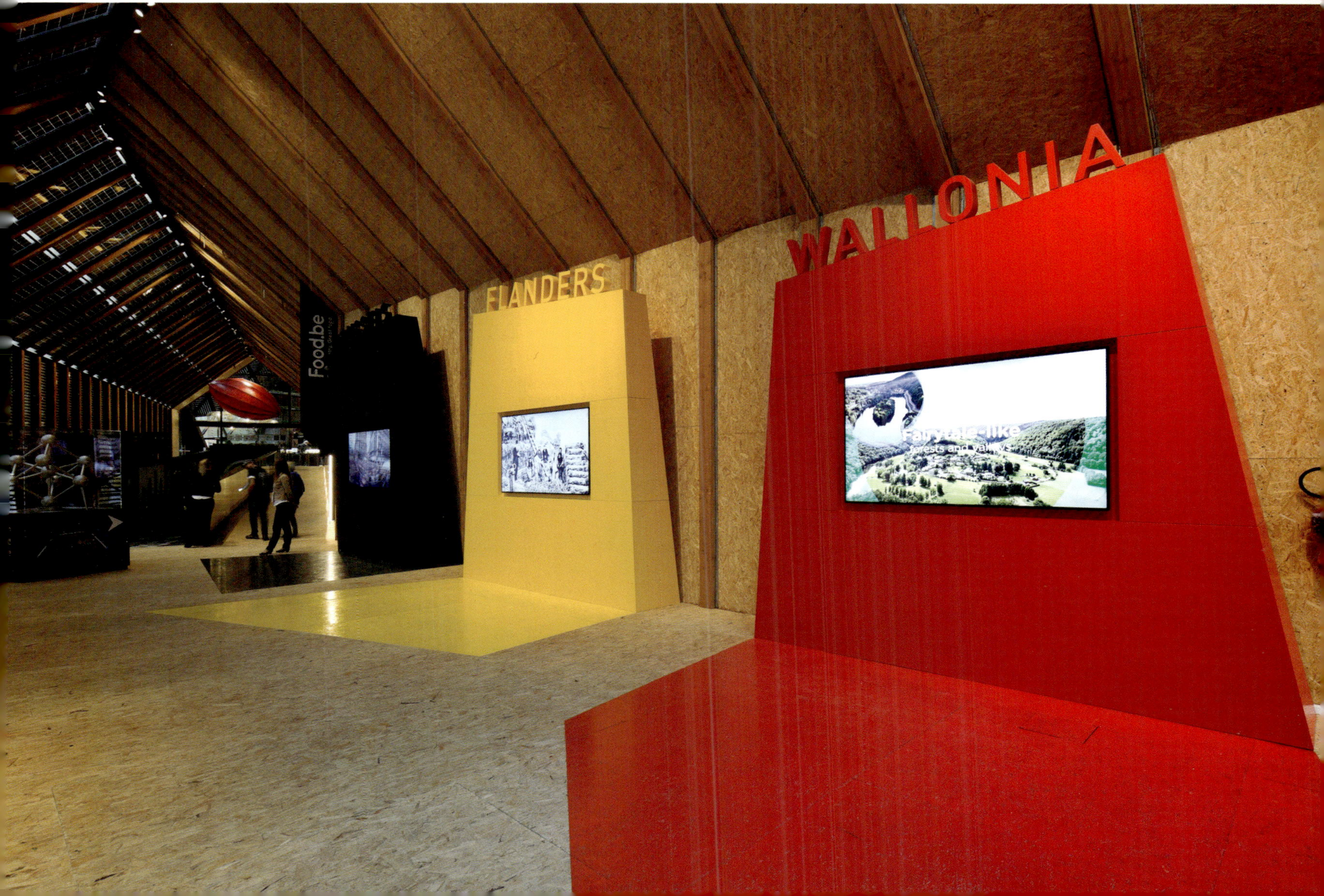
WALLONIA

HOLY SEE PAVILION
梵蒂冈馆

Not only Bread Alone. At the Lord's Table with all Mankind
上帝的餐桌供全人类享用

建筑设计：Quattro Associati / 项目面积：747 平方米

Architectural Design: Quattro Associati / Project Area: 747 m²

梵蒂冈馆在白色的外立面上用13种语言各镶嵌着两句话，这其中用到了中文，它们分别是：“人的生活不能只靠饼”和“求你今天赏给我们日常的粮食”。这两句话富含深意，启发人们思考。馆内空间则像一个大餐厅。这是一个理想的交互空间，它提供了一处让我们探索日常生活和满足不同饮食文化背景而创造的共同空间。馆内的墙面上有一组组图片，有些是固定的照片，有些则是变化的投影。这些图片传递出来的讯息引发我们对“全球无差异化”进行思考。

The Holy See Pavilion welcomes visitors with two phrases translated into 13 languages and displayed on the outer walls of the pavilion: “Not by bread alone” and “Give us this day our daily bread” which is meaningful and thought-provoking.

The interior of the pavilion is set out as a large refectory: it is interactive and offers an itinerary exploring the tables of our everyday lives and the bond of solidarity that is created in order to satisfy the different forms of hunger among humanity. On the side walls, there is firstly a series of photographic images, fixed or projected, that reinforce condemnation of the “globalization of indifference”.

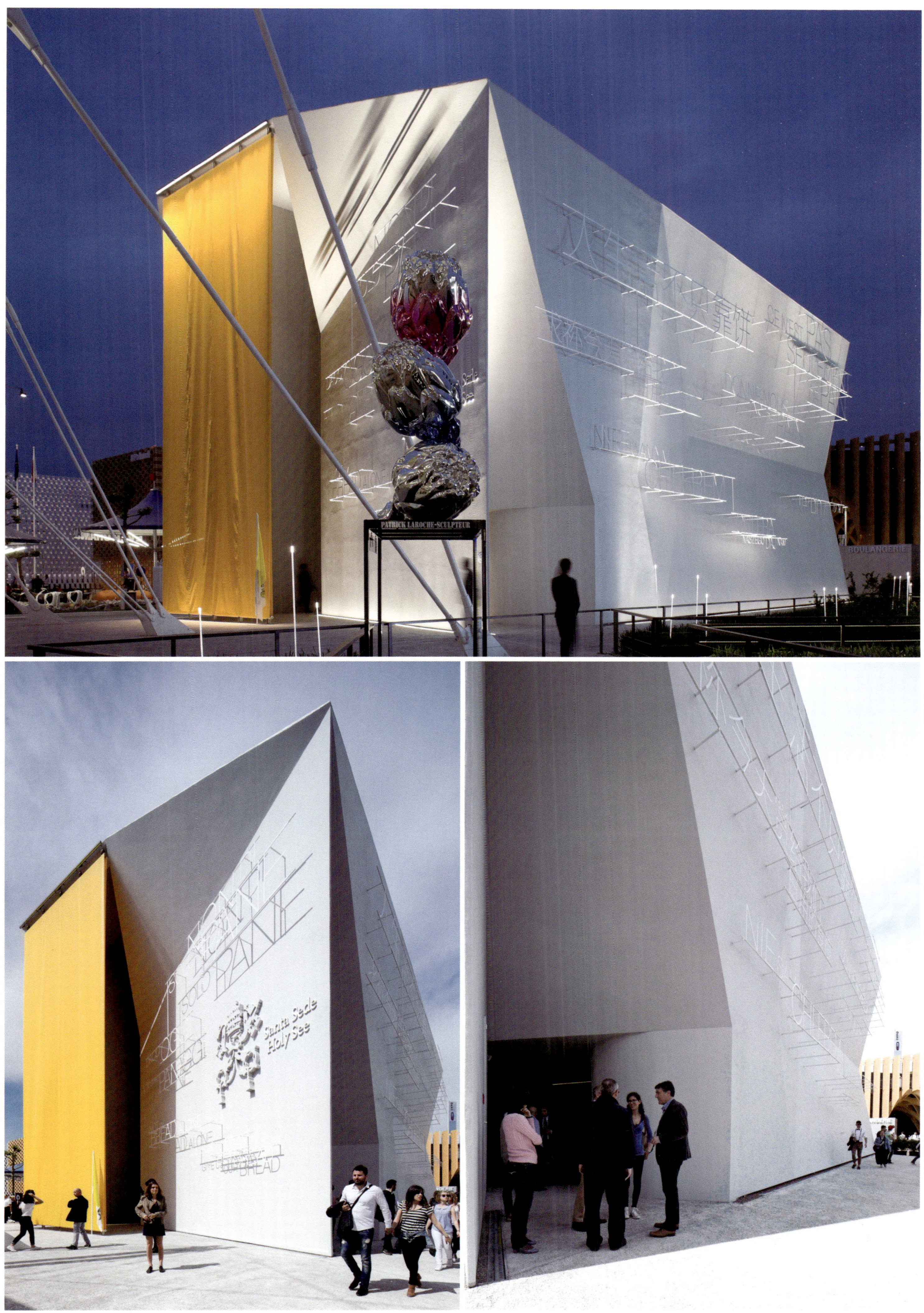
PATRICK LAROCHE-SCULPTEUR
BOULANGERIE
Santa Sede
Holy See

POLAND PAVILION
波兰馆

A Treasure Box
百宝箱

建筑设计：Piotr Musialowski, 2PM Studio / 项目面积：2 369 平方米

Architectural Design: Piotr Musiałowski, 2PM Studio / Project Area: 2,369 m²

波兰馆造型简单，是一个四四方方的木盒的形状，远看像一个藏着宝藏的宝箱。镂空的结构呼应世博会生态保护和简约的宗旨。

波兰馆的经典之处在于它有一个神秘的花园。设计使得展馆变成了一座迷宫，而花园就是迷宫的核心。花园里种满了苹果树，苹果林被对面的银镜做的休息区反射出来，延展出无限的空间，让人联想起波兰广袤的农业景象。

波兰展馆前的露天市场被塑造成了万花筒的视觉效果。游客走在世博会主干道上都会被这纷繁的景象所吸引。大家纷纷来到这个丰富多彩的波兰集市，并不自觉地被神奇的通道引入波兰展馆内。

在离开展馆前，游客可以在展馆内所设的商店里购买到波兰各地的传统特色商品，也可以在布置得既浪漫又愉悦的餐馆里品尝到地道的波兰美食。

The Pavilion is a simple, rectangular solid wooden box, hiding valuable "gems" within its interior spaces. The openwork structure refers to the ecological and simple form of apple boxes.

One of the attractions of the Pavilion is its magical garden. The design creates a symbolic maze, with a magical garden as its focal point – a Polish orchard, full of apple trees. The hidden garden becomes a resting place on the other side of the mirror. An apple orchard reflected in infinite space is clearly associated with the Polish agriculture.

On the piazza in front of the Pavilion will be featured scenery that combine to represent a solid "kaleidoscope" art installation, leaving the Decumanus to visit the Pavilion. Encouraged by its many attractions, vistors can see the Polish Marchés – and discover the "mysterious gap" at the entrance to Poland's Pavilion.

Along the corridor that leads into the Pavilion, visitors come to a magical garden symbolizing an unusual and intriguing Poland and through its center follow a narrow, winding path interspersed at irregular intervals by apple trees.

On leaving this interactive and fun space, visitors can find an on-site store to browse Poland's regional products. The last attraction of the Pavilion is a restaurant in which visitors can taste delicious Polish cuisine in a romantic and pleasant setting that certainly makes this one of the best and most relaxing places to be.

#Poland

#Poland

AUSTRIA PAVILION
奥地利馆

Breathe. Austria
呼吸·奥地利

设计公司：Penda, Alex Daxböck / 项目面积： 1 910 平方米

Design Company: Penda, Alex Daxböck / Project Area: 1,910 m²

BREATHE AUSTRIA
EXPLORE THE NATURE
BENVENUTO! RESPIRA & GODITI
IL PADIGLIONE AUSTRIA
D' ATMOSFERA
FOREST
BAR D'ATMOS

奥地利馆“出自你手”的设计灵感来自于建筑公司penda与alex daxböck的合作。他们的设计构想获得了米兰2015年世博会的第一名。以“给养地球”为主题，奥地利馆让参观者有机会在场馆内亲手种下种子，并期待它们的发育成熟。奥地利馆将高品质就地种植的概念展示在场馆的建筑结构中，当世博会结束时，奥地利馆将变成一座有机食物的城堡。

奥地利的展馆外部框架高3.6米，采用模式化网格系统，这样方便容纳更多参观者，同时也有利于后期的拆装和重组。

随着种子的发芽，生长，直到成熟结果，奥地利馆在为期7个月的展期中将不断变化，最终木质框架将慢慢被蔬菜，水果和草本植物填满。

在展馆入口，参观者将拿到一盆植物，他们可以把这些植物种在沿途的坡道上，坡道的一部分是向外开放的，沿着主结构框架这些植物将按照自己的生长周期开始自由生长。不同植物生根发芽的全过程将慢慢呈现，采摘也会在后期展示出来。在坡道的末尾将会有一个餐厅把已完成了整个生长周期的食物进行烹煮，加上同样“出自你手”的奥地利的特色调料，制作出一份份传统奥地利美食，其中葡萄架和杜松子就是不可或缺的美食搭配。

奥地利展馆创造出一座森林公园，平均每小时能释放出62.5千克新鲜氧气来代替过滤器和空调。它能同时容纳1 800名参观者，并提供舒适的气温环境。这个巨大的绿肺展馆源源不断地提供氧气，吸收二氧化碳，给参观者一个清新的世界。同时，奥地利馆也给出了一个很好的范例，展示出造林政策在有限绿地空间的城市里所带来的各种益处。

The design for the austrian pavilion ‘naturally yours’ by architectural firm penda in collaboration with alex daxböck has won 1st runner up for the milan expo 2015, themed ‘feeding the planet’. The winning idea provides visitors with the opportunity to plant seeds and then directly eat the food grown on the pavilion. Based on Austria’s high quality, locally grown produce the concept for the pavilion lies within its structural framework – at the end of the expo it will be fully taken over by organic food.

At the beginning of the expo the 3.6 m structural grid will be fully exposed, the pavilion will constantly change during the 7 months due to the seeding, growing and harvesting of the plants, and its timber frames eventually are filled with seeds of vegetables, fruits or herbs.

The pavilion is based on a modular grid system, which enables it to flexibly adapt to increasing numbers of visitors and also easily deconstructed and reused afterwards.

At the entrance people will be given pots to plant along a ramp that is partly open to the outside. Running through the main structure, it will be lined with local plants and seeds to help communicate the full lifecycle of growing food. Examples of different ways natural produce is treated while it grows, how it is picked and harvested will be on display. At the end of the ramp a restaurant will complete the full lifecycle of food with the ingredients combined to make traditional austrian cuisine accompanied by wine or schnapps.

The pavilion creates a small scale Austrian forest that provides 62.5 kg of fresh oxygen every hour, without filters or conditioners, which is enough for 1,800 people in an ideal climate, providing wellness and absorbing CO_2. It is a green lung that induces the desire for a cleaner world, offering a model for urban practices that can ensure a higher quality of life and demonstrating the benefits of a reforestation policy against the global decline of green areas.

Austrija
Дишай Австрия
lélegezzen Austria
nefes Avusturya
Αυστρία
WHEN YOU TAKE A BREATH,
humeka Autriche
humeka Austria
fresh air for the planet
O_2
produces
62,5 kg O_2/h
32°C
43.200 m2 leaf surface
smell
EVAPOTRANSPIRATION
comfortable climate
CO_2
humidity
26°C
PHOTOSYNTHESIS
circulation
1800 visitors /h
A hybride?
Yes, a teamplay of nature and technology!
HYBRIDE
PV modules
41 kWp
wooden shell
48 fog nossels
27 ventilators
12 fog stela
TECHNOLOGY
+
H_2O
O_2
CO_2
NATURE
12600 plants
54 trees
2550 m² soil
10,6 to microorganism

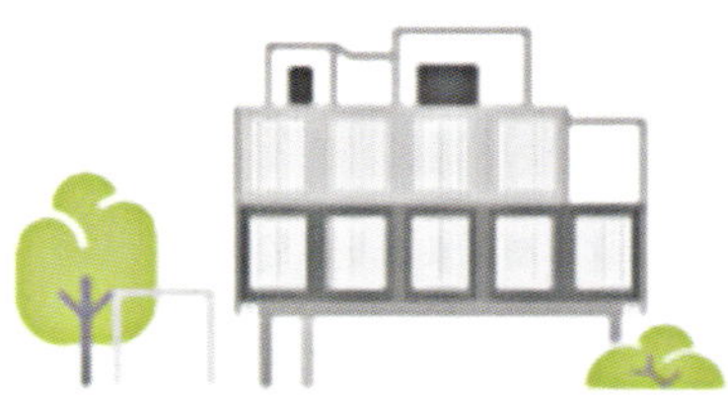

CZECH REPUBLIC PAVILION
捷克馆

Laboratory of Life
生命实验室

建筑设计: Chybik + Kristof Associated Architects
设计团队: Ondrej Chybik, Michal Kristof, Krystof Foltyn, Pavel Hruza, Vojtech Kouril, Veronika Mikulkova, Radim Musil
项目面积: 3 200 平方米

Architects: Chybik + Kristof Associated Architects
Design Team: Ondrej Chybik, Michal Kristof, Krystof Foltyn, Pavel Hruza, Vojtech Kouril, Veronika Mikulkova, Radim Musil
Project Area: 3,200 m^2

Republic

Czech Republic

以水作为本次捷克参与米兰世博会展览的核心元素对捷克人来说是一件顺理成章的事。多条著名的河流流经捷克境内，比如易北河，奥德河还有多瑙河，同时捷克还拥有丰富的温泉。20世纪30年代，捷克建造的游泳池更是闻名全球。另外很重要的一点是，捷克在净水技术方面在世界领先。

为迎合此次大会的能源保护主题，捷克馆的设计就围绕捷克人民与水生生不息的关系，在建筑中央设置了一个公共游泳池，泳池的设计展示了捷克在水资源管理与使用方面的创新，以及生物化学和纳米技术对水源净化的研究成果。纯白色的外观让捷克馆看起来格外清新简明。建筑首层有一间餐厅和一个小型圆形剧场；展馆的二层也有一间餐厅还有许多展示空间让参观者了解大自然，了解我们所生活的世界；屋顶是公共绿化平台，在这里参观者可以休息并欣赏这座纯白建筑的美丽。

捷克展馆各个矩形模块将在捷克本国预制，运往米兰后再进行组装。为遮挡展馆建筑的玻璃外墙，各模块将包裹在垂直遮光栅格屏中。展览结束后，捷克馆各模块将被赋予新的使命。低层的模块建筑可继续作为餐厅使用，而上层部分将改建为公共浴池，幼儿园或其他有用的建筑。

The Czech Republic pavilion makes special reference to Water, which is not altogether surprising, since the country features three important rivers, the Elbe, Oder, and the Danube, as well as a number of thermal springs. The country also boasts many impressive swimming pools constructed in the 1930s. Last but not least, the Czech Republic is a world leader in water-purification technology.

Responding to the Expo's energy conservation theme, the Czech Republic pavilion is centered around the Czech Republic's unique relationship to water, featuring a public swimming pool at the center of the design and presenting the latest progress in nanotechnology for water purification. The clean, simple design also includes a restaurant and a small amphitheater on the ground floor, a second restaurant and exhibition spaces on the first floor, and a public green roof.

The modular design also takes the closing of the Expo into account; the individual modules can be removed and transported back to the Czech Republic for reuse, and the leftover structure in Milan can be repurposed into a permanent public baths, a kindergarten, or other useful building.

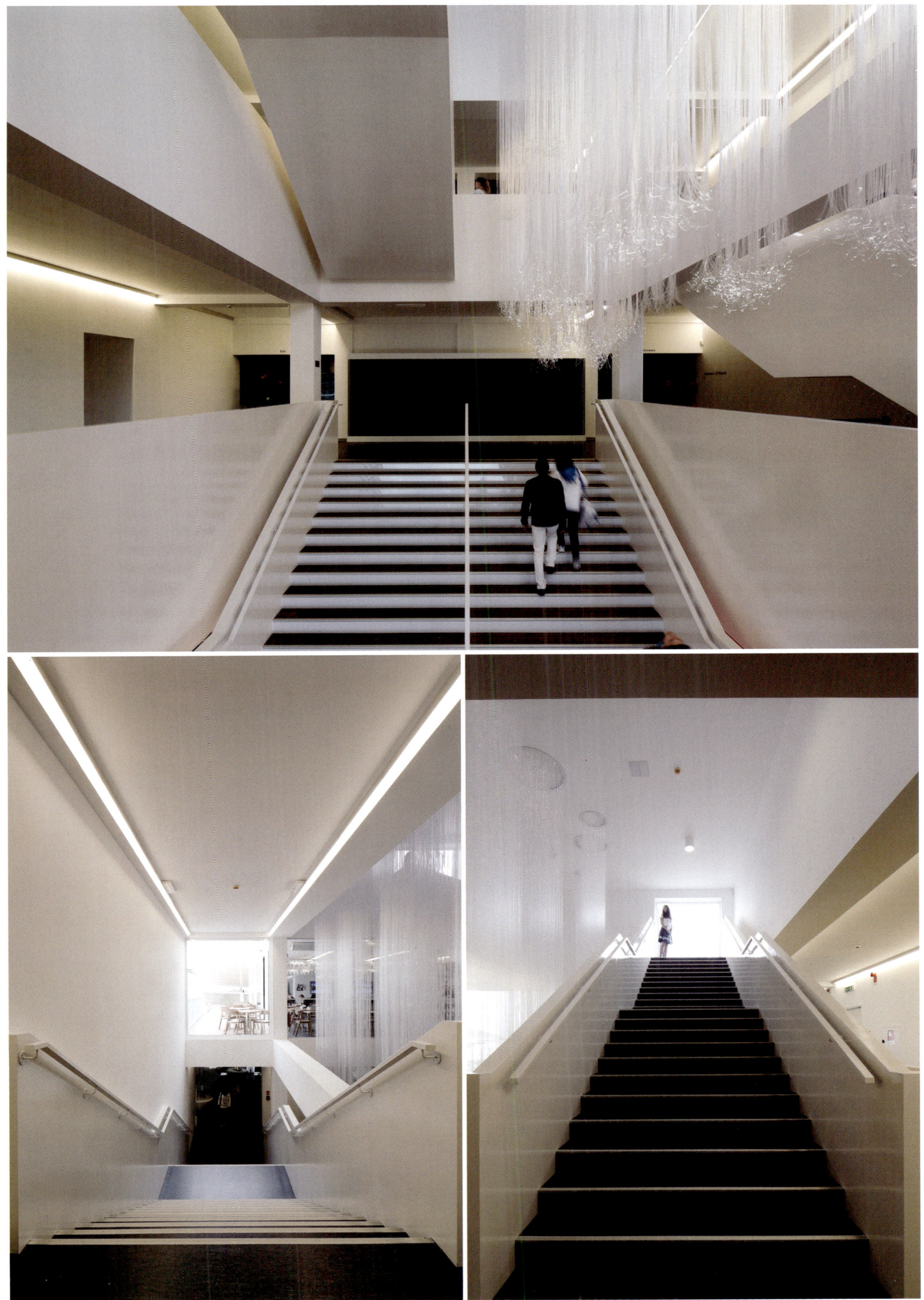

Pilsner Urquell
TANK BEER
1842
TANKOVNA

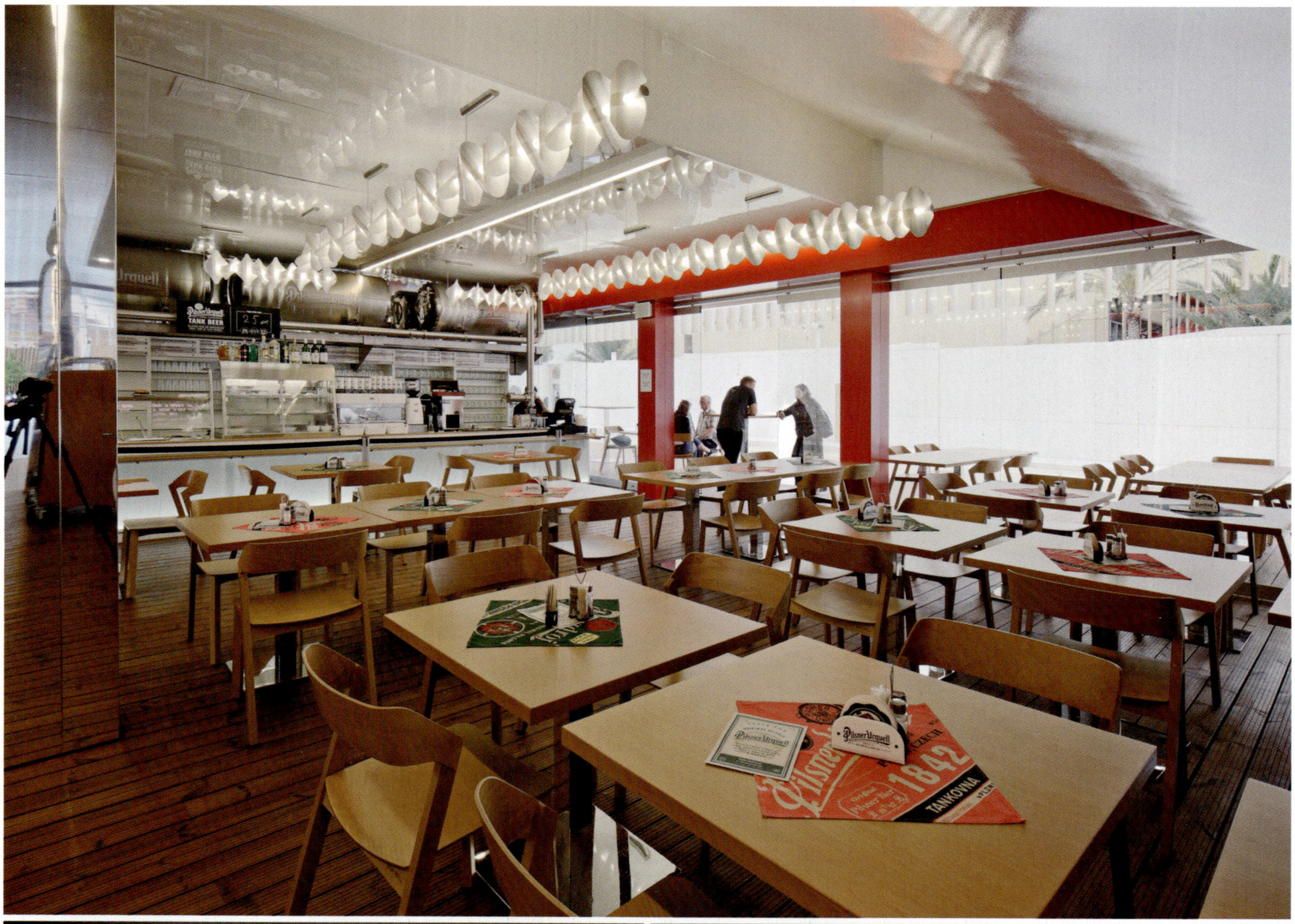

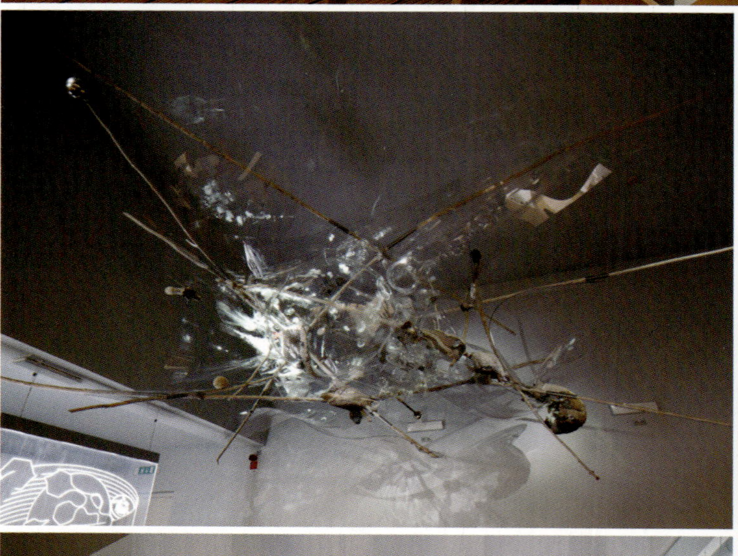

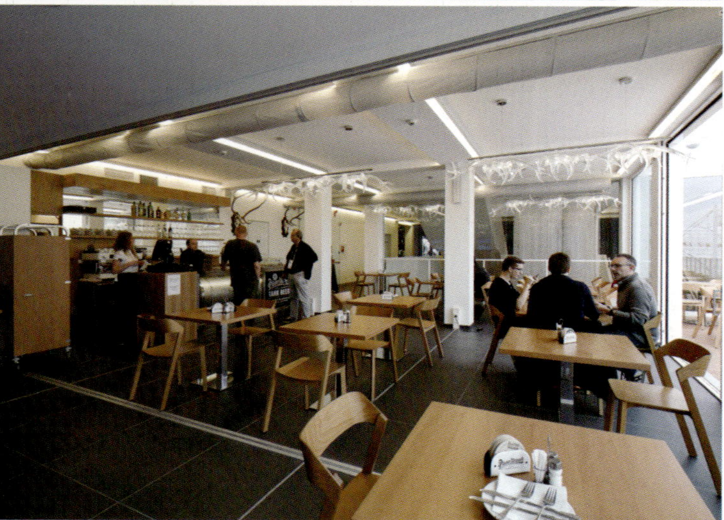

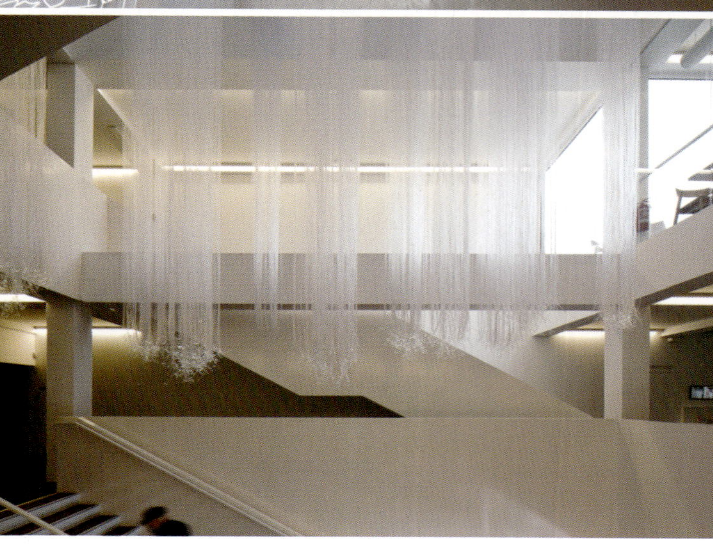

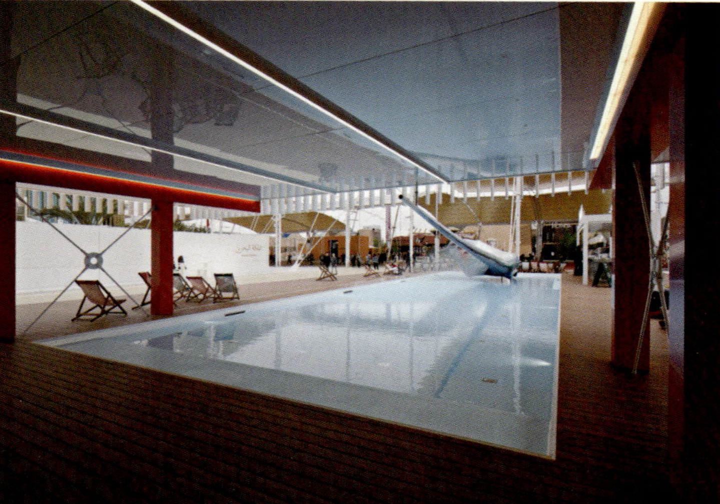

HUNGARY PAVILION
匈牙利馆

From The Purest Sources
取自最纯净的资源

建筑师：Attila Ertsey, Herczeg Ágnes Sándor Sárkány / 项目面积：1 910 平方米

Architects: Attila Ertsey, Herczeg Ágnes Sándor Sárkány / Project Area: 1,910 m²

匈牙利馆占地1 910平方米，共有三层。它的设计造型（包括一个谷仓，一些筒仓和马厩）和建筑材料突出了典型的匈牙利风格。设计综合了各方面的因素，包括20世纪中期开始盛行的有机建筑及匈牙利的当地建筑传统，对自然法则的理解以及人类与宇宙的关系。而场馆中心的设计灵感来源于诺亚方舟，它是生命和救赎的象征。

匈牙利馆的两端放置了萨满鼓，体现出匈牙利古老的根基和与自然的神秘关系。在萨满鼓上装饰着“生命之树”的古老象征，里边流动的清水代表着匈牙利的精神，也体现了它的地热特点。进入展馆后，参观者能通过一系列展览和活动了解匈牙利的食物传统，匈牙利与意大利的历史渊源以及匈牙利现代文化的各方各面。展馆的顶层有一个露天花园，馆外的绿地上栽植了33种不同种类的水果、蔬菜和草药。

大部分的建筑材料都是可回收再利用的，比如木材，胶合板和纤维板。在世博会结束后，匈牙利馆将被拆除并被带去松博特海伊，并在老的Hussar Barracks景点重新组装，并将其用作新创意遗产保护和价值发展中心的一个不可或缺的组成部分。

The Hungary Pavilion comprises three floors and covers 1,910 m^2. The shapes and materials composing the main features are typically Hungarian (including a barn, silos and stables). They have been designed according to the principles of organic architecture that was developed in the mid-twentieth century and is based on local traditions, the understanding of the laws of nature, and on the celebration of the relationship between man and the universe. The central area of the pavilion is inspired by Noah's Ark , the symbol of salvation of living beings.

The two end points take the form of shamanic drums, representing Hungary's ancient roots and highlighting its mystical relationship with nature. The drums are adorned with the ancient symbol of the “tree of life” that flows with fresh water, being the Hungarian one celebrated for its thermal properties. Inside the pavilion visitors can find organized exhibitions and events on topics such as food traditions of the country, the historical relations between Italy and Hungary and other aspects of contemporary Hungarian culture. The top floor houses an open-air garden, and outside the pavilion a green area can be found, planted with 33 kinds of fruits, vegetables and medicinal herbs.

Most of the materials used for construction are renewable (wood, laminated wood, cellulose) and the entire building will be dismantled, reconstructed and re-used as a research center in Hungary.

ROMANIA PAVILION
罗马尼亚馆

Living with Nature
与自然共存

设计方：SC Prospect SRL, Collective East Architects
设计团队：Gabriel Costachescu, Tudor Costachescu, Alexandre Motora, Ioana Nastase, Livia Palmadeala, Horia Tas
项目面积：887平方米

Design: SC Prospect SRL, Collective East Architects
Design Team: Gabriel Costachescu, Tudor Costachescu, Alexandre Motora, Ioana Nastase, Livia Palmadeala, Horia Tas
Project Area: 887 m²

罗马尼亚馆是对坐落在多瑙河洲古老村落的现代诠释，在这里参观者将可探索罗马尼亚的深厚文化，自然食物资源和为可持续发展采取的生态平衡解决方案。随着参观者的深入，一个微缩版的罗马尼亚将慢慢呈现在眼前。

罗马尼亚馆占地887平方米，建筑部分共两层。首层展示的是现代罗马尼亚丰富的自然资源；二层一幢典型罗马尼亚房屋覆盖着芦苇屋顶充分展示了罗马尼亚的建筑传统。在展馆的主入口处是一排类似排箫的巨型篱笆，“罗马尼亚”几个大字嵌入其中，有两层楼高。

罗马尼亚馆展出空间将被划分成8个不同的主题区域：“生物多样性”“文化与绿色能源”以及“水果和蔬菜”在一楼，“文化和传统”“烹饪的艺术”“花园”“门廊与房屋”与餐厅一道设在二楼。

这些区域象征着罗马尼亚的村庄已经超越自然，通过旅游，农业，生态发展和罗马尼亚的饮食来体现自身价值。餐厅里提供的食物素材来自罗马尼亚的各个区域，同时也展现了各区域的独特性。罗马尼亚的民间传说人物Lia（Ciocârlia）将由演员扮演并在全息影像中出现，他将传达来自罗马尼亚的讯息：传统与现代融合并和谐存在于自然之中。

The Romanian pavilion is a contemporary interpretation of a traditional village house situated on the delta of the Danube, where visitors are invited to discover the Country's rich culture, its natural food resources, and its ecological solutions adopted to promote sustainable development. It has been designed to provide a unique experience that is finely attuned to the micro-universe of Romania, gradually revealed over the course of the visit.

The Pavilion, which occupies a total space of 887 m², is structured on two levels: the ground floor, a present-day interpretation of the richness and variety of the natural resources of Romania, and the first floor, dedicated to tradition, represented by a typical Romanian house with a roof made of reeds. A wooden palisade, which resembles a large pan flute containing the word "Romania", marks the main entrance.

The exhibitions are grouped in eight areas. On the ground floor "Biodiversity", "Culture and Green Energy" and "Fruit and Vegetables" are on the ground floor; "Culture and Tradition", "Culinary Arts", "Garden", "Porch" and "House" where the restaurant is situated are on the first floor.

These areas represent - beyond a relationship with nature - the symbol of the "Romanian village," which has the ability to revive and restore its values through tourism, agriculture, ecological produce and Romanian cuisine. The restaurant offers dishes and produce from different parts of the Country, presenting the uniqueness of each region. The unifying symbol of this experience is Lia (Ciocârlia), the Romanian folklore character who, played by actors or represented by a hologram, spreads the bright message of Romania, of a fusion of tradition and modernity living in harmony with nature.

IRELAND PAVILION
爱尔兰馆

Origin Green Ireland; Working with Nature
绿色爱尔兰 与自然协作

建筑设计：爱尔兰公共工程办公室
项目面积：1 175 平方米

Architectural Design: Office of Public Works Ireland
Project Area: 1,175 m²

爱尔兰馆采用当地木材作为环保材料，以此来保证较低的碳排放量。就如爱尔兰人的食物由人工精致而作并一直传承下来却不失现代标准，爱尔兰馆的设计正如其所制之食，精致、环保且具现代性。爱尔兰偏居欧洲东隅，曲线的展馆立于一汪池水中，像极一条木质小船航于水面。清澈的池水和曲面墙体的微小空隙把意大利的炙热阳光雕塑成精致轻盈的光影。屋顶的绿色花圃可供游客一览整个世博展美景。

一进入爱尔兰展馆，参观者将开启一段难忘旅程：穿越爱尔兰的乡野以及原始的大西洋领地。各种爱尔兰美景分别在五块电子屏幕上展示着，体现了爱尔兰土地上的各种美以及难得一见的景致。爱尔兰人对自然的守护，以及爱尔兰的高品质自然环境，这种高品质是其发源于绿地的最好证明。五块电子屏幕分别置于象征爱尔兰不同地域风貌的景观区，展现着爱尔兰各地优越的粮食生长自然条件。

参观者走出爱尔兰馆便进入爱尔兰活动广场，此处闹中取静，是一处绝佳露天活动场所，这里展示着爱尔兰的文化，传统，现代音乐和设计。

The Ireland Pavilion is using local wood for a sustainable design with a very low carbon footprint. In the same way that Irish food is both handcrafted, sustainable and made to modern standards, the Ireland Pavilion is an architectural abstraction of these same goals. Ireland is a lush green island on the edge of Europe. The curved shaped pavilion is set within a water pool with a sail like wood wall of boat like construction. Delicate and etheareal light is modulated by the water pool and small gaps in the curved wall, such that the strong Italian light is softened like Irish light. A green roof garden gives views over the whole Expo site.

On entering the Ireland Pavilion, visitors embark on an unforgettable journey through the Irish countryside and along its wild Atlantic coast. Five screens present a choreographed sequence that illustrates different aspects of Ireland's beauty, her unmistakable landscapes and the care for nature and attention to quality that are the hallmarks of the Irish Origin Green programme. Each of the screens rests on an evocation of the Irish landscape, which contributes so much to Ireland's natural advantage in food productivity.

Above visitors' heads, a sculptural installation shot through with light represents the famously variable Irish weather and the beauty of the continuously changing skies-which contribute an important ingredient to Ireland's distinctive agricultural landscape.

ÉIRE
IRLANDA
ÉIRE
IRLANDA

BELARUS PAVILION
白俄罗斯馆

The Wheel of Life
生命之轮

建筑设计：Kola Zhitsya / 项目面积：1 147 平方米

Architectural Design: Kola Zhitsya / Project Area: 1,147 m²

代表白俄罗斯参与2015年米兰世博会的白俄罗斯馆，名为“生命之轮”，该展馆代表并促进了该国的主要自然资源：面包、盐和水。该展馆被设计成一个种满草皮的山丘状构筑物，一个轮子从中间切开，形成缺口，作为主要入口路径。这种穿越景观的交通流线，就似一条穿境而过的河流，大型水轮高居其上，成为该展馆的动态象征。展馆内展出的内容主要为未来要面对的农业问题和国家发展策略。

在整个展馆的中心，从地面隆起的巨大引水轮制造了一挂瀑布把展馆分成两边。主展区通过交互式显示器和LED屏幕展示着一组组不同的盐井地，而另外一边则作为展示白俄罗斯历史，文化和传统的空间。

景观构筑物使用了木框架结构，光线洒落并照入室内。连绵不断的地形指引游客走进长满草的小山丘。展区内设有开放座位区，为游客提供了吃饭和休息的场所，并提供可饮用水。游客还有机会品尝白俄罗斯的特色菜肴和饮料。

For its participation in Expo Milano 2015, the republic of belarus presents a pavilion titled, 'wheel of life', which represents and promotes the country's primary natural resources: bread, salt, and water. The design is organized as a constructed grassy hill, with a slice cutting through the center producing the primary pathway. This circulation through the landscape resembles a river passing through the landscape, while a large water wheel is elevated above to serve as a dynamic symbol for the structure. Galleries beneath the curving forms present content aimed at agricultural issues and the country's strategies for the future.

At the center, a large elevated water wheel creates a waterfall at the ground level, which directs circulation to either of the galleries. The main area features an arrangement of diverse salts well information displayed on interactive monitors and LED screens. On the other side of the pathway, a secondary presentation space is dedicated to the history, culture, and traditions of belarus.

The constructed landscape structure is composed of a wood frame, with skylights scattered throughout the surface providing daylight to the interiors. The continuity of the terrain allows visitors to walk upon the grassy hills. The exhibition areas are complemented by an open seating area providing an area for eating and relaxation, and featuring a spring of potable water. Visitors have the opportunity to taste belarusian drinks and dishes.

ESTONIA PAVILION
爱沙尼亚馆

Gallery of
艺术展廊

建筑设计：Kadarik Tüür Arhitektid / 项目面积：1 010平方米

Architectural Design: Kadarik Tüür Arhitektid / Project Area: 1,010 m^2

GALLERY OF
ESTONIA
GALLERY OF
ESTONIA
GALLERY OF
ESTONIA

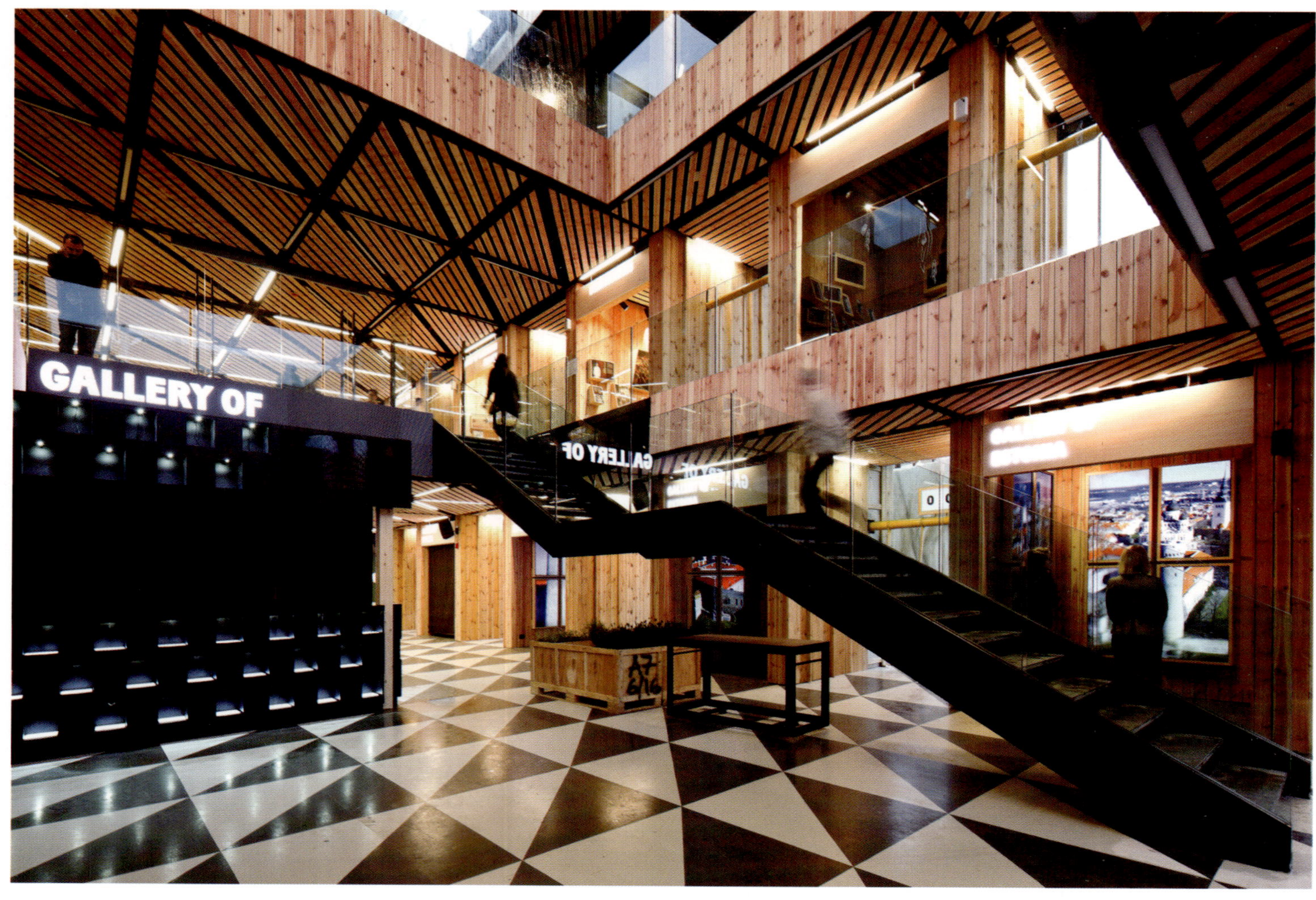

爱沙尼亚馆“艺术展廊”的设计将着重体现这个年轻的北欧国家充满活力和迅猛的发展态势。展馆由三层层叠木板拼堆而成的一个个“巢箱”空间组成。首层临街一面的巢箱之间嵌有秋千，游客在荡秋千的同时可以把动能转化成电能，这些电能可以供日常所用，如给手机充电，给电灯供电或做其他用途。

展馆首层有六个“巢箱”，分别作为报刊亭，纪念品商店，街边小吃馆等等，让参观者自行去探究关于爱沙尼亚的各方各面。

展馆二层是集中展厅区域。在这里，参观者能了解到爱沙尼亚在各方面取得的成就，其中有一个区域被设置成一处吧台，提供爱沙尼亚的特色美食——黑麦啤酒。

展馆三层种植了北美国家的特色花卉和树木，体现了爱沙尼亚的自然一面。在这一层参观者能观赏到爱沙尼亚的各种鸟禽，并通过隐蔽的摄像机来观察动物们在爱沙尼亚美丽的自然环境中的日常活动。

Estonian pavilion “Gallery of” is designed to introduce it as a young, dynamic and rapidly developing country in northern Europe. The pavilion comprises three floors of shifting wooden blocks stacked on top of one another as modules – ‘nesting boxes’ which together make up the Estonian gallery. It is filled with swings hanging between the boxes. Visitors can transform the kinetic energy created by themselves into electrical energy by using these energy swings on the ground floor and will give people an idea of how much energy is required for simple, everyday things – recharging a phone, turning on a light and more.

On the ground floor will be an Estonian street food restaurant, an information kiosk and a souvenir stand. Six ‘nesting boxes’ will make up a gallery which gives visitors the chance to find out essential information about Estonia.

On the first floor will be an exhibition showcasing fields that are important to Estonia. Here visitors will have the chance to find out all about Estonian achievements and success stories in a range of areas. The first floor will also host a bar dedicated to rye and craft beer – Ryebar: Estonian craft beer and spirits.

The second floor will feature a slice of Estonian nature, including plants and trees characteristic of the Nordic countries. On this floor visitors will also have the chance to find out about Estonian birds and observe the day-to-day lives of animals in Estonian nature through hidden cameras.

GALLERY OF

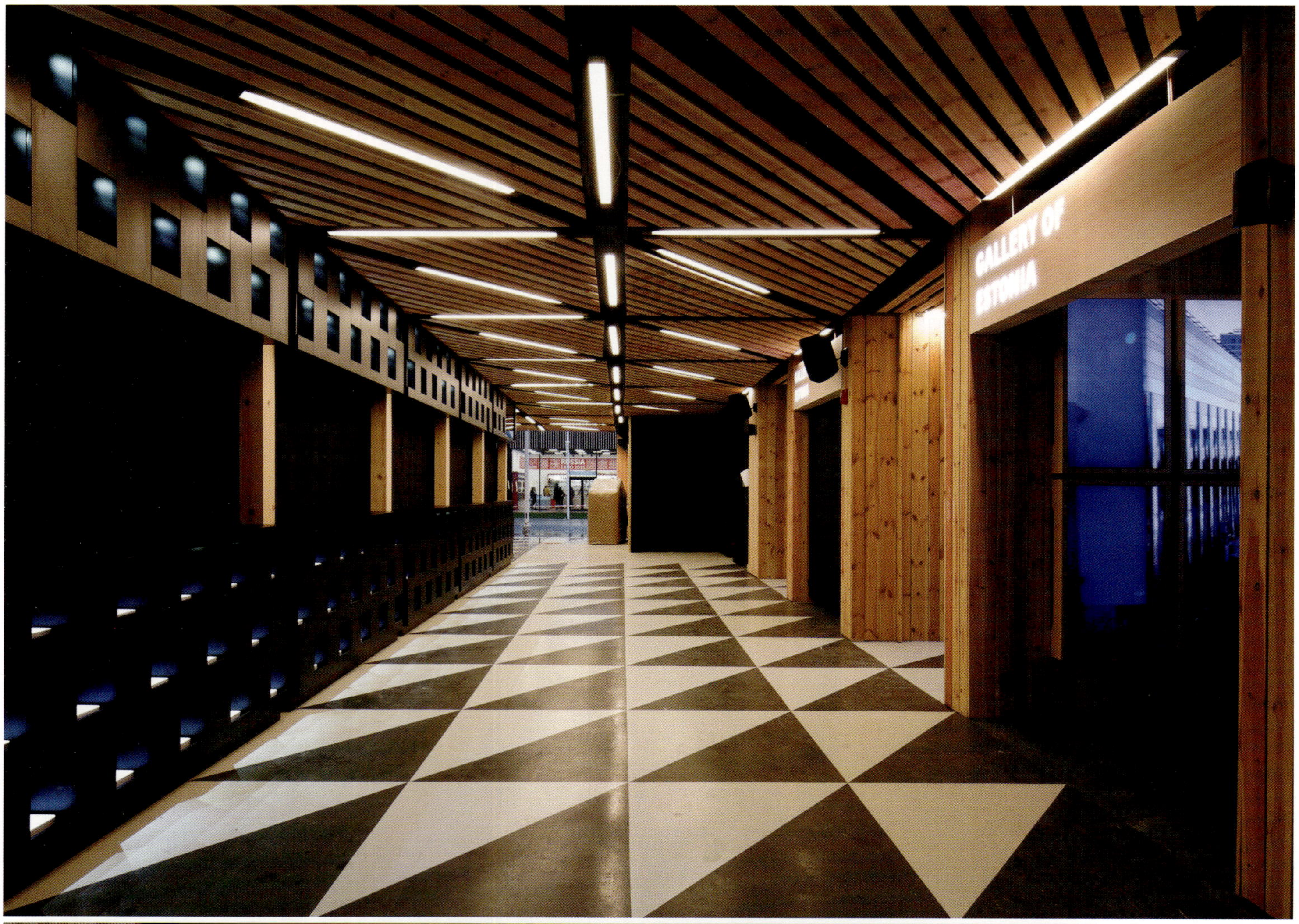
GALLERY OF
ESTONIA

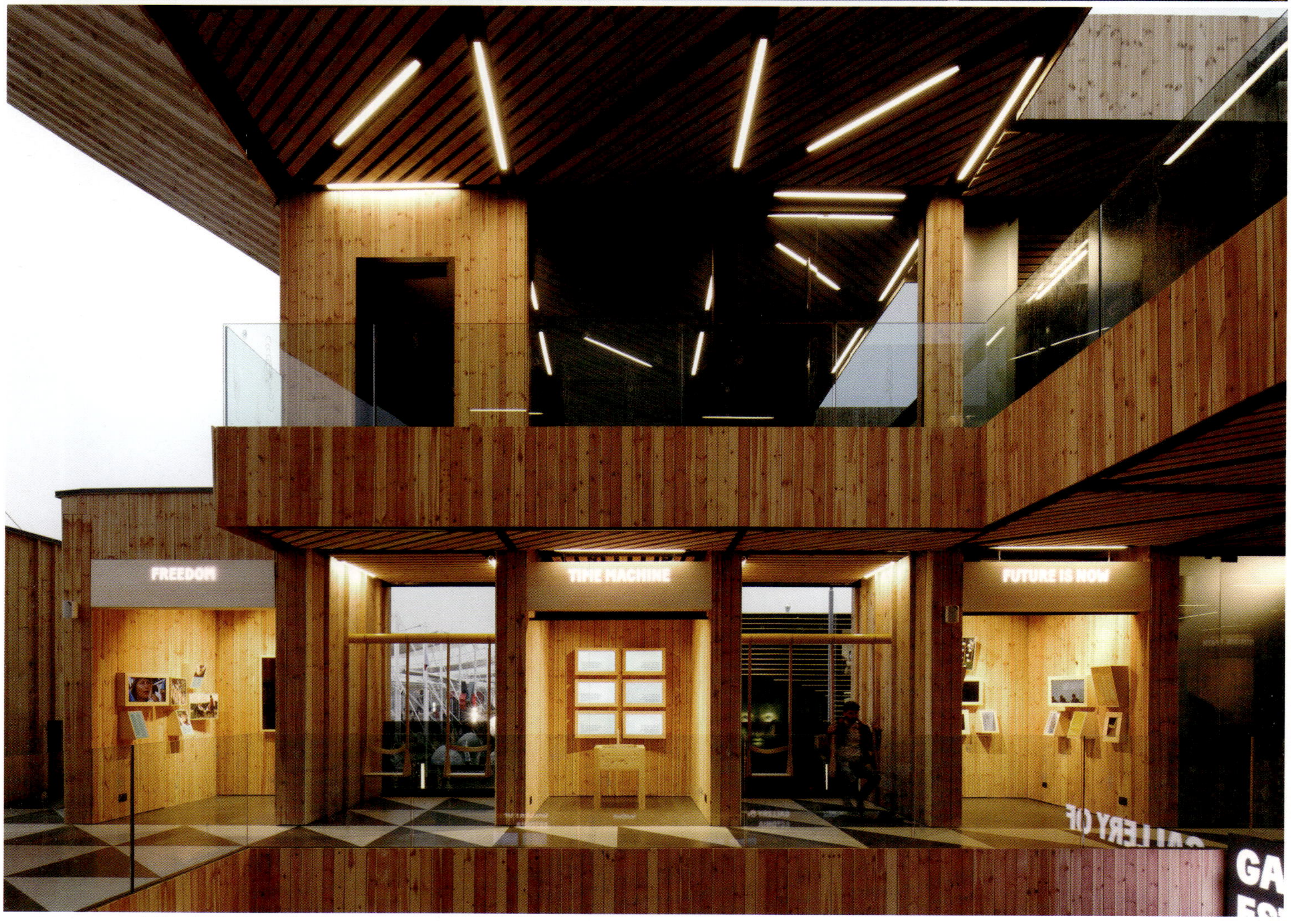
FREEDOM
TIME MACHINE
FUTURE IS NOW

MYSTERIOUS PATH
COAST OF NORTHERN
BEAUTY

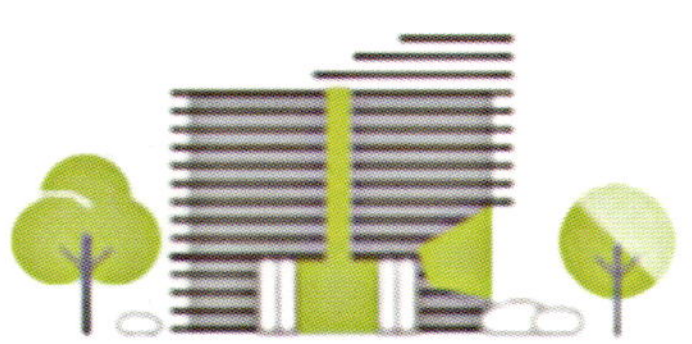

SLOVAKIA PAVILION
斯洛伐克馆

The World in Your Pocket
袖珍世界

建筑设计：Agent ú ra EVKA & Karol K á llay / 项目面积：1 010 平方米

Architectural Design: Agentúra EVKA & Karol Kállay / Project Area: 1,010 m²

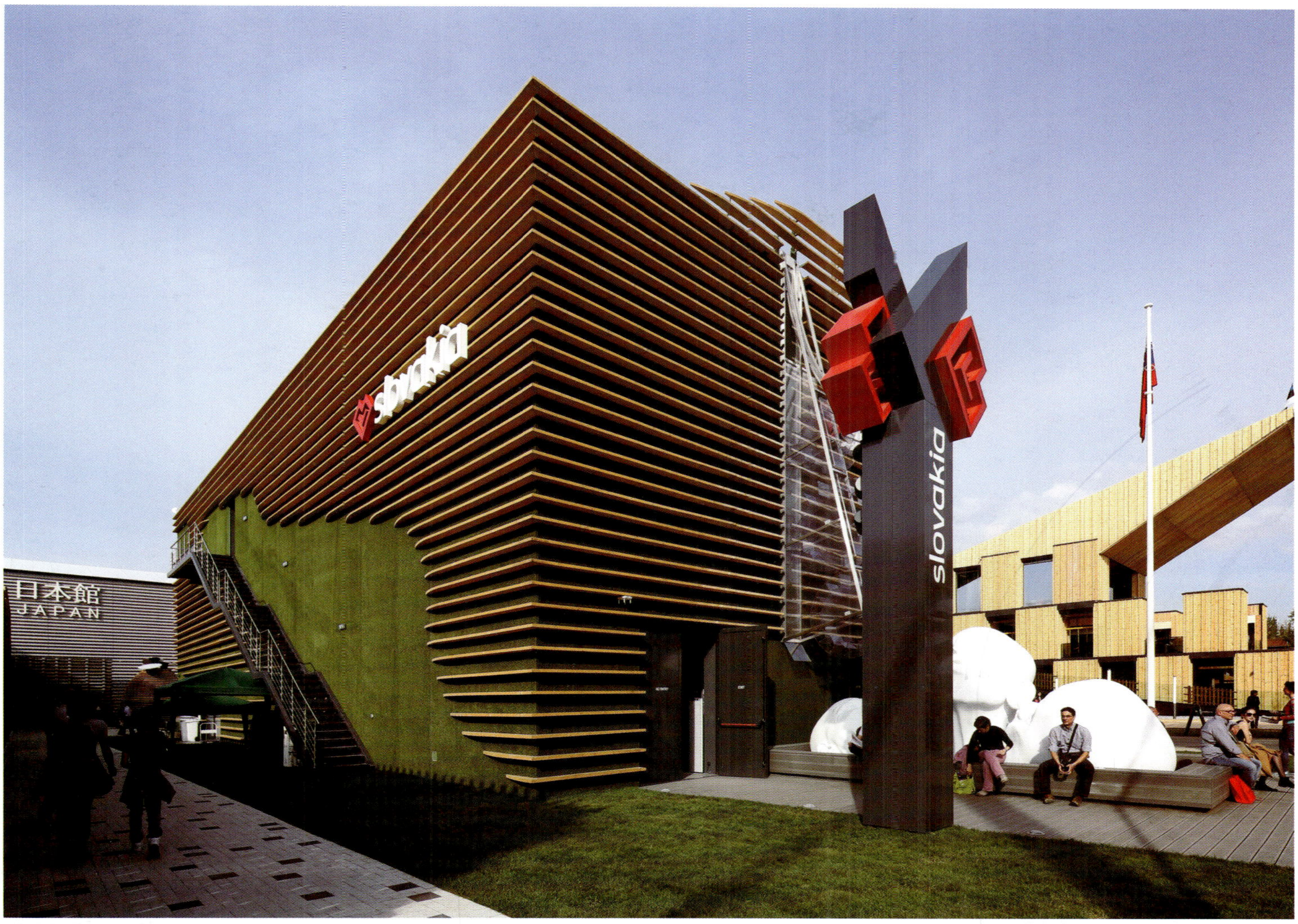
slovakia
slovakia
日本館
JAPAN

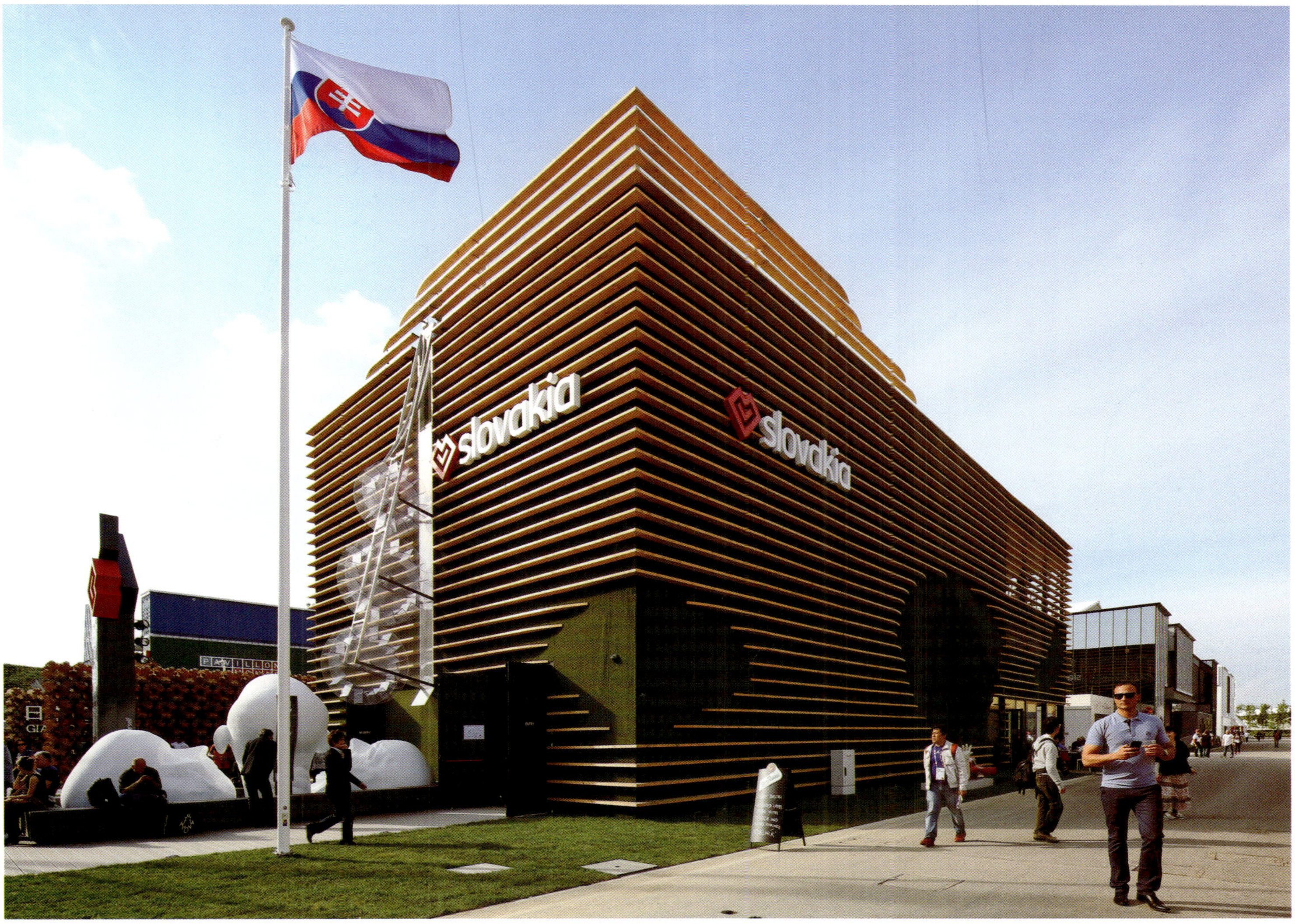
slovakia
slovakia

slovakia
ILLON
MONACO

slovakia
GELATINA DI CARNE
HALUŠKY DI BRYNZA
slovakia

本次参与米兰世博展，斯洛伐克是带着两大宗旨而来，一是展现她的历史，文化和自然多样性；另一个是展示其社会，文化和自然环境的协同性。如何给生活注入能量？斯洛伐克的回答是：在分类，竞争和差异化方面保持生物共生多样性。因为生物多样性能滋养地球也能给我们的生活提供能量。斯洛伐克的农业生态系统以小麦为主，然而她利用小农场和大型发电厂等各种能量场的协同共生从而保证了食物链的完整和稳固。

由斯洛伐克建筑师Karol Kállay设计的斯洛伐克馆，其灵感来自创意概念“斯洛伐克，给自己充电”。这种设计体现斯洛伐克不仅是个自然能源资源的富饶之国，也体现出她丰富的文化遗产，传统和卓拔的经验。这个创意概念在场馆的建设体现在两个部分：一部分是能源补给区，它设在展馆外部。能源塔就矗立于休息地带，游客可以在这里休息，在Tuli坐垫（该国品牌）上放松一会，同时也可以给自己的手机、平板电脑或笔记本充充电。

另一部分位于展馆内，这里体现了斯洛伐克的能量和多样性。游客将探索到能量的概念贯穿于现在生活和文化传统的各方各面，它们通过六个主题分别体现出来：传统、创新、运动、文化、经验和食物。展馆内处处可见具有代表性的心形标志。展馆里设有餐厅，游客可以品尝到一系列传统的斯洛伐克美食和改良的现代特色菜品；商店里可以买到斯洛伐克的纪念品和手信，或者寄一张斯洛伐克明信片，还可以买到斯洛伐克独创开发的USB充电器。

Slovakia's participation at Expo Milano 2015 is based on two pillars: historical, cultural, natural variety, and the symbiotic synergy of a number of social, cultural and natural environments. How can we provide energy for life? Slovakia responds with the symbiosis of biodiversity in place of specialization, competition and differentiation, since biological abundance can feed the world and provide energy for life. Even in the agricultural ecosystem of a country renowned for endless fields of wheat, there is a coexistence of all elements of the food chain, from small farms to large power plants.

Designed by the Slovak architect, Karol Kállay, Slovakia's Pavilion is inspired by the creative concept of “Slovakia. Recharge yourself”. It is imbued with the spirit of “a country that is rich in natural energy resources, but also a country full of the energy, cultural heritage, traditions and extraordinary experiences.” This concept is articulated by its Pavilion in two basic sections: the first, the Recharging Zone, is an external relax area dominated by an energy pylon. Here, visitors can take a break, relaxing on a Tuli bag, and recharge their mobile phones, tablet or laptop.

The second represents the energy and diversity of Slovakia and is located within the Pavilion as an area where visitors can discover the idea of energy linking modernity and cultural traditions across six themes of Traditions, Innovation, Sports, Culture, Experiences, and Nutrition and made visible throughout the exposition by a symbolized heart logo. At the Pavilion's restaurant, visitors can enjoy a selection of Slovak dishes and modern reinterpretations of traditional specialties, or call in at its shop, where they can find souvenirs and gifts of Slovakia, send a postcard from Slovakia, or buy a unique USB charger developed in Slovakia.

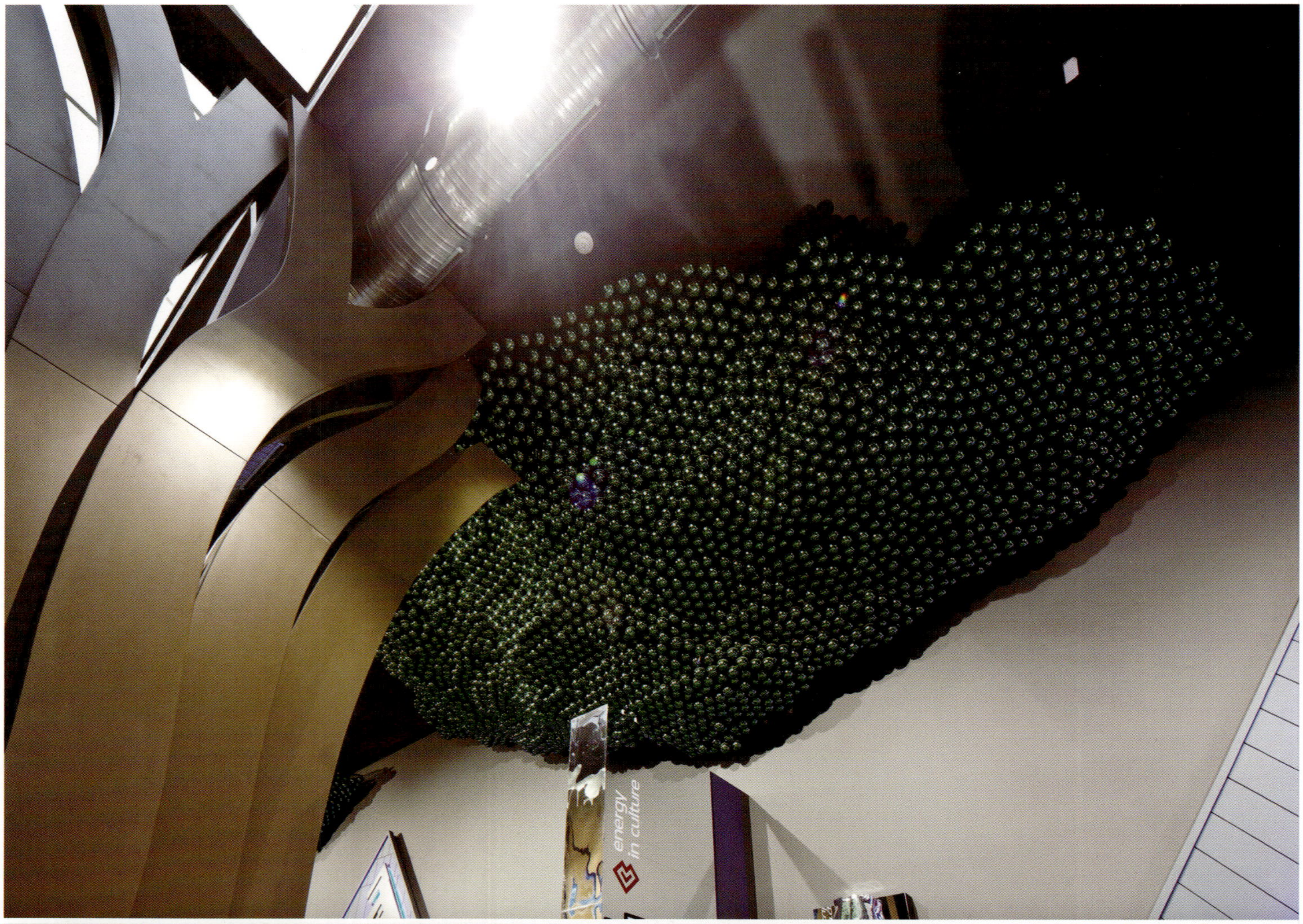
energy
in culture

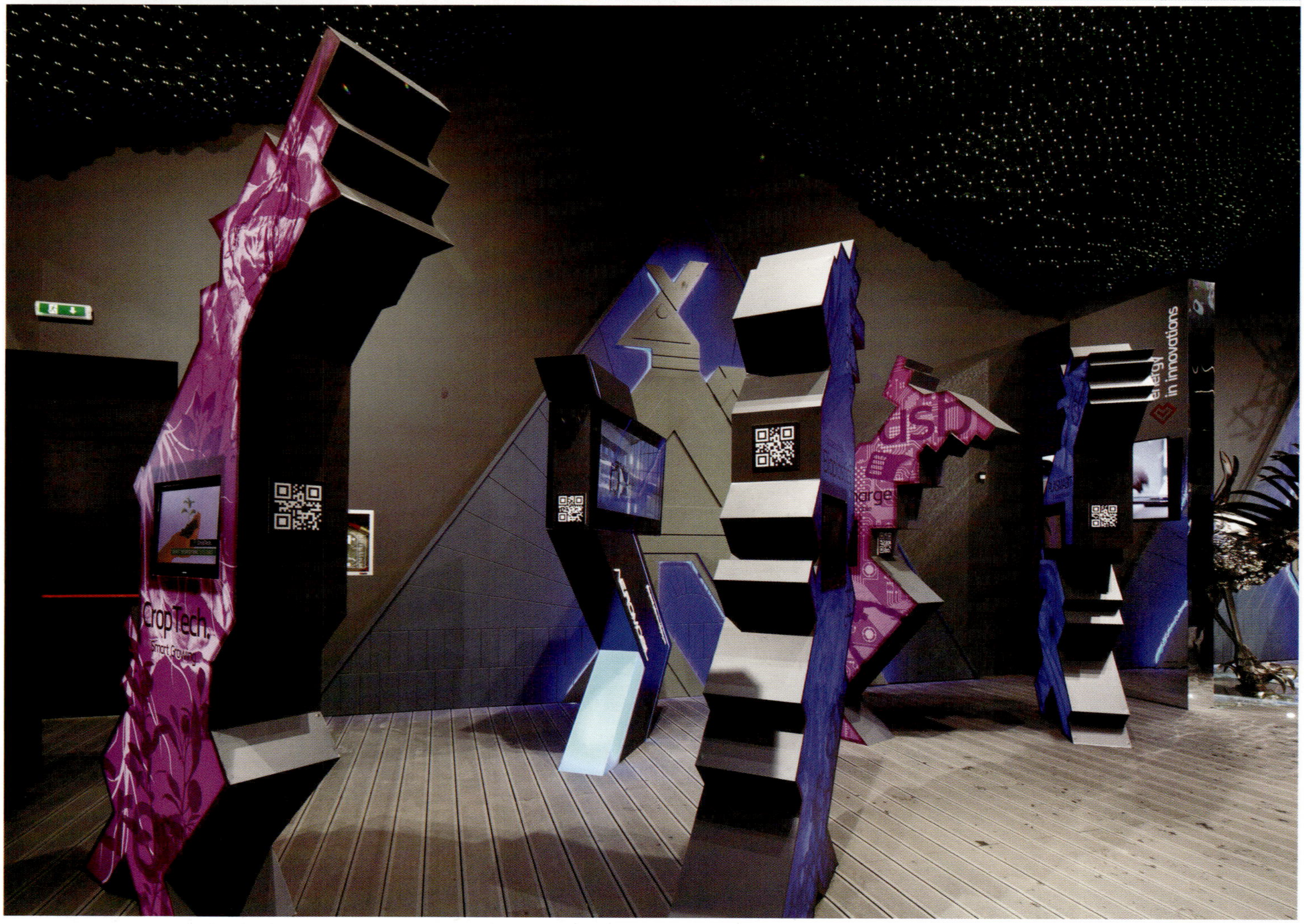
CropTech.
energy
in innovations

Biodegradable
Bioplastics
AEROMOBIL
the most advanced flying car
Water for
Mining
Machinery

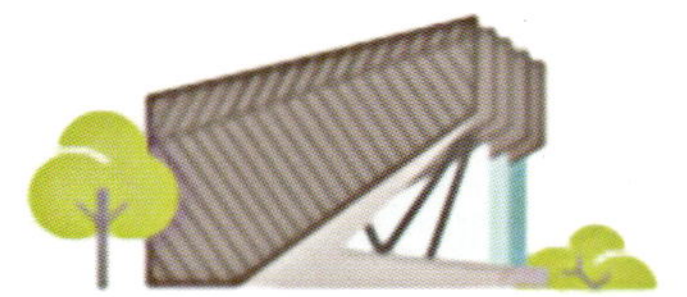

SLOVENIA PAVILION
斯洛文尼亚馆

I Feel Slovenia. Green. Active. Healthy
感受斯洛文尼亚：绿色·积极·健康

建筑设计：SoNo Arhitekti / 建筑施工：Lumar IG / 项目面积：1 910 平方米

Architectural Design: SoNo Arhitekti / Construction: Lumar IG / Project Area: 1,910 m²

I FEEL SLOVENIA
during a visit to
the Slovenian Pavilion
you will gather
of Slovenian grains
TRACCE

斯洛文尼亚馆以金字塔形状示人，采取几何造型的立面分别代表斯洛文尼亚丰富的地貌景观：如阿尔卑斯山脉和潘诺尼亚山，地中海的耕地平原，盆地，山谷以及被瑰丽的钟乳石和石笋装饰的地下山洞。建筑师设计了五个棱柱状结构，赋之予几何形状的动感外观，使人联想到田地，它们代表着斯洛文尼亚多样的地理景观和可持续发展的根本理念。

以"感受斯洛文尼亚：绿色·积极·健康"为主题，展馆选择采用自然材料来构筑，木料和玻璃也被大量采用。斯洛文尼亚的森林覆盖率达60%，因此木材是其战略性和可持续使用的资源，也是其最重要的可再生能源的来源。本次世博展，斯洛文尼亚将通过展览和互动来鼓励人们保护我们赖以生存的地球。

The Pavilion of Slovenia features pyramid shapes placed on a geometrically varied surface, the objects reflecting the diversity of the landscapes of the territory of Slovenia: the Alps and the hills of Pannonia and the Mediterranean, the arable land in the plains; the basins and valleys and the underground world of caves decorated with stalactites and stalagmites. Five prismatical structures, positioned on the geometrically and dynamically designed surface, whose shape is reminiscent of a cultivated field, will represent Slovenian diverse geographical landscape and symbolize fundamental ideas of sustainable development.

The Pavilion, whose concept is "I feel Slovenia. Green, active and healthy" will be made with natural materials, especially wood and glass. In Slovenia, where the forest covers 60% of the territory of the country, wood is a strategic and sustainable resource, as well as being one of the most important renewable energy sources. During Expo Milano 2015, Slovenia will dedicate space to projects and interactive shows that will provide visitors with educational content on the main theme of the Exhibition and will encourage them to contribute to the preservation of our planet.

KRŠA DO MORSKIH PLITVIN,
M, JE KRALJESTVO SOLIN.
BURJA, BORIN, MAESTRAL,
GRE SLANICA V KRISTAL.
AVČEK

Guardatevi nello specchio
Le vostre azioni si riflettono
nell'ambiente e hanno un impatto
sulla vita delle api
Senza l'ape, la vita umana come
apiterapia
concedetevi un po'
nella dimora dell'ape

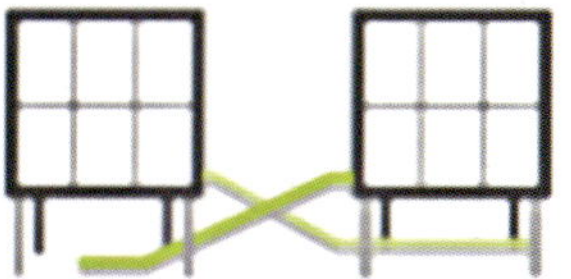

LITHUANIA PAVILION
立陶宛馆

A Fusion of Traditions and Innovations for a Balanced Future
传统与现代结合只为和谐未来

建筑设计：Vilnius Architecture Studio / 项目面积：1 147 平方米

Architectural Design: Vilnius Architecture Studio / Project Area: 1,147 m²

LITHUANIA

立陶宛馆采用简约设计，在1 147平方米的范围内用相互连接的通道承托着两个简单的白色立方体建筑。设计的经典之处在于这样的建筑让人联想起代表平衡的天平，此建筑造型也表达了立陶宛在农业和食物平衡发展问题上的一种态度。

在进入展馆前，游客可以看到蔬菜园，种的是立陶宛的传统食物。入口和出口处有广场，比较阴凉，游客可在此休息、交谈和用餐。沿着小路走，是展览大厅，为人们呈现出立陶宛未来的发展前景。中间的环形设计可将游客带到上面的平台，那里视野开阔，可以看到世博会的全景。这里还通向多功能区、餐厅和商店，为游客提供便利。展馆后面是行政区，附近有很多热门景点。

Inspired by minimalist architecture, the Lithuania Pavilion is composed of two cubic buildings joined by a series of interconnecting walkways, covering a total of 1,147 m². In its essence the design brings to mind the image a set of scales and is intended to represent the balance between tradition and innovation, both key characteristics of the country's agri-food sector.

The exhibition starts even before entering the pavilion: the vegetables garden shows the main elements of the lithuanian traditional alimentation. A fresh and shaded square at the ground level is the starting and ending point of the entire pavilion experience: a place for relaxing, sharing knowledge, and tasting dishes as well. Following the circulation path's one way route, one continues to the first floor the exhibition main halls focusing on the future of lithuanian growth. Then a central circular element works as a vertical distributor bringing the visitors to the upper terrace, which offers a special view on the entire Expo. It can also bring guests to the multifunctional space or to the restaurant and shop at the entry. All the administrative functions are located in the backside, directly connected with all the pavilion hot spots.

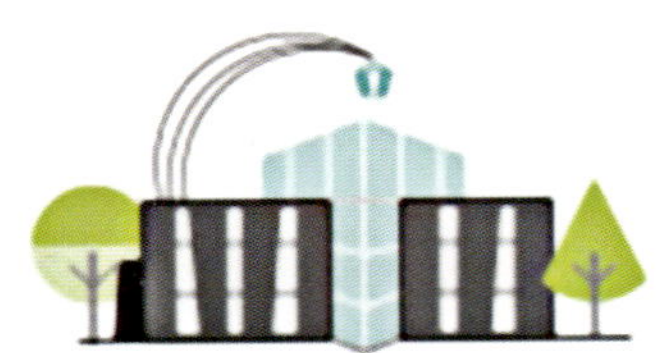

MOLDOVA PAVILION
摩尔多瓦馆

Shine the Light-Energy of Sun, Energy of Earth, Food for People
来自阳光和土地的食物

建筑设计：Gorgona Architecture & Design Studio, Pavel Braila / 项目面积：250 平方米

Architectural Design: Gorgona Architecture & Design Studio, Pavel Braila / Project Area: 250 m²

摩尔多瓦馆的一大特色是它翠绿的苹果瓣造型。在整个展览室内面积达747平方米的空间里，从室内装饰和家私到整个展厅梁柱无一不采用苹果绿作为装点，呈现出一个鲜活的摩尔多瓦。

进入展馆后，参观者能够看到一个特殊的天体，它是在黑色塑料上安装霓虹灯做的星座图。展馆的核心元素是一个太阳能之花，此装置安置在一个大型的透明玻璃房顶，无数小平面组成的三棱镜构成的多面体吸收和反射阳光，形成无数光斑环绕整个室内空间。

绿植覆盖的长长的走廊一直延伸穿过玻璃房，体现了摩尔多瓦人对环境、自然和人类的关怀，走廊一直延伸带领参观者进入摩尔多瓦传统农业生态区，这里有各种生态农业产品和极品葡萄酒，其中很多还未被世界所熟知。

An enticing and inspiring shade of apple green is the key feature of the project. From its furnishings to the large colored beams that surround the structure, extending over a total exhibition space of 747 square meters, everything is modeled to recall the shapes of a large sliced apple, evoking the idea of freshness, as a flavor and characteristic that Moldova wishes to share with its visitors.

The central element of the pavilion is a solar flower, placed on top of a large glass cube. It is an installation of mirrors consisting of thousands of facets that capture and reflect sunlight, re-projected in thousands of bright spots. Other highly evocative elements include: planetary constellations that visitors encounter upon entering the pavilion.

The long corridor flanked by green plants, crosses a large glass cube to convey care for the environment, innovation and humanity, and leads visitors to the biozone of Moldovan agriculture, where they can learn about Moldova's traditions, food and local wines.

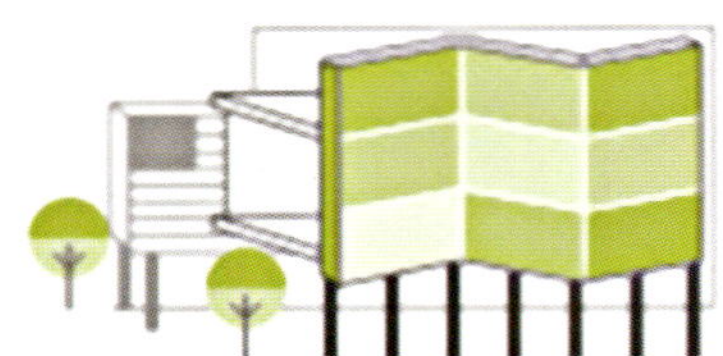

UNITED STATES OF AMERICA PAVILION
美国馆

American Food 2.0: United to Feed the Planet
美国食物2.0：联合起来滋养地球

建筑设计：Biber Architects / 工程：ESA Engineering / 结构和系统：SCE Project
灯光设计：Tillotson Design Associates / 景观设计：Dlandstudio / 平面设计：Pentagram / 面积：3 251.6平方米

Architects: Biber Architects / Engineering: ESA Engineering / Structures and Systems: SCE Project
Lighting Design: Tillotson Design Associates / Landscape Design: Dlandstudio / Graphic Design: Pentagram / Area: 3, 251.6m²

美国馆由纽约本土建筑事务所Biber Architects设计，成谷仓型，这与“美国食物2.0”的建筑概念主题是一致的，同时也是对2015年米兰世博会主题“滋养地球，生命能源”的创新表达。展馆将会向参观者呈现解决全球目前面临的两个挑战（食品安全和健康生活方式的提升）的工具和方法。

展馆入口向主要人行木板道敞开，木板全是可回收再次利用的。木板道延伸到二楼，指引参观者向上参观，而且在下面隐藏了一个展示空间。顶层包括一个屋顶露台，并安装了可产生能源的嵌板和半透明的地板。

展馆的主要特色在于覆盖展馆其中一个长形立面的漂浮垂直式农场。农场采用营养液栽培灌溉系统和雨水收集系统种植各种作物。同时，还使用了旋转式花园面板来跟踪太阳走向。整个立面启发性地展示了美国农场和食物的过去、现在和将来。 展馆的覆板成为各种互动展示、最先进的数字媒体和现场表演的背景幕布，而农场也成为一个动态的奇观——空中舞者在此表演一段段庆祝丰收的芭蕾舞。在展馆的另外一面，穿孔的生锈镀锌蓝色钢铁结构的设计略微参考了美国国旗。

The American pavilion by New York-based firm Biber Architects has been designed to look like a granary in keeping with the architectural concept American Food 2.0 and will offer an innovative exploration of the theme of “Feeding the planet, Energy for Life”. Visitors will be provided with tools and solutions that can respond to two of the challenges faced by the worldwide population on a daily basis: food safety and the promotion of a healthy lifestyle.

The pavilion’s door opens up to the main pedestrian path and a symbol of American food: the boardwalk. Made of recycled wood from US boardwalks, the walkway extends to the second floor, serving as a pathway for self-guided tour and concealing an exhibition space below. The top floor will contain a rooftop terrace with energy generating panels and a translucent floor.

The main architectural feature is a floating vertical farm running the length of one side of the pavilion. The hydroponic facade will feature a variety of harvestable crops, set into panels that will track the motion of the sun, which are sustained by a rainwater irrigation system. The wall is a didactic display talking about the past, present and future of the American farm and the American diet. With the pavilion doubling as a backdrop for interactive exhibits, state-of-the-art digital media and live performances, the farm will also become a dynamic spectacle where aerial performers will act out a harvest ballet. Meanwhile, on the other side of the pavilion, a perforated metal structure in rusted, galvanized and blued steel will create a subtle reference to Old Glory.

Walgreens

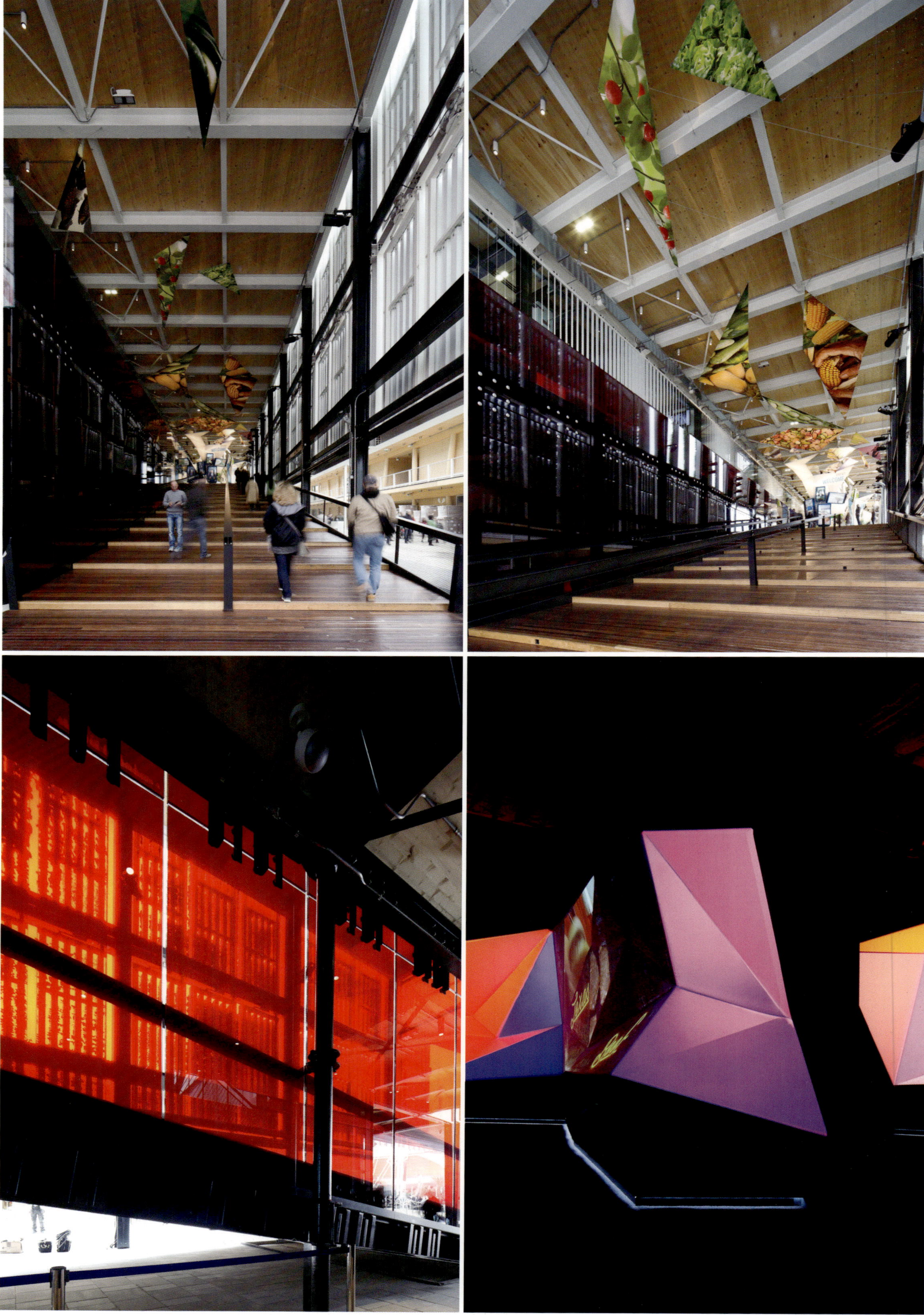

OD 2.0

BRAZIL PAVILION
巴西馆

Feeding the World with Solutions
粮食危机的解决方案

建筑、室内以及家具设计：亚瑟萨斯工作室 / 创意指导：亚瑟萨斯
展览和舞美：马尔科画室 / 平面设计：Estudia Design / 占地面积：4 133平方米 / 建筑面积：2 388平方米

Architecture, Interior and Furniture Design: Studio Arthur Casas Team / Creative Director: Arthur Casas
Exhibition and Stage: Atelier Marko Brajovic / Plane Design: Estudia Design / Site Area: 4,133 m² / Building Area: 2,388 m²

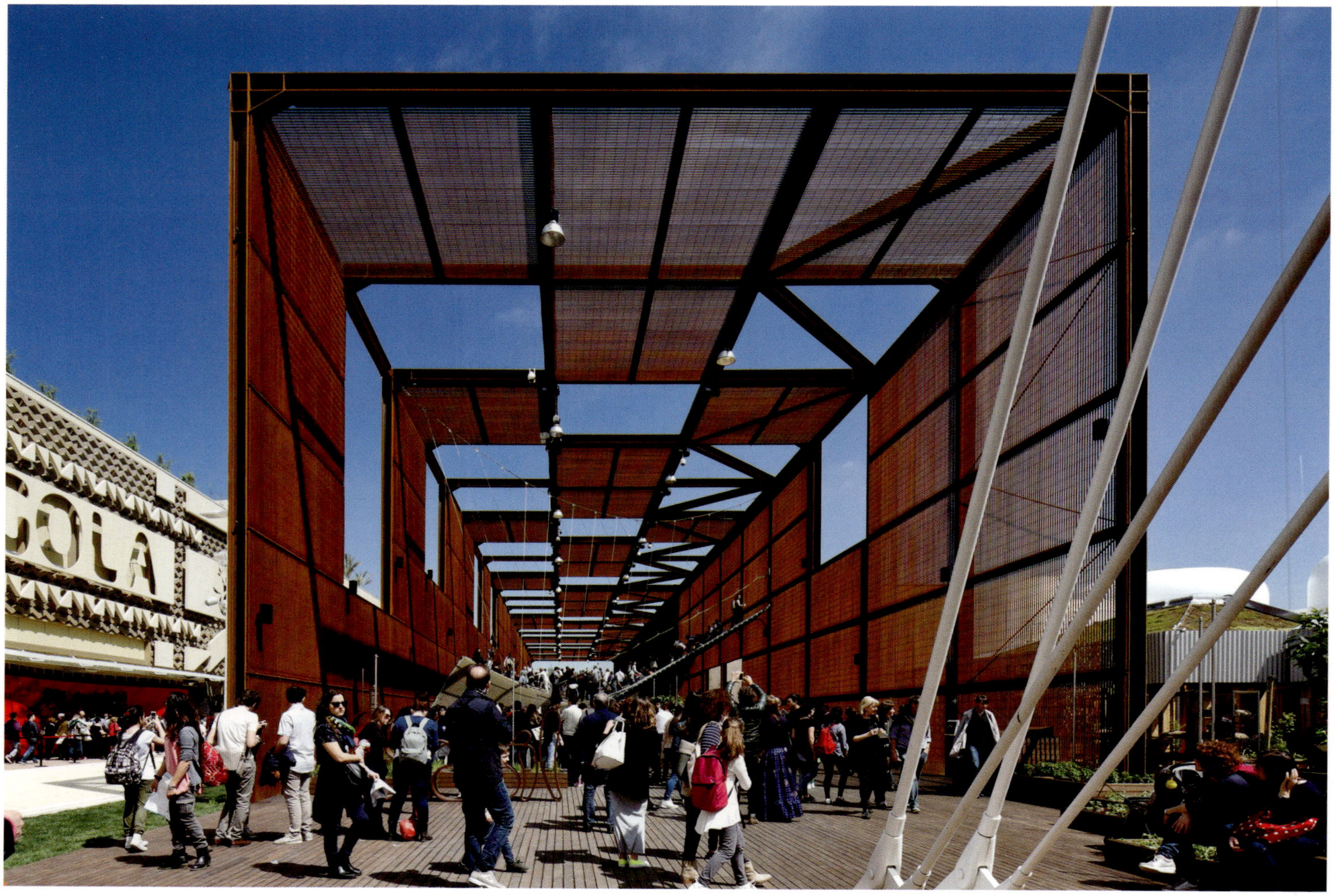

为了在2015 米兰世博会呈现出巴西的多样性，这个多彩的国家委托亚瑟萨斯工作室和马尔科画室进行巴西馆的设计，以表现和传递他们的价值观。巴西馆的主题是“粮食危机的解决方案”，目标是在展馆中利用互动式的学习和科技带给观众沉浸式的直观感受，向世界展示出巴西的的价值观及其对农业的期望。巴西馆的空间将成为把人们聚集在一起的中心，它的广场也激发了人们的好奇心。

巴西馆的设计方案消除了边界的概念。泥土的颜色和由铁构件固定的材料多孔性将在张力结构中完全展现，为游客创造出意想不到的社交空间，游客们可以坐下休息，也可以谈天交流。坡道系统使空间由外向内平滑地过渡，同时也反映了巴西展馆一贯具有的传统巴西现代风格。

展馆设计有四个关键主题：自然的智慧、色彩的王国、人类的力量和创造性的融合。马尔科工作室设计的展览空间突出了巴西的过去、兴旺的现在以及对未来的乐观预期。建筑中与弹出式商店、餐厅、咖啡厅和酒吧相连的展览空间位于展馆后部，而所有空间都与中庭相联系，以此来最大化地利用自然光。

Aiming to bring Brazil's diversity to the Expo Milan 2015, the colorful country has commissioned studio arthur casas and atelier marko brajovic to represent and transmit their values into the design of their pavilion. The theme for this year's expo is 'feeding the world in solutions' and Brazil's aim is to highlight the country's values and agricultural aspirations through the architecture of their pavilion by using sensorial immersion through interactive learning and technology. The space aspires to be a hub that brings people together and is accentuated by the proposed public square to attract curiosity.

The construction suggests the concept of erasing boundaries. The earthy colored and porous nature made of iron will be fully open with the tensile structure creating unexpected niches for visitors to sit and socialize. A ramp systems encourages a smooth and gradual transition from exterior to interior, but also reflects the traditional Brazilian modernism of previous pavilions.

Dictated by four key themes: natural wisdom, empire of colors, human power and creative fusion, the exhibition itself, developed by atelier marko brajovic will highlight Brazil's past, exuberant present and optimistic development for the future. The exhibition spaces along with a pop-up store, restaurant, cafe and bar will be located at the rear of the pavilion, all interconnected through an atrium to maximize natural light.

ARGENTINA PAVILION
阿根廷馆

Argentina Feeds You
养育你的阿根廷

建筑设计：阿根廷政府 / 项目面积：1 907 平方米

Architectural Design: Argentine Government / Project Area: 1,907 m²

Argentina

在阿根廷国家政策背景下设置的场馆主题“养育你的阿根廷”响应了2015年米兰世博会的中心主题“滋养地球，生命能源”。阿根廷馆为游客提供体验阿根廷的丰富性和多样性的展示空间，具体体现在阿根廷馆四部分主体内容：第一，探讨在过去十年的社会融合基础上，粮食安全和社会经济发展问题；第二，描述了在阿根廷广袤肥沃的土地上的各种基础作物的生产情况，如谷物、水果、蔬菜以及肉类和海产品等，它们广泛富于较高价值并被全球的消费者所认同；第三，阿根廷重视知识，因此展馆为游客展示了她在持续创新道路上的兼容并蓄，着力推动研究与科技发展，使阿根廷的产品在世界舞台上极具市场竞争力和附加值；最后，着眼于全球发展模式，探讨资本主义面临的挑战，粮食主权和平等发展等问题。

在此背景下，阿根廷寻求公开辩论如下议题：如农业保护主义，自由贸易协定，动植物检疫措施，全球价值链和粮食商品投机。内容通过视听资源，模拟器，交互系统，多感官空间，文化活动和丰盛的特色美食精选来展现。通过这些战略支柱，阿根廷馆的主题体现她作为一个发展中国家在推动社会包容性，减少饥饿，并努力为全球提供优质食品方面的能力和信念。同时，也体现出阿根廷在全球多边探讨关于未来10亿人面临的全球食物危机挑战中在科技创新方面所作出承诺。

With its theme “Argentina feeds you” Argentina showcases its country set against a backdrop of national policies that are closely aligned with the central theme of Expo Milano 2015, “Feeding the Planet, Energy for Life.” It is a theme that offers visitors experiences that feed their understanding of Argentina's richness and diversity in a space that reflects four subtopics. The first, Argentina feeds its people, explores the question of food security within its economic development policies of the past ten years based on social inclusion; the second, Argentina feeds the world, describes the vastness and fertility of its land that produces a wide variety of primary products such as cereals, fruits, vegetables, meat, products from the sea but also a wide range of value-added products consumed and recognized all around the world; the third, Argentina feeds knowledge, offers visitors a view of its inclusive and sustainable innovation, that facilitates and promotes research and technologic development, boosting the development of highest competitiveness and value-added to Argentina's production. The last, Argentina feeds debate, looks at the global paradigm and the challenges of capitalism, food sovereignty and equal development.

In this context, Argentina seeks to open debates on issues such as agricultural protectionism, free trade agreements, sanitary and phyto-sanitary measures, global value chains and speculation on food commodities. Contents are shared through audiovisual resources, simulators, interactive systems, multisensory spaces, cultural events and a varied and characteristic gastronomic selection, among other offerings. Articulated through these strategic pillars, the overall theme embodies Argentina's power and energy as a developing country that promotes social inclusion policies to relieve hunger, and as a global supplier of quality and value-added food and beverages goods. It also captures Argentina's commitment to scientific-technological innovations for a frank and multilateral debate on future global food challenges facing a billion people in years to come.

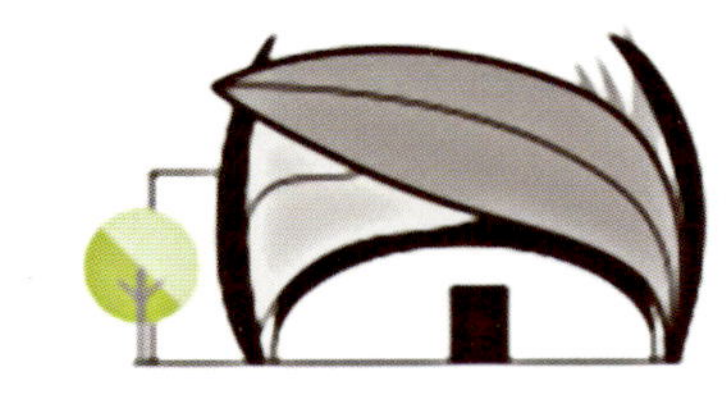

MEXICO PAVILION
墨西哥馆

Mexico, the Seed for the New World: Food, Diversity and Heritage
新世界的种子

设计公司：Loguer / 项目面积：1 910 平方米

Design Company: Loguer / Project Area: 1,910 m²

从第一次在费城参与世博展开始（1876），墨西哥馆就给人们留下了深刻的印象，并让人产生无限遐想。结合2015年米兰世博会可持续发展的宗旨，该展馆的造型设计模仿了堆叠的玉米苞，借此向墨西哥最重要的食物致敬，同时回应了2015年世博会的主题——“滋养地球，生命能源”。

在本次米兰世博展的两条主参观道轴线上，你很难忽视外形像一个大玉米穗的墨西哥展馆，此展馆占地1 910平方米，地理位置在整个世博会中十分优越。展馆里有全方位的食品生产展示，沿着一条溪水，它在浇灌花园的同时也会带领你随着盘旋的坡道去探索墨西哥丰富的烹饪美食，生态和文化。

在墨西哥地区，玉米有着重要的文化、社会和经济作用。因此展馆中的玉米壳状外观有着象征意义，同时有助过滤日光，避免刺目阳光直射室内。每个弯曲的PVC膜重量轻，其预制的设计易于安装。坡道会引导游客参观各种室内园林、水景和博物馆空间。展馆还包括入口广场、中央庭院和餐厅。

Since its first participation in a Universal Exhibition (Philadelphia in 1876), Mexico has always delivered an impressive pavilion that captures the imagination. The fundamental theme of Expo Milano 2015 is sustainability, being as much a driving principle for feeding the world's population as a criteria for architectural design, the shape is from typical Mexican food: corn.

Indeed, its large external structure, inspired by the shape of a big corn cob, covers the 1,910 m^2 pavilion, set in a prime location at the intersection of the two main avenues. The interior offers an all-encompassing exhibition of typical produce, edged by a stream of water that gives life to the gardens and takes visitors along spiral ramps, to explore the gastronomic, ecological and cultural riches of Mexico.

In Mexico region, corns play a vital role in cultural, social and economic perspectives. The shape of corn cob symbolizes the meaning within, and meanwhile the corn leaves can filter the sunlight. The curved PVC film is light and of easy installation. Along with the ramp, visitiors will experience an interior garden, waterscapes and a museum space. The Mexico Pavilion also has a welcoming plaza, a central courtyard and a restaurant.

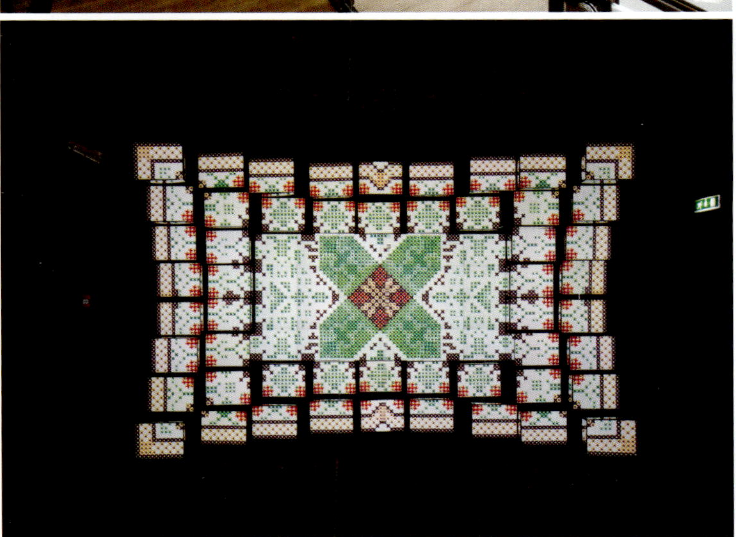

Michoacán
MEXICO

ANCIENT HEALING PLANTS
TOAD HERB
Eryngium heterophyllum

CHILE PAVILION
智利馆

A Country Rich in Variety
富饶的国度

建筑设计：Cristián Undurraga / 项目面积：1 910 平方米

Architectural Design: Cristián Undurraga / Project Area: 1,910 m²

Chile
Cile

从阿卡塔马沙漠到巴塔哥尼亚高原，从中央苍翠的大峡谷到东部诸岛，各种极端地貌遍布智利，这些地域特色将在2015米兰世博会的智利展馆里一一展示。智利馆面积有1 910平方米，一入其内便让人感觉舒适备至。展馆采用悬挂结构，中间巨型木质过梁由一圈横梁围拱，下方是四根混凝土柱作为支撑形成中部空间，视野开阔，具有典型的智利建筑风格。场馆的入口处为休闲区域，设有桌椅条凳供游客休息。进入馆内，抬眼便能看到智利人的“餐桌”，尽显智利风情。沿步道装饰着一组红色雕塑，描绘出智利的农民形象。一条走道巧妙地连接起展厅，食物品尝区和活动区域。

馆内的一条隧道通道里，设置了24架实时投影设备，游客行走于其内会有一种置身于虚境的感觉，或泛舟海面或游赏于卡曼尼的葡萄架下。投影设备带领游客领略智利不同地区的特色农作，像一场盛宴似的把智利地域的多样性，智利的人，智利的果园向世界展示出来。

From the Atacama Desert to Patagonia, from its central green valleys to its eastern islands, extreme geographical diversity will be a key feature of Chile's showcase at Expo Milano 2015. The architecture of the pavilion, which is spread over an area of 1,910 m², focuses on the art of hospitality. It is a suspended structure, a large wooden lintel enclosed by a frame of crossed beams and supported by four concrete pillars that create an intermediate space, a clear horizon, typical of Chilean architecture. The access point is a relaxation area with tables and benches. On entering the pavilion visitors will find the Chilean "dinner table," with all its flavors and colors. A group of red statues, depicting Chilean farmers, indicates the path to follow. A corridor connects the exhibition hall with an area for tastings and events.

As for the decoration of the Chile Pavalion, a tunnel surrounded by twenty-four synchronized projectors immerse visitors in a virtual reality experience, on a fishing boat at sea or in the vineyards of Carmenere. All these elements combine to illustrate the various regions and typical crops, communicating the diversity of its territory, the people, the fruits of the land, the imagery and the banquet that Chile offers to the world.

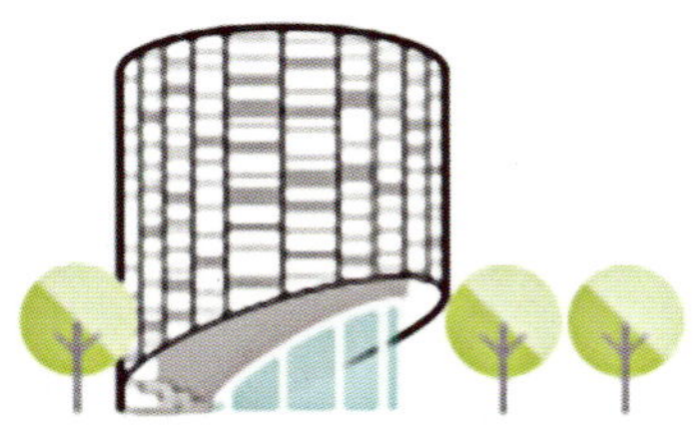

URUGUAY PAVILION
乌拉圭馆

Life Grows in Uruguay
乌拉圭的生活

建筑设计：Javier Diaz, INAC / 项目面积：747 平方米

Architectural Design: Javier Diaz, INAC / Project Area: 747 m²

URUGUAY

URU

GUAY

本次米兰世博会是乌拉圭首次以独立展馆的形式参展，其展馆由乌拉圭本土建筑师亲手操刀，展馆面积747平方米，创新的设计将给参观者带来多感官的体验。

为了保证展馆建筑用地与周围环境的平衡，乌拉圭馆的建造完全采用再利用和可回收材料，并以螺旋状造型来吸引眼球。

乌拉圭馆给参观者创造了一场涵盖不同主题的声音之旅。一楼展馆作为视听展区，参观者沿着声音坡道慢慢而行将聆听到各种声音，这些声音来自土地，来自海岸，来自牛排餐馆，来自街头乐队等等。展馆还设置了美食区，参观者能够品尝到乌拉圭的当地美食和特色烤肉。

Uruguay will participate for the first time with its own pavilion, designed by Uruguayan architects. Built in an area of 747 m^2, the pavilion will exhibit an innovative design that will house various interpretative spaces that will offer visitors a multisensory experience of the country.

Its architecture has been designed in order to achieve a perfect environmental balance between green spaces and built areas. It has a spiral structure to be made of entirely reusable and recyclable materials.

The pavilion offers visitors a journey of sensory immersion through its various thematic areas. The core of the didactic proposal will be the audiovisual area housed on the first floor. To get there, visitors must travel a sound ramp where they will experience different sound landscapes typical of the country, from its fields and beaches to its steak restaurants and bands of street musicians. In addition to the display areas, the pavilion will feature a gastronomic area that will offer specialties from the Uruguayan cuisine and "parrilla".

LA VITA CRESCE IN
URUGUAY

ECUADOR PAVILION
厄瓜多尔馆

The Land of Evolution
演变之地

建筑设计：Zorrozua Asociados Consultoria de diseño
项目面积：747 平方米

Architectural Design: Zorrozua Asociados Consultoria de diseño
Project Area: 747 m²

厄瓜多尔首次以独立国家馆的形式参与世博会，她将给来自世界各地的游客展示自己的自然和人文资源以及环境和文化遗产。

厄瓜多尔馆的设计依据主题的不同分为四个部分：第一个主题是“多样的国家”，着重介绍了厄瓜多尔的各种地貌景观；第二个主题是“食物作为社会的集合”，这个主题内容丰富，通过精选具有代表性的传统厄瓜多尔美食深入浅出地道出了每道菜背后的意义；第三块区域命名为“美好生活”，这里提供了供参观者坐下来休息的一个空间，回忆前面看到和听到的信息；第四个区域是厄瓜多尔馆最有趣味的部分，这里有一个餐馆和一个多功能空间。

For the first time, Ecuador participates with its own pavilion at a Universal Exposition, with the commitment and responsibility to show the world the essence of the people of Ecuador, the value of its natural and human resources and its cultural and environmental heritage.

The Pavilion's design is divided into four themes: the first, A Diverse Country, highlights the different regional landscapes as a core of the country's identity. The second area, Food as a Social Collective, is richer in content and information, and works to explain what is behind its dishes through a selection of representative products of traditional Ecuadorian food. The third area is entitled, Live Well, (in Quechua Sumak Kawsay) it offers a space for reflection, where the visitor can rest and think about the message just received in an area full of images, sounds and sensations. Finally the fourth area, Amor, is the most fun part of the Pavilion, in the form of a restaurant and a multifunctional space.

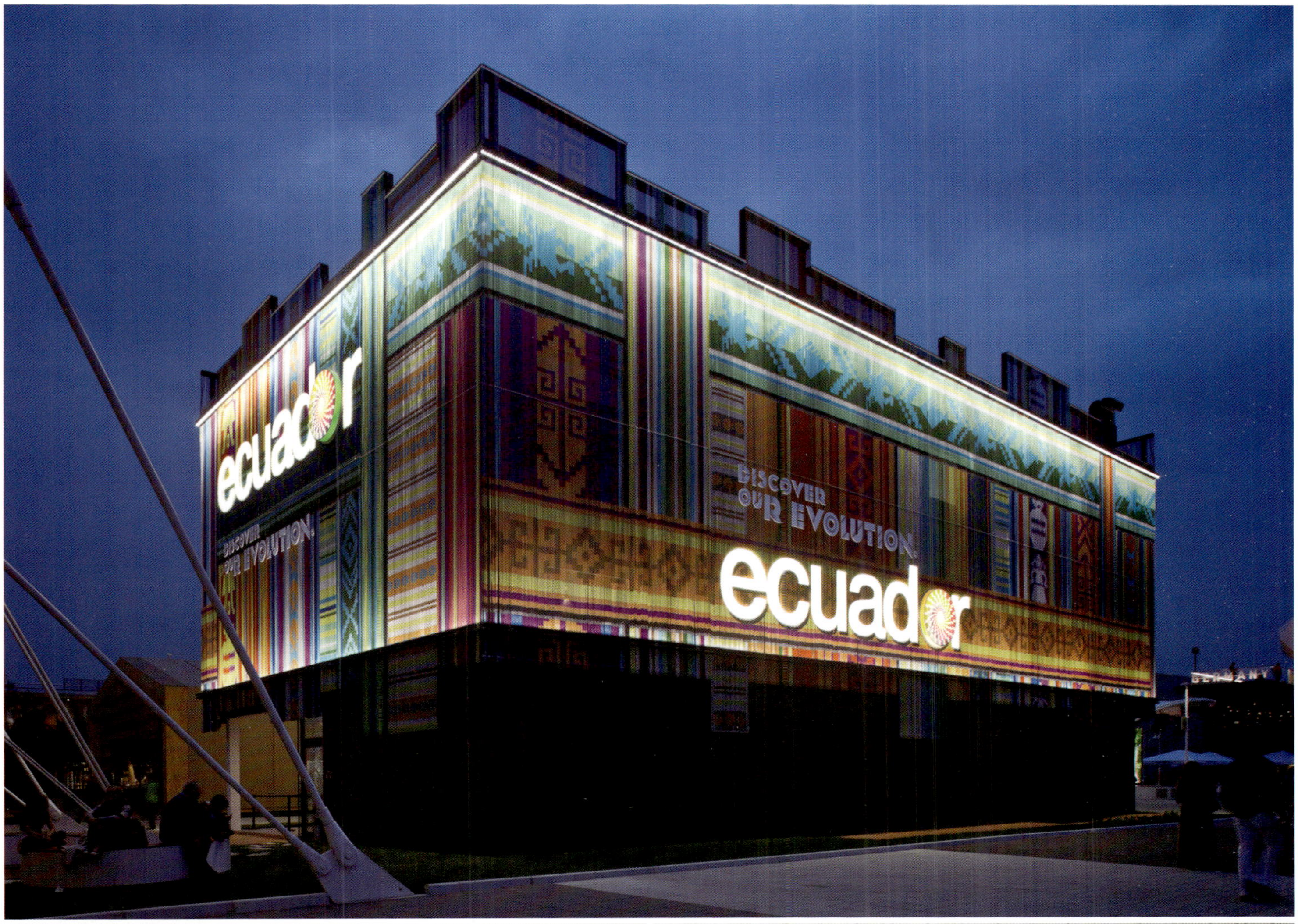

ECUADOR
DISCOVER
OUR EVOLUTION

COLOMBIA PAVILION
哥伦比亚馆

Naturally Sustainable
自然的可持续发展

建筑设计：Marivel Villa Arquitectos–Studio Cardenas Conscious Design / 项目面积：1 907 平方米

Architectural Design: Marivel Villa Arquitectos-Studio Cardenas Conscious Design / Project Area: 1,907 m²

COLOMBIA
NATURALLY SUSTAINABLE
COLOMBIA

COLOMBIA
COLOMBIA
NATURALLY SUSTAINABLE

2015米兰世博会将再次肯定哥伦比亚作为世界粮仓大国和在避免饥饿方面做出的贡献。由于哥伦比亚在纬度上接近赤道，她的气候不受季节更迭影响，相反，这里的气候变化随着海拔、温度、湿度、风力和降雨情况而变化。从海平面至5 000米高的海拔范围内依次呈现五个气候带：热带、温带、寒带、高沼地和常年积雪地带。

哥伦比亚馆的设计理念就是遵循这五个气候带而设计。展馆分为四块区域来展示哥伦比亚不同的地貌特色，让参观者逐一了解从热带到常年积雪地带的旖旎风光。

动感的立面设计使得参观者在不同的角度能获得不同的视觉感受。建筑材料主要采用枞木，不但保证了对环境的保护，也吻合哥伦比亚馆的主题“自然的可持续发展”。

Expo Milano 2015 is the platform for Columbia to reaffirm its position as one of the granaries of the world and a key player in the prevention of hunger. Given its proximity to the equator, Colombia is not subject to the changing seasons. Instead, it has a tropical climate with variations depending on altitude, temperature, humidity, winds and rainfall. The country varies in altitude between zero and 5,000 m above sea level and has five climatic zones with constant average temperatures throughout the year: warm, temperate, cold, moorland and perennial snow.

The architectural concept interprets the five climate zones, diving the building into four areas that represent the Colombian landscape, from the warm floor up to the perennial snow floor.

The facade is dynamic, with a visual effect that changes in relation to viewpoint. The main material used in the constuction is fir wood, recognized as environmental friendly in line with country's chosen theme: Naturally Sustainable.

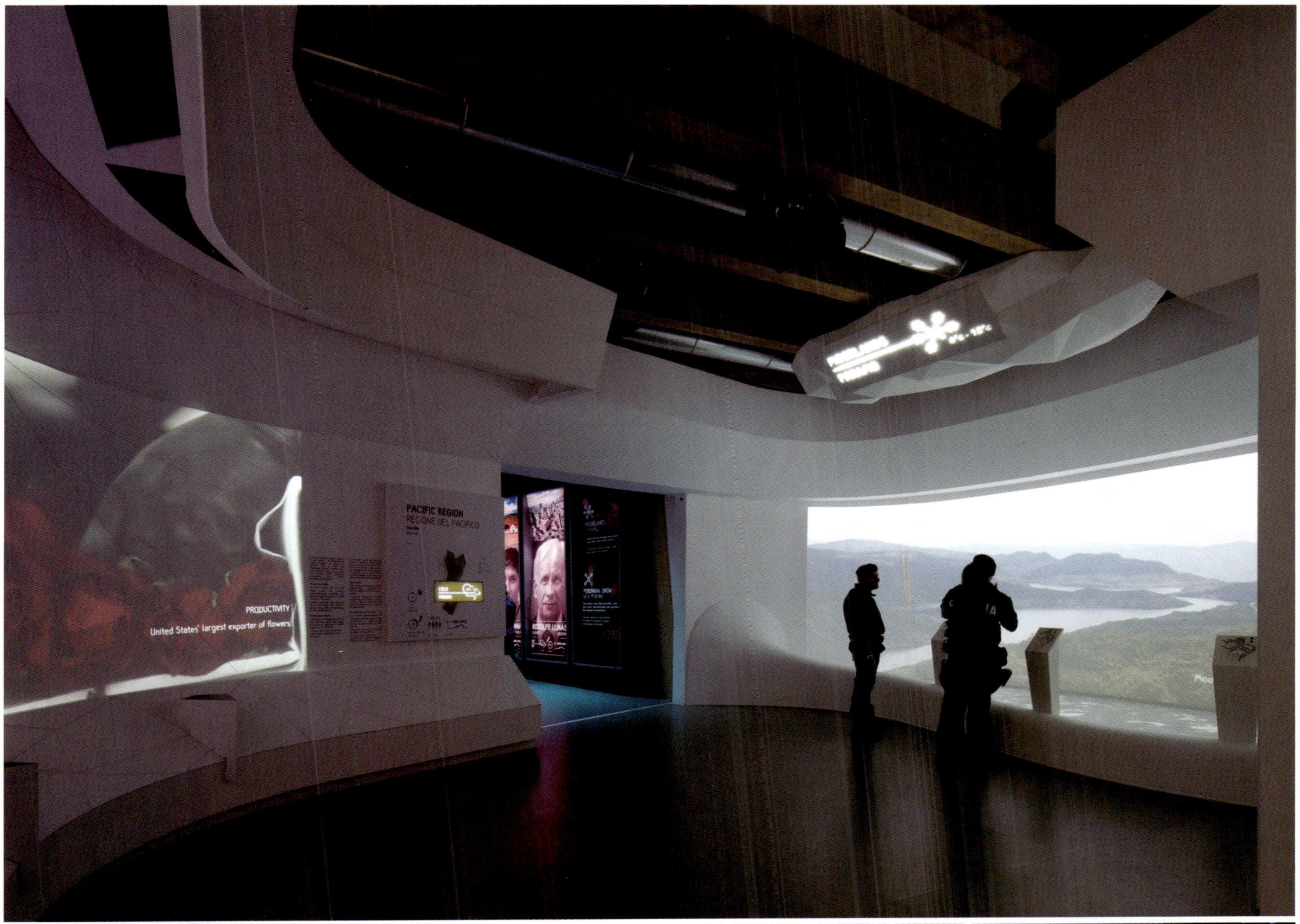
PRODUCTIVITY
United States' largest exporter of flowers
PACIFIC REGION
REGIONE DEL PACIFICO

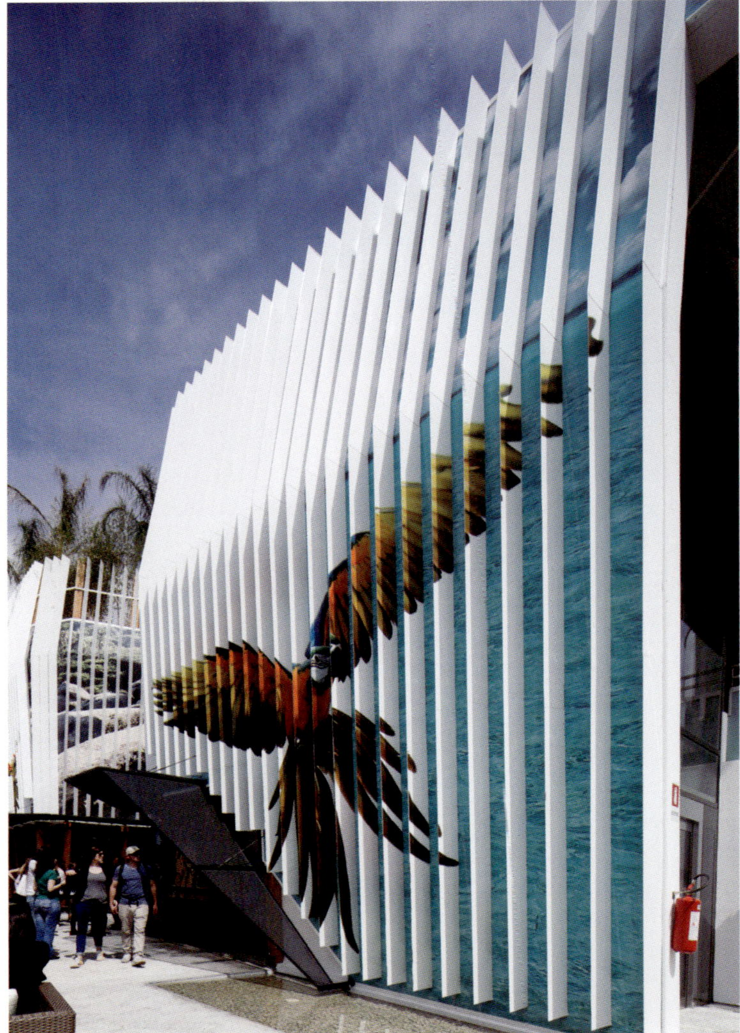

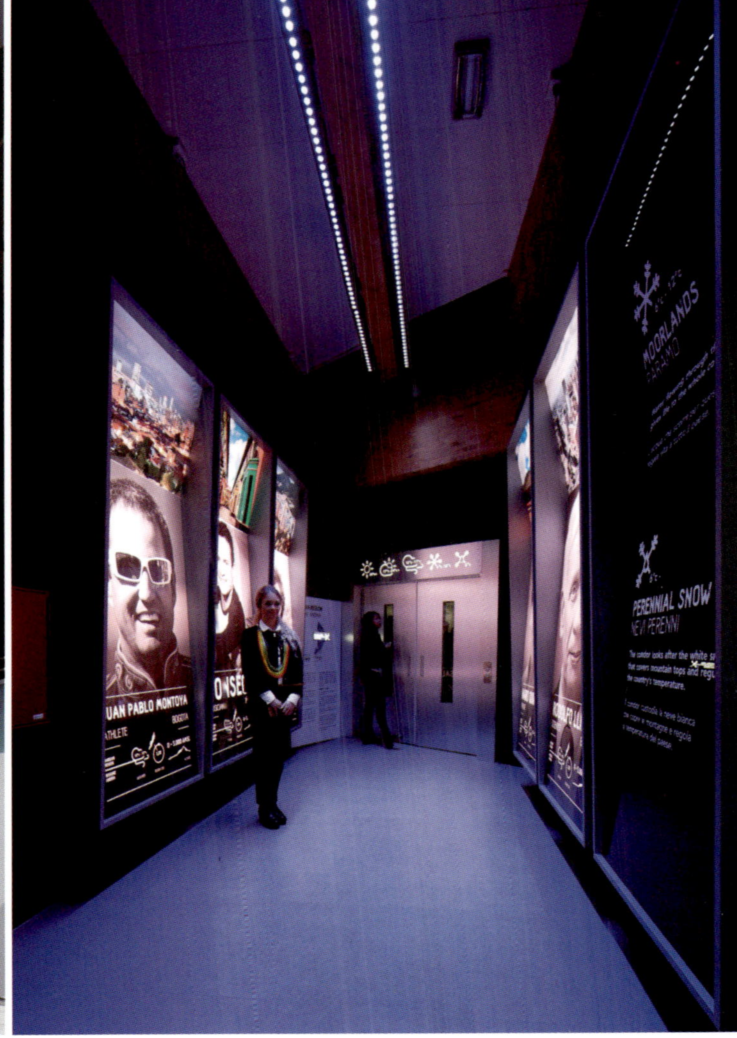

MOORLANDS
PERENNIAL SNOW
NEVI PERENNI
UAN PABLO MONTOYA
ATHLETE

JUAN PABLO MONTOYA
ATHLETE
MOORLANDS
PARAMO
PERENNIAL SNOW
NEVI PERENNI
Il condor custodia la neve bianca
che copre le montagne e regola
la temperatura del paese.

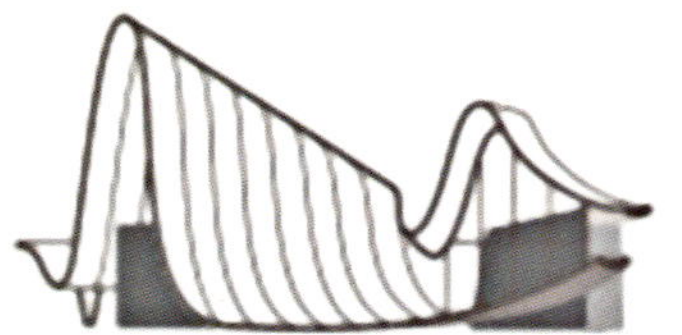

CHINA PAVILION
中国馆

Land of Hope, Food for Life
希望的田野

建筑设计：清华大学美术学院与Studio Link-Arc工作室 / 首席建筑师：陆轶辰 / 副主管：Kenneth Namkung, Qinwen Cai, Ching-Tsung Huang (Studio Link-Arc)
项目团队：Mario Bastianelli, Alban Denic, Ivi Diamantopoulou, Shuning Fan, Zachary Grzybowski, Elvira Hoxha,
Dongyul Kim, Hyunjoo Lee, Aymar Mariño-Maza (Studio Link-Arc)
结构工程师：Simpson Gumpertz & Heger / 附件工程师：Elite Facade Consultants + ATLV
机电工程师：Beijing Qingshang Environmental Art & Architectural Design / 面积：4 590平方米

Architect: Tsinghua University & Studio Link-Arc / Chief Architect: Yichen Lu (Tsinghua University + Studio Link-Arc) / Associate In Charge: Kenneth Namkung, Qinwen Cai, Ching-Tsung Huang (Studio Link-Arc)
Project Team: Mario Bastianelli, Alban Denic, Ivi Diamantopoulou, Shuning Fan, Zachary Grzybowski, Elvira Hoxha, Dongyul Kim, Hyunjoo Lee, Aymar Mariño-Maza (Studio Link-Arc)
Architect and Engineer of Record: F&M Ingegneria
Structural Engineer: Simpson Gumpertz & Heger / Enclosure Engineer: Elite Facade Consultants + ATLV
MEP Engineer: Beijing Qingshang Environmental Art & Architectural Design / Area: 4,590m²

Staggered Panels
Rough Edge

2 panels = 3 bays
Running Bond
900 x 3600

板材长度：1.5跨
交错排布
900 X 3600

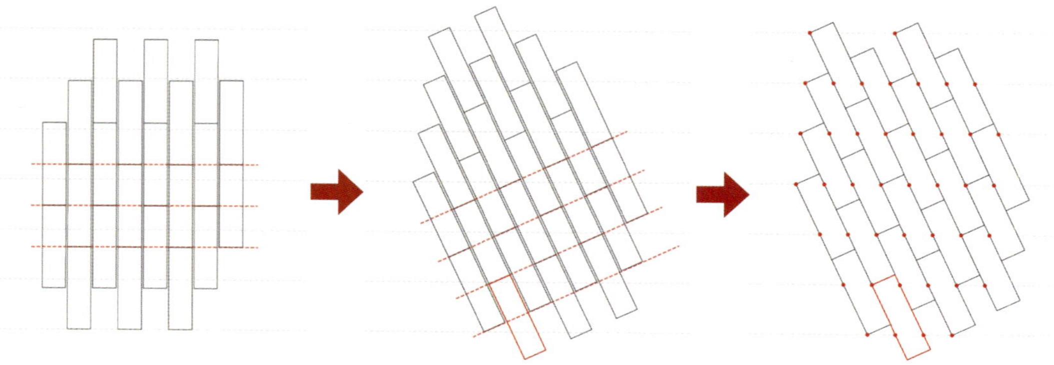

Each panel has three connections to structure
板材有三个节点锚固于结构

CONCEPTUAL PANELING GEOMETRY

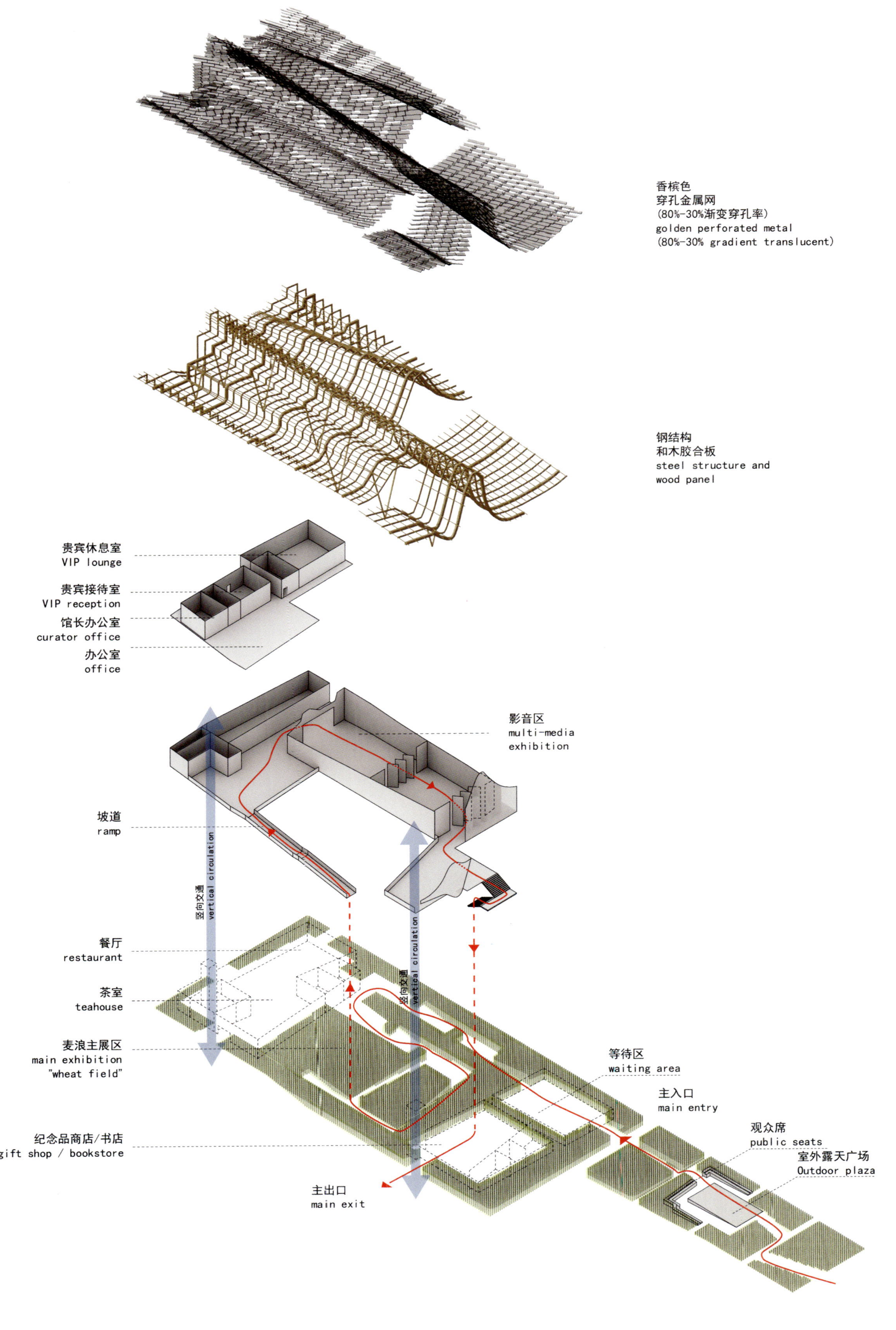

香槟色
穿孔金属网
(80%-30%渐变穿孔率)
golden perforated metal
(80%-30% gradient translucent)
钢结构
和木胶合板
steel structure and
wood panel
贵宾休息室
VIP lounge
贵宾接待室
VIP reception
馆长办公室
curator office
办公室
office
影音区
multi-media
exhibition
坡道
ramp
竖向交通
vertical circulation
餐厅
restaurant
茶室
teahouse
麦浪主展区
main exhibition
"wheat field"
竖向交通
vertical circulation
等待区
waiting area
主入口
main entry
观众席
public seats
室外露天广场
Outdoor plaza
纪念品商店/书店
gift shop / bookstore
主出口
main exit

中国馆以“希望的田野”为主题，以4 590平方米的第二大外国自建馆精彩亮相2015年米兰世博会。展馆被设计成一朵漂浮在“希望的田野”上空的云。悬浮屋顶之下是一系列展览项目，这种独一无二的设计为中国馆创造了标志性的形象，也为世博会营造了一处别具一格的风景。

悬浮屋顶参考了中国传统建筑中的抬梁，设计成木架构，并运用现代建造技术创造大跨度以突出建筑的自然特性。屋顶借鉴传统的中国陶瓦屋顶架构覆以木瓦，并被重新诠释成大型的竹叶，在提升了屋顶的轮廓的同时，也为下面的公共空间提供了阴凉。

展馆的展览和文化产品被设计成一系列的空间体验，始于外部景观等候区，通往包括互动设施和来自中国40多个省份的文化产品的主题展示区。随后，参观者可通过一部微倾的公共楼梯到达多媒体设施上方的全景观赏平台。紧接着，他们会跟随指引进入一个多媒体空间，欣赏一部聚焦中国春节家庭团聚的短片。最后参观者可到达竹屋顶上方的室外平台，饱览世博会址广阔的景色。

中国国家馆设计方案紧扣“希望的田野，生命的源泉”的主题，以“天、地、人、和”为核心概念贯穿设计。建筑从正面看是自然的天际线，从背面看是城市的天际线。建筑方案通过建筑的屋顶、地面和空间，将“天、地、人”的概念和水稻、小麦的元素融入其中，如同希望田野上的一片“麦浪”。“希望的田野”意喻中国广袤的土地，隐喻中国古老的文明。展馆充分吸收中国传统建筑的结构和形态，结合现代技术，形成具有强烈中国传统建筑意向的中国馆形象。屋顶采用具有中国象征意义的竹编材料覆盖，大幅度降低了材料成本。在意大利灿烂阳光的照射下，将折射出金色的光芒。

中国国家馆展陈设计由五部分组成，主题分别为：“序、天、人、地、和。”“序”主题展区：该区为观众等候区。“天”主题展区：24节气汇集了中国人对于自然的尊重及顺应自然求发展的哲学观。“人”主题展区：是中国馆具体展项的集中展区，将围绕农业文明，民以食为天，面向未来的智慧三大板块进行展示。“地”主题展区：展示华夏大地山川河流地貌的多样性，以及农民劳作丰收的壮观场景。“和”主题影像厅：将以鲜明的故事线描述中国人在发展农业，获取粮食和食品的同时，寻找与自然和谐平衡，推动可持续发展的思索。

中国国家馆的标志(logo)，用线与面勾勒出大自然的轮廓和曲线，蓝色代表天空，绿色代表田野，金色代表粮食，红色代表人和生命。图形透叠寓意世间万物和谐共生、天人合一的传统思想。将中国传统书法和绘画元素融入现代图形设计，强化中国传统文化特色。

China Pavilion, second only to Germany in size, will welcome visitors with the theme “The Land of Hope”. Rejecting the typical notion of a cultural pavilion as an object in a plaza, the China Pavilion is instead conceived as a field of spaces. Envisioned as a cloud hovering over a “land of hope”, the Pavilion is experienced as a series of public programs located beneath a floating roof, the unique design of which creates an iconic image for the project and a unique presence within the Expo grounds.

Conceived as a timber structure that references the “raised-beam” system found in traditional Chinese architecture, the Pavilion roof also uses modern technology to create long spans appropriate to the building’s public nature. The roof is covered in shingled panels that reference traditional terra-cotta roof construction, but are reinterpreted as large bamboo leaves that enhance the roof profile while shading the public spaces below.

The Pavilion’s full exhibition and cultural offerings are experienced as a sequence of spaces, beginning with an exterior waiting area in the landscape, leading to a themed exhibition space with interactive installations and cultural offerings from forty Chinese provinces. After this, visitors are guided up a gently sloped public stair to a panoramic viewing platform above the multimedia installation, after which they are guided into a multimedia space featuring a short film focusing on family reunions during China’s annual Spring Festival. This sequence concludes with visitors stepping outside the building onto a platform above the bamboo roof that enjoys expansive views of the Expo grounds.

China Pavilion’s design focuses on the theme of “Land of Hope, Food for Life”, and takes Heaven, Earth, Human and Harmony as core design concepts. From the front the pavilion appears a natural skyline, while a city skyline forms from a rear view. The core concept of heaven, earth and human and the elements of rice and wheat are expressed on roof, ground and spaces, just like a wheat wave on the land of hope which means the vast land of China and imply our ancient civilization. The China Pavilion fully absorbs Chinese traditional architectural structure and form, meanwhile incorporates modern technologies to display the China image. The roof is clad in bamboo panels which reduce the material costs and refract golden light under Italian brilliant sunshine.

The China Pavilion is composed of five exhibition sections, namely the Preface, Heaven, Earth, Human and Harmony. The Preface exhibition section is a visitor waiting area. Heaven exhibition section displays Chinese traditional 24-solor-terms which embodies the philosophy of Chinese respecting for nature and complying with natural development. The "Human" hall is the major exhibiting space of China Pavilion where creative exhibits agricultural civilization, food as the paramount and facing the future themes. Earth exhibition section demonstrates the topographic diversity of mountains, hills and rivers as well as spectacular scenes of farmer harvest. The Harmony exhibition hall shows a short film to depict how Chinese people develop agriculture and search a balance with nature and sustinble development simultaneously.

China Pavilion Logo adopts lines and faces to outline natural contours and curves. Blue stands for sky, green for field, gold for food and red for human and life. All the figures overlap in transparent form that conveys a traditional thought that everything exists harmoniously with one another and heaven and human are also in a harmony. As for the logo design method, it blends in Chinese caligraphy and painting elements and modern graphic design to intensify the characteristics of Chinese traditional culture.

中国
China

桂炉烤鸭
全聚德

JAPAN PAVILION
日本馆

Harmonious Diversity
和谐多样性

设计: Atsushi Kitagawara Architects / 规划执行: Ishimoto Architectural & Engineering Firm
结构工程: Arup / 面积: 4 170 平方米

Design: Atsushi Kitagawara Architects / Execution Planning: Ishimoto Architectural & Engineering Firm
Structural Engineering: Arup / Area: 4,170 m²

日本館
GIAPPONE
slovakia

坐拥4 170平方米面积的日本馆将成为2015米兰世博会上最大的展馆之一。该馆的主题是“共存的多样性”，展馆正中央的木头不仅是建筑结构的一部分，更象征了植被、森林等自然元素。

日本馆将以一根简洁的筷子形状来呈现，从世博会缩写EXPO中的E字母铺陈开来，从意识上简单而形象地传递了其与食物的关联。这座双层建筑的基座是一个三维木质网格，象征着日本多样性的起源。一层是和食和日本农业展示区，二层为提供和食的日式餐馆及活动广场，地方政府将在这里宣传各自的特产。

该展馆旨在成为一个“包容多样性的碗”，在这里植根于日本的多样性元素能在全球性危机中被视为一个强大的潜在贡献力量，这也符合世博会的主题，例如食品安全。展馆的建造方式将融合日本传统建造技艺，该技艺表现在建于7世纪的佛教寺庙法隆寺，这座寺庙完全由木头制成，没有任何金属链接或支撑，并结合了日本如今在城市建筑中使用的反地震技术。日本展馆将会是迄今为止第一个将传统建造技术与现代研究、应用技术充分结合的展馆，旨在打造一个融合日本传统文化和先进技术的创意建筑。

The Japan Pavilion spreads over an exhibition area of 4,170 m² and it is one of the largest pavilions in the Expo Milano 2015. With the exhibition theme of “Harmonious Diversity”, it takes a wooden pillar in the center of its pavilion as a component of the architecture, which also symbolizes natural elements of vegetation and forest.

The Japan Pavilion appears to be a piece of chopstick shape in letter E form deriving from the abbreviation of “Expo” to exprss a connection with food. The architecture is of two levels on foundation support of a three-dimensional wooden grid that will symbolizes the origin of Japan’s diversity.The ground floor is an exhibition hall for Japanese food and agriculture, and the second level is Japanese restaurants and activity areas where Japanese provincial governments will propaganda their featured products.

The Pavilion will take the shape of a “bowl of diversity”, and the “diversity” cultivated in Japan is a great potential for contribution to global issues in relation to the Expo’s theme, such as food security. The traditional wooden construction techniques of Japan — epitomized in Horyuji Temple — use “a compressive strain method” in which pieces of wood are connected together with couplers and joints for support. This results in constructions that are extremely resistant to earthquakes; a kind of building that has sometimes been called “living construction (or life theory construction)”.The pavilion,created from a three-dimensional wooden grid, will be the first ever to use both traditional construction knowledge about wooden frameworks and the modern analysis and application techniques used for “the compressive strain method”. This will result in truly innovative construction that fuses Japan’s traditional culture and advanced technology.

PAVILLON
MONACO
日本館
GIAPPONE

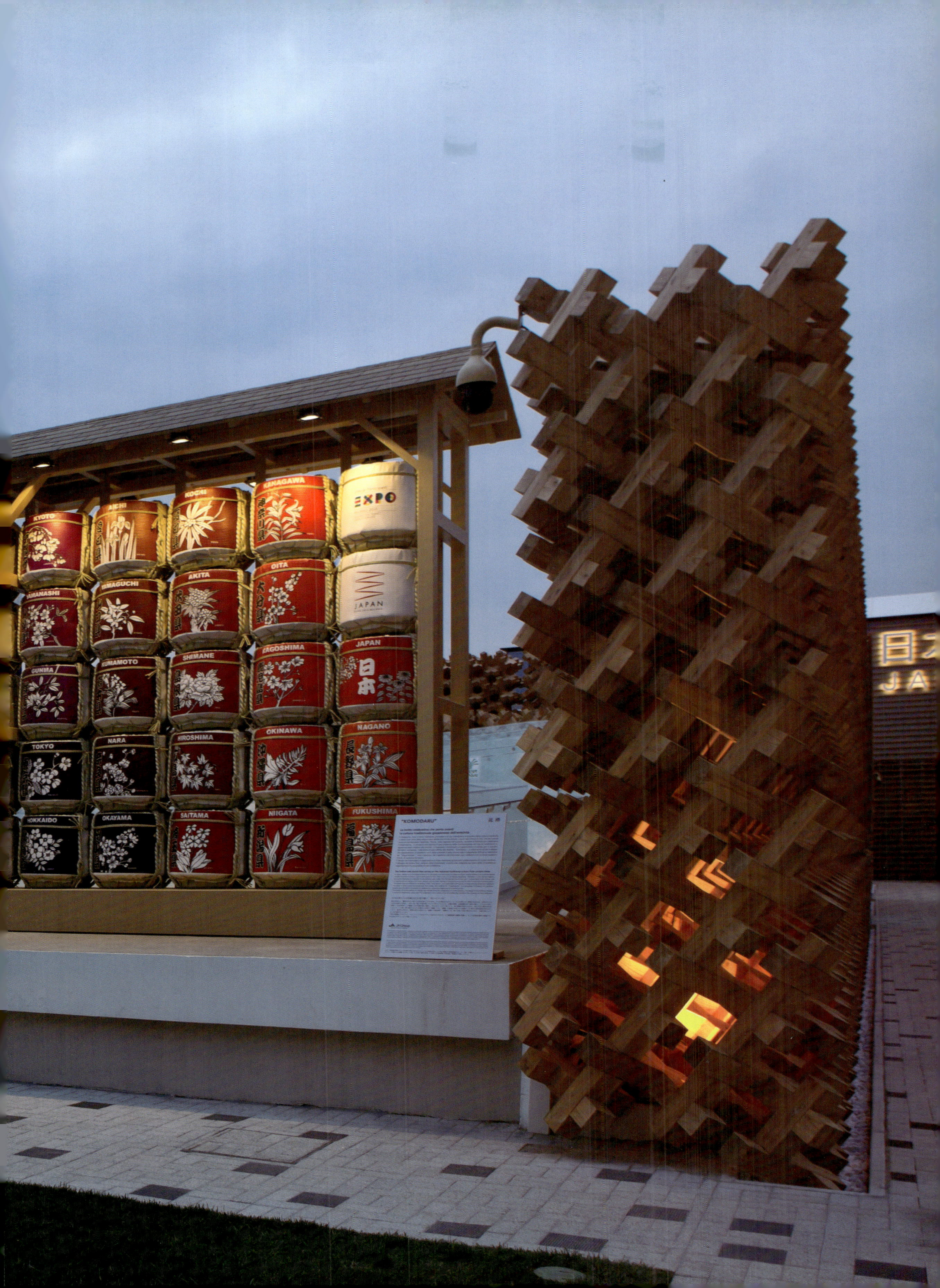

KYOTO
AICHI
KOCHI
KANAGAWA
EXPO
AKITA
OITA
JAPAN
SHIMANE
GUNMA
JAPAN
日本
NAGANO
TOKYO
NARA
HIROSHIMA
OKINAWA
OKAYAMA
SAITAMA
NIIGATA
FUKUSHIMA
"KOMODARU"

生を知らず

Panasonic
Panasonic

野
菜
Soia e derivati
Soy beans and related food

主菜: Portate principali
魚
Pesce
Fish
principali
Carne
Meat
副菜: 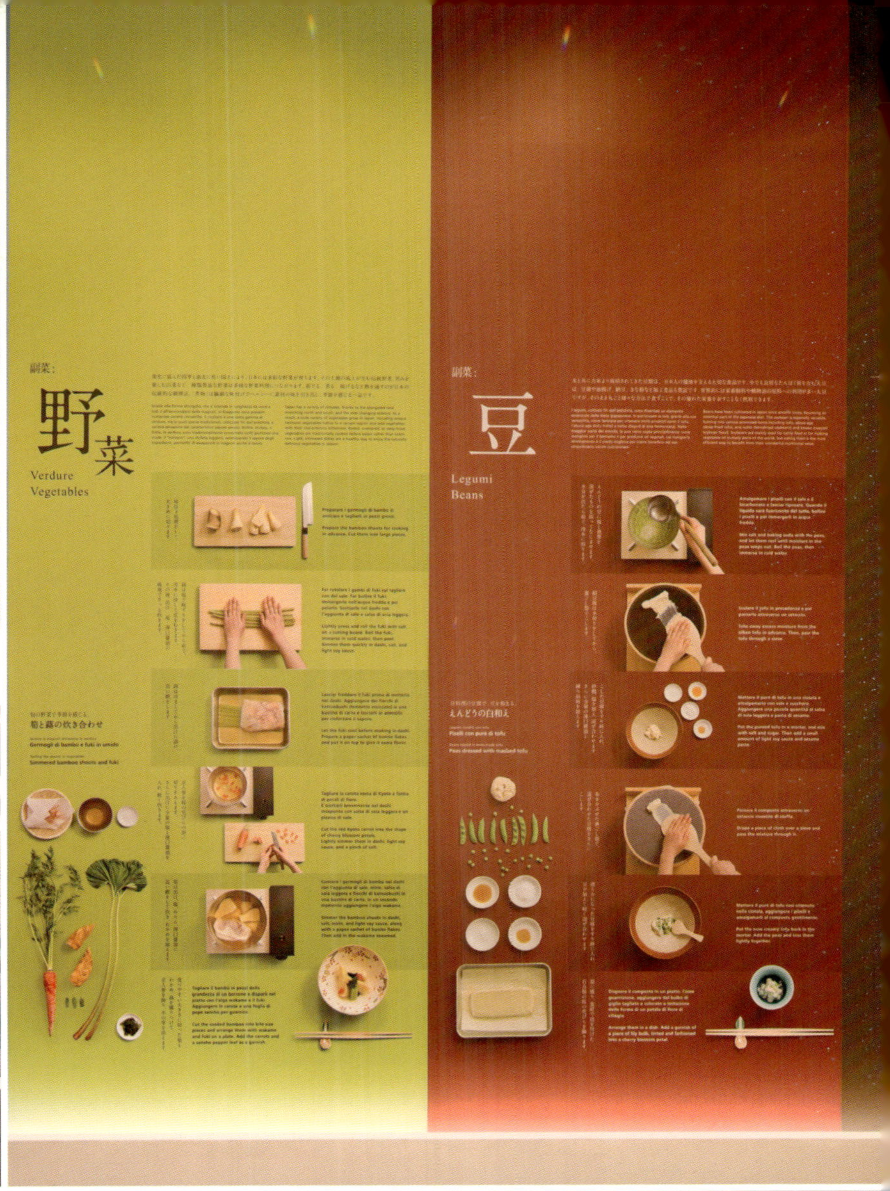
野菜
Verdure
Vegetables
副菜:
豆
Legumi
Beans

REPUBLIC OF KOREA PAVILION
韩国馆

You are what you eat
人如其食

建筑设计：Archiban / 项目面积：3 880 平方米

Architectural Design: Archiban / Project Area: 3,880 m²

COREA

COREA
Republic of Korea
대한민국

COREA

韩国馆将以“月亮罐”作为建筑主题，展馆优美的曲线和微妙起伏的外形既简单雅致，又能与周围环境和谐贴合，看起来像是浮在空中的一轮满月。这种满月形状源于韩国传统的一种陶制器皿。韩国的陶器经历了从简单的粗制陶碗到青瓷和釉瓷的发展过程，而这些陶瓷碗成为了本届米兰世博会韩国馆的主题。

韩国馆本次的主题将是展示本国传统的烹饪习俗，突出他们饮食的优良性和可延续性。展览将提供更大视角来探索烹饪创新和日常饮食调和，在保证传统的同时给未来的烹饪发展提供可持续的发展。韩国馆的展览主题核心在于推进可持续发展的健康饮食。在打出“寒食节，食在未来，人如其食 ”的标语下，展览将演绎健康的饮食是如何影响我们未来的生活以及我们自己的面貌。吃什么以及怎么吃都将反映我们自己是何种状况。健康的饮食习惯不仅能帮助我们自身做到最好，而且能帮我们保护我们赖以生存的环境。

本届韩国馆将举办三个主题展，它们分别是：食物交响曲，科学的饮食时间和土地的智慧，关注我们人类在饮食方面面临的问题。

The pavilion will be constructed with the architectural theme of the "Moon Jar", a traditional pottery vessel in the shape of the full moon. During the past, pottery in Korea was transformed from simple ceramic grain bowls into beautiful celadons and porcelains. These bowls represent Republic of Korea's theme of Expo Milano 2015.

The Korea Pavilion will showcase the culinary practices of Korea founded on its indigenous traditions, highlighting their benefits and sustainable properties. The pavilion aims to provide a much broader scope of the cultural creativity and adaptability of Korean cuisine into everyday life, providing a sustainable alternative for the future while preserving tradition. The overarching theme of the Korea Pavilion is to promote a more sustainable way of life through healthy eating. Under the banner "Hansik, Food for the Future: You are What You Eat" the exhibition will showcase how a healthy diet can affect one's outlook and appearance on life. What we eat and how we eat all reflect the way we are. A healthier diet will not only help us make the most out of life but also preserve the environment around us.

The Korea Pavilion will address three issues of food that the human kind is confronted with: symphony of food, science of time and wisdom of the earth.

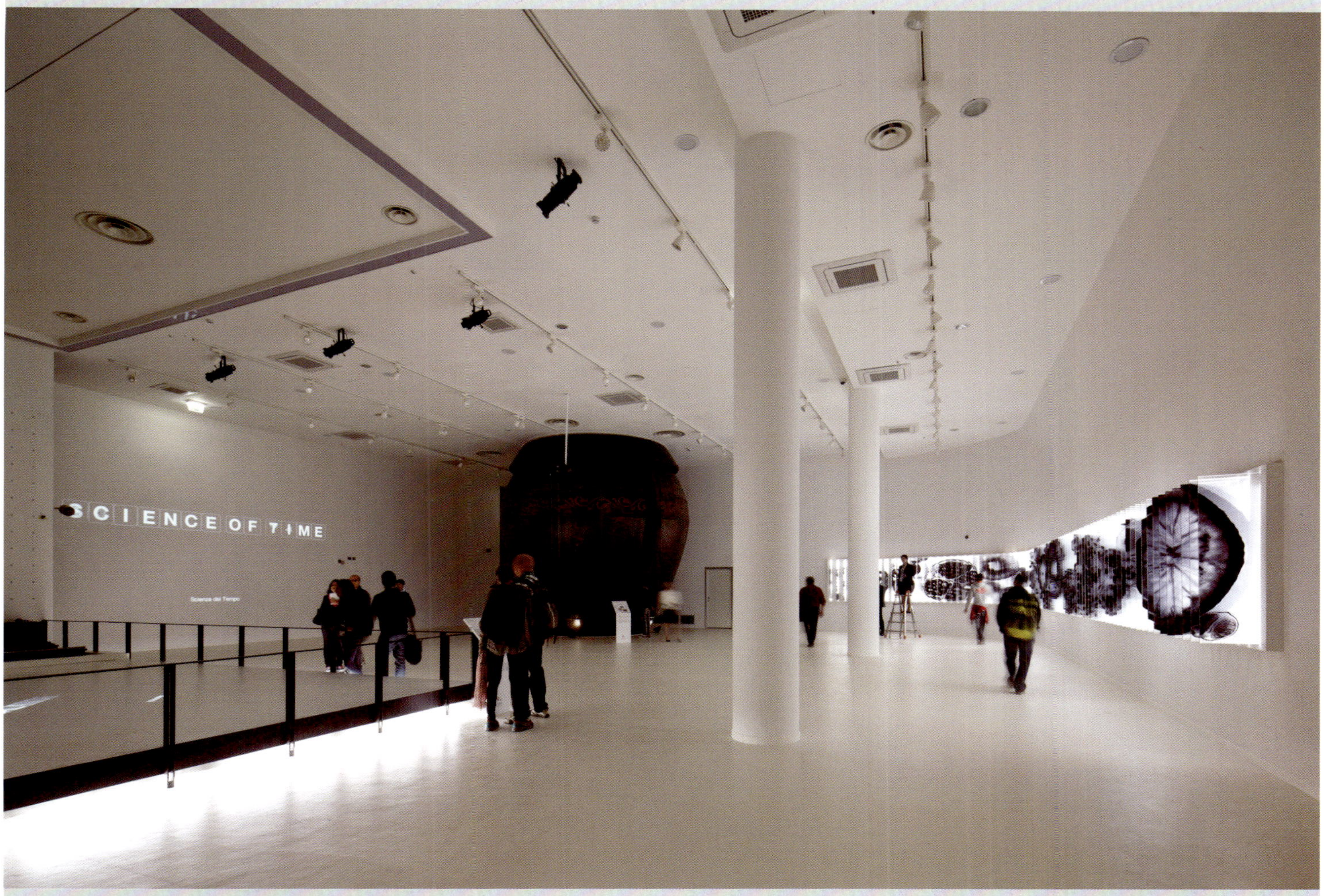
SCIENCE OF TIME
Scienza del Tempo

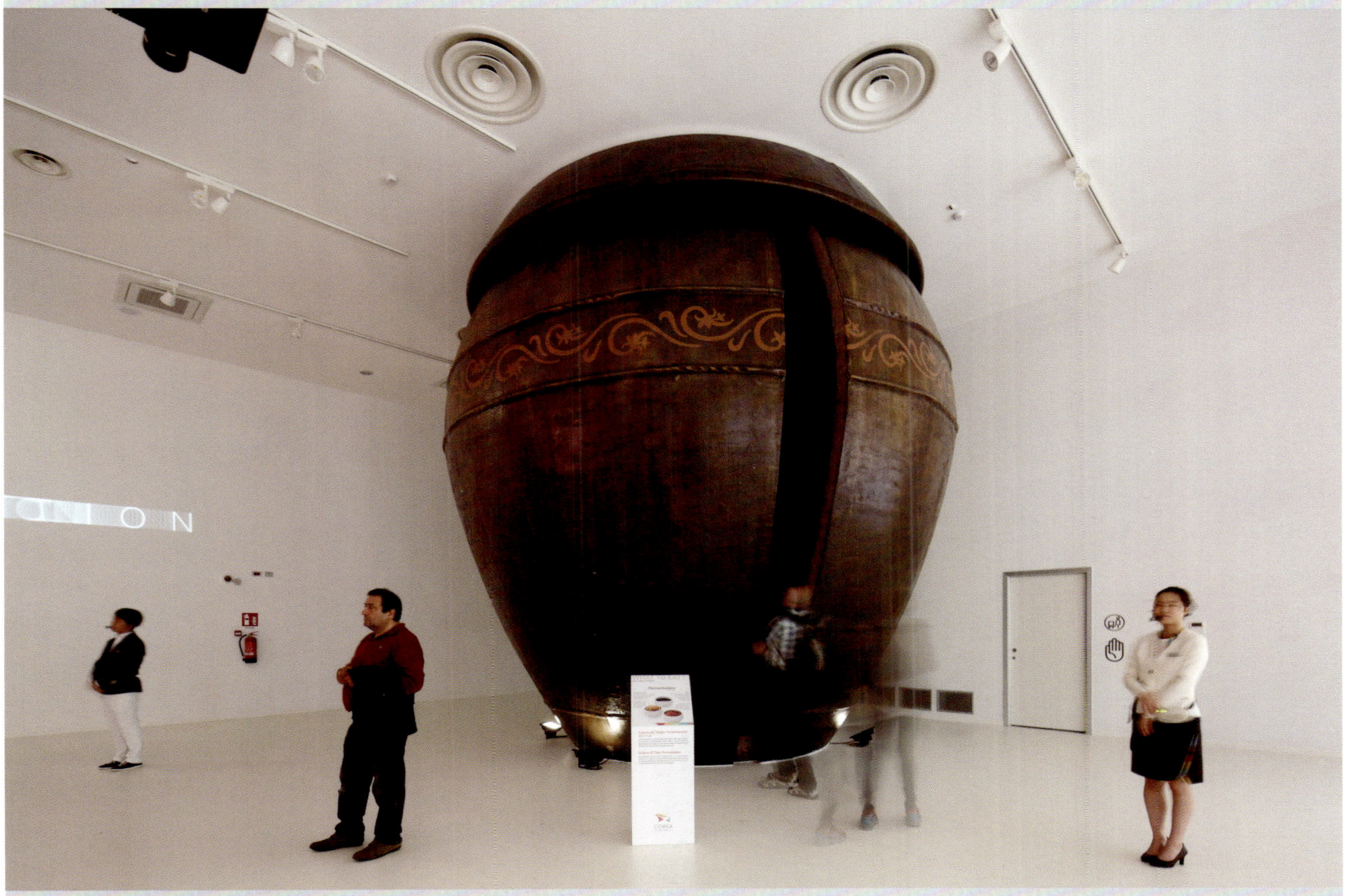

Pad thai
Sausage Stew
Budaejjigae
Kimchijjigae
Massamancurry
sandwich
noodle
Seafood
Jokbal
Beefsteak
Loach Soup
Cheeseburger
Gimbap
PineNutPorridge
AssamLaksa
duck
Stir-friedPork
Bulgogi with Rice
Dried Pollack Soup
Haemulpajeon

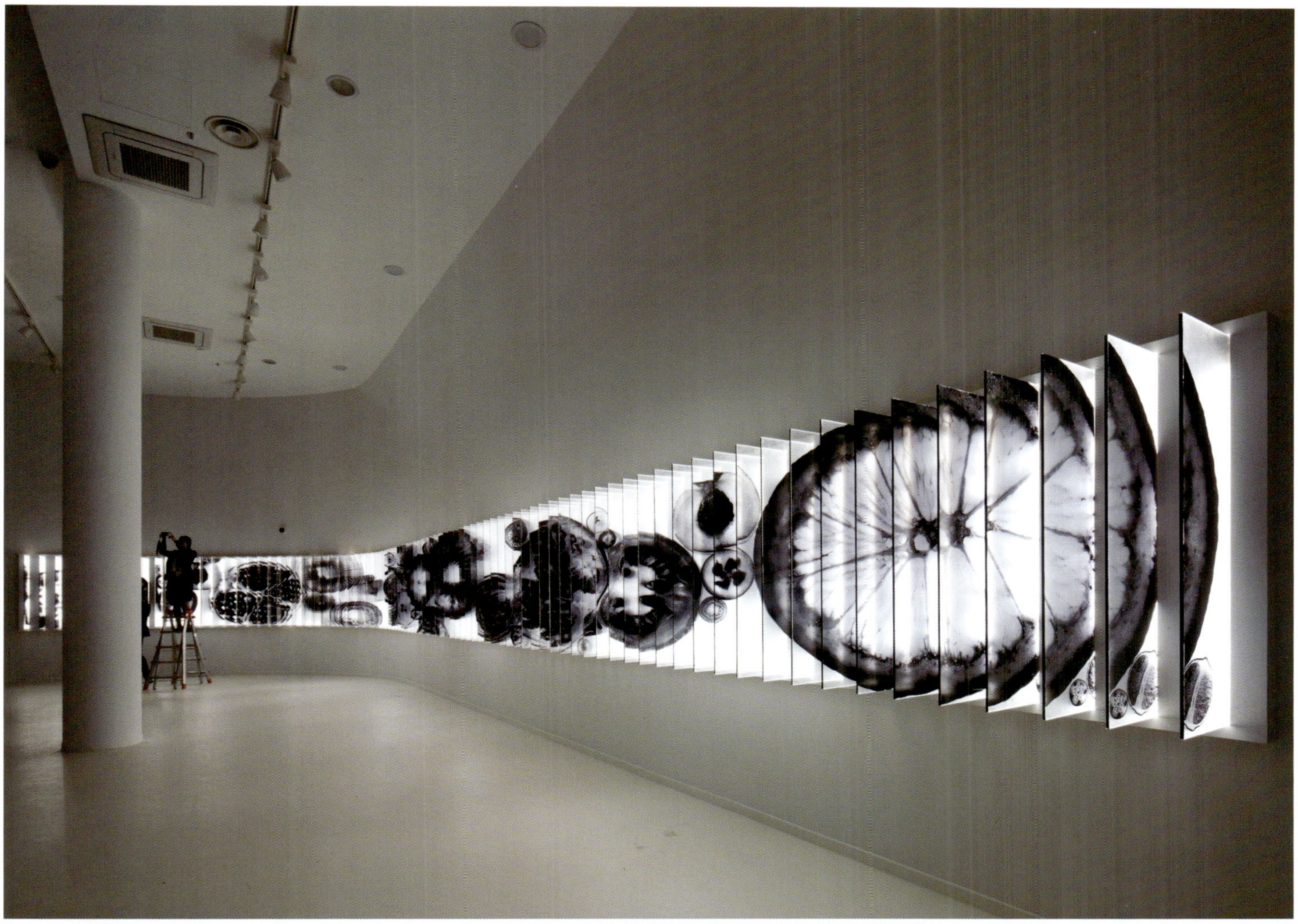

ESTINTORE
CIBO COREANO
HANSIK
Chiedi e la Tradizione Risponderà
Ask and Tradition Shall Answer

COREA
Republic of Korea
PIANO TERRA
GROUND FLOOR
RISTORANTE HANSIK
HANSIK RESTAURANT
DESSERT COREANI
KOREAN DESSERTS
NEGOZIO DI SOUVENIR
SOUVENIR SHOP
COREA

THAILAND PAVILION
泰国馆

Nourishing and Delighting the World
滋养地球，欢乐世界

建筑设计：曼谷建筑事务所 / 主设计师：Smith Obayawat / 总建筑师：Francesc Domingo / 设计总监：Waroon Limpchalerm
设计团队：Chris Singshinsuk, Nattakit Jeerapatmaitree, Khongphak Pansoongnern, Natchaya Promsuwan, Margot Therond, Elodie Artieres
结构，机电工程师：Meinhardt / 景观顾问：Landprocess- Kotch Voraakhom / 首席顾问：Work and Right Joint Venture

Architect: The Office of Bangkok Architects / Design Principal:
Smith Obayawat / Architect In Charge: Francesc Domingo / Design Director: Waroon Limpchalerm
Design Team: Chris Singshinsuk, Nattakit Jeerapatmaitree, Khongphak Pansoongnern, Natchaya Promsuwan, Margot Therond, Elodie Artieres
Structural, Mechanical and Electrical Engineer: Meinhardt / Landscape Consultant:
Landprocess- Kotch Voraakhom / Lead Consultant: Work and Right Joint Venture

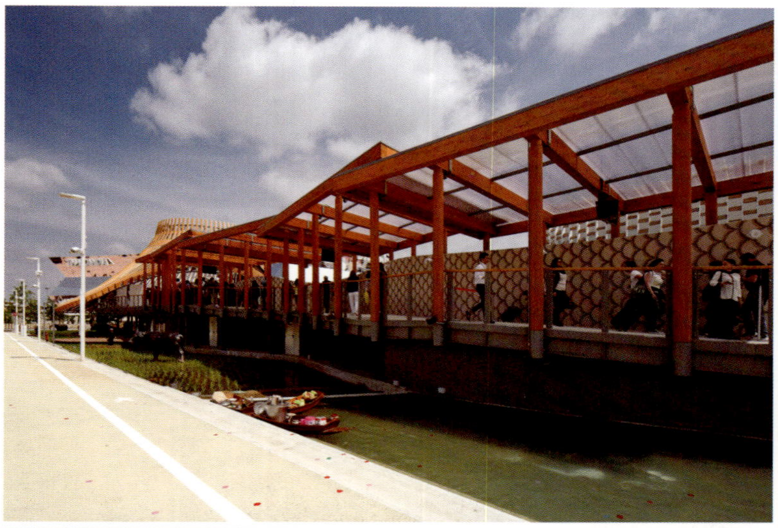

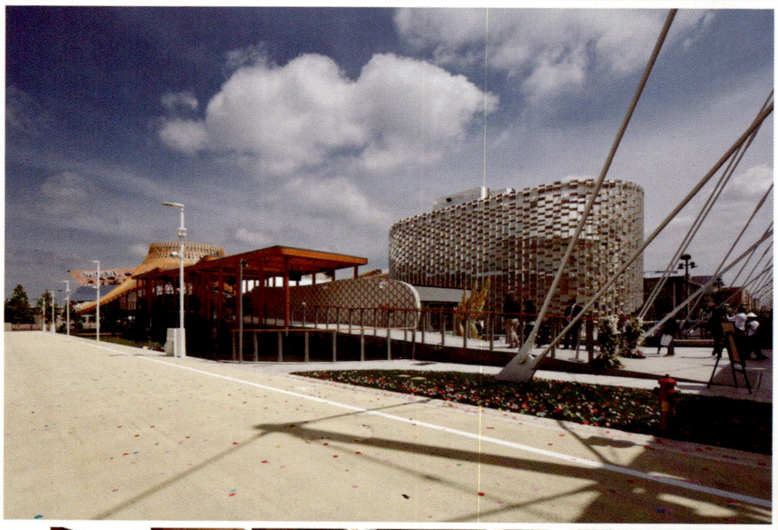

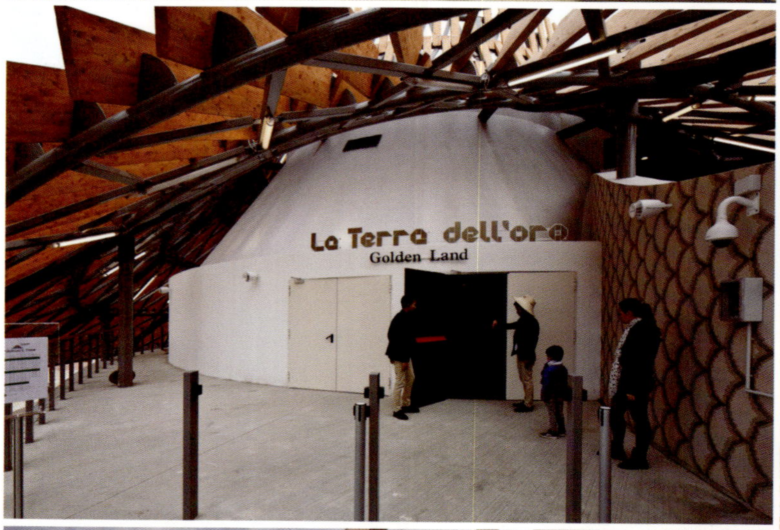
La Terra dell'oro
Golden Land

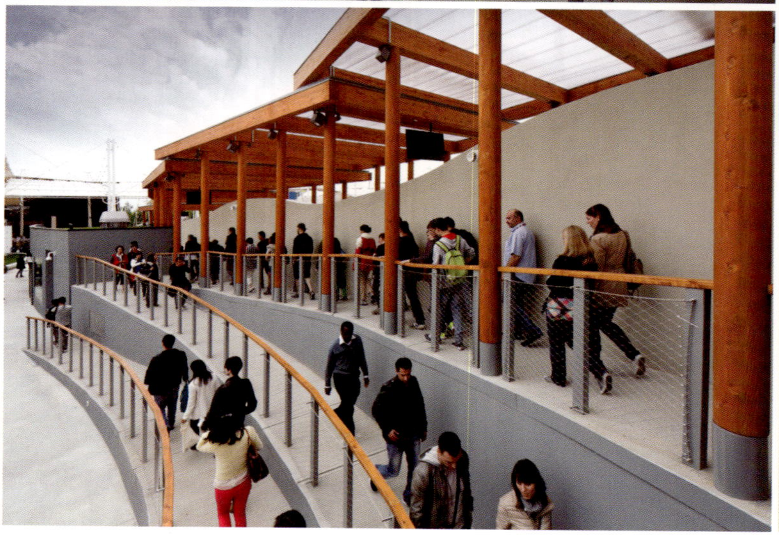

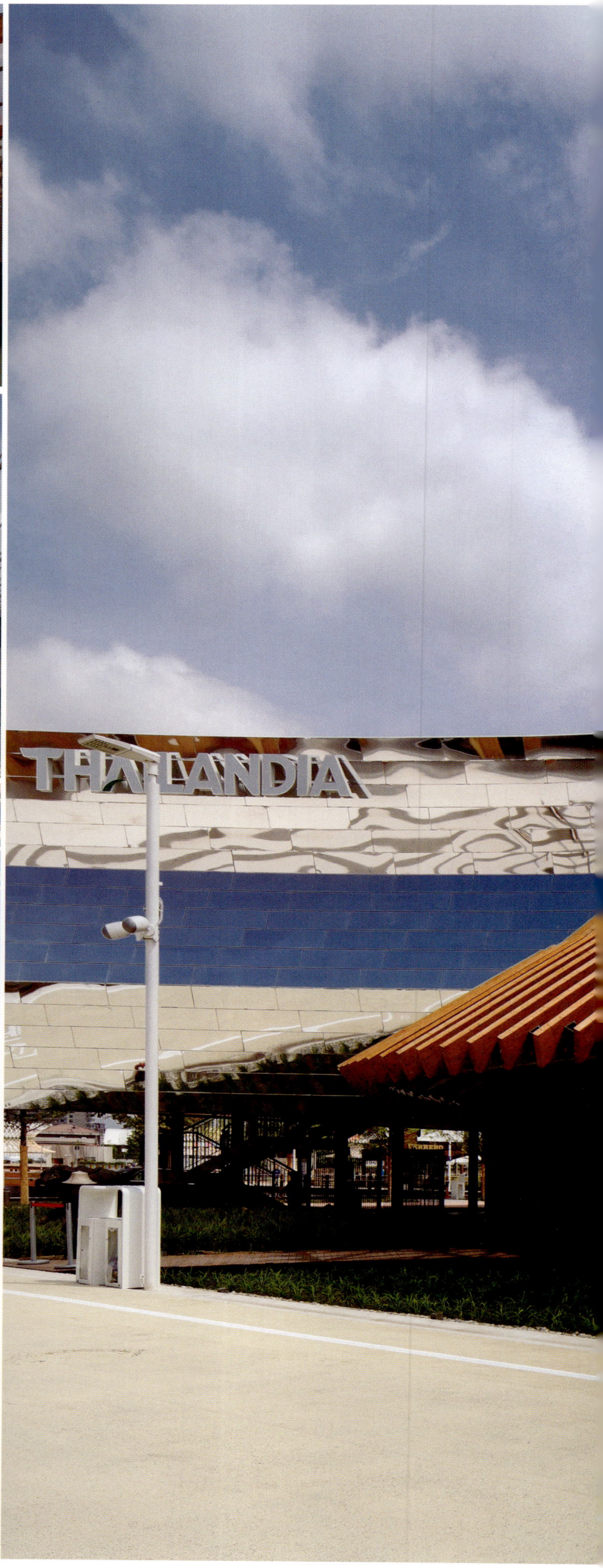
THAILANDIA

Golden Land

曼谷建筑事务所（OBA）设计的泰国馆运用农业和宗教特质诠释了泰国。展馆坐落于世博会的主干道中央，与其毗邻的人工河也将作为展览的一部分，正好呼应了曼谷“亚洲威尼斯”的美称。

水资源对泰国农业起到了很大的作用，泰国馆一直强调这一点。一进入泰国馆的通道处，就可以看到来自泰国神话传说中的水蛇娜迦（Naga）的生动描写。这条通道将会带领游客穿过一块稻田，通过不同生长阶段的水稻充分展示了泰国农业的发展。

泰国馆的入口本身是一个巨大的木质结构，模仿泰国农民和小摊贩戴的一种叫做ngob的传统帽子，很具有泰国文化气息。泰国馆最突出的元素ngob的设计成为该国家农产品展示的一个象征。该馆的建造也非常具有文化气息，一道砖砌墙很好地模仿了泰国寺庙的传统墙壁构造。每块砖都有三个不同的倾斜角度，表面镀有一层闪闪的镀面。稻田、游人和天空在这面墙上都能反射出来。通过这种方式，将泰国的农业、自然和人民有机地融合在一起。

The honor of designing Thailand's pavilion for the 2015 Milan Exposition has officially been awarded to The Office of Bangkok Architects (OBA). The firm's winning design incorporates the Expo's theme of "Feeding the Planet, Energy for Life" with the agrarian and religious qualities that define the Kingdom of Thailand. Located centrally on the Expo's main avenue, the pavilion will be adjacent to a canal that will be used as a part of the exhibition, relating back to Bangkok's informal title as the "Venice of Asia."

The pavilion will emphasize the crucial aspect that water plays in Thai agriculture in a number of ways. A depiction of Naga, the legendary water snake from Thai mythology, will greet visitors at the beginning of the pavilion's walkway. This walkway will take visitors across a rice field that has been planted in various stages of cultivation, displaying the foundation of agriculture in Thailand.

The entrance to the pavilion itself is a large wood-frame replica of a ngob, the traditional hat worn by farmers and vendors in Thailand. The most prominent element of the pavilion, the ngob becomes a symbol of the country's agricultural identity. The pavilion building proper will be framed by a brick wall modeled after the traditional walls of Thai temples. Sloped at the three different angles and clad in a reflective surface, the wall will reflect the rice fields of the pavilion, the visitors to the Expo, and the sky. In this way, the wall will represent the agriculture, nature, and people of Thailand.

From various fertility of national
to the continuously developed
SCIENCE
Dalle varietà fertili delle risorse nazionali
al continuo sviluppo della
RESEARCH
SUSTAINABLE

VEITNAM PAVILION 越南馆

Water and Lotus 水和莲

设计公司：Vo Trong Nghia Architects / 建筑师：Vo Trong Nghia
设计团队：Takashi Niwa, Raffaello Rosselli, Marek Obtulovic, Nguyen Viet Hung, Dau Nhat Quang, Hoang Quoc Bao

Design Company: Vo Trong Nghia Architects / Architect: Vo Trong Nghia
Design Team: Takashi Niwa, Raffaello Rosselli, Marek Obtulovic, Nguyen Viet Hung, Dau Nhat Quang, Hoang Quoc Bao

越南馆的设计灵感来自莲花，该展馆由一些坐落于水池上的用竹木包裹的伞状结构组成，上方种有植物。建筑师提到，莲花是越南的国花，象征着纯洁、承诺和对未来的乐观。

除了莲花的美，它还与越南的菜肴有着紧密的联系。所有植物都可以是美味的食物。作为一个临时展馆，建筑师的角色是将展馆对环境的影响力减到最低。为了达到这一点，该设计广泛使用了竹材，这是一种快速增长、低碳的建筑材料。该展馆还能被拆解，以重复使用其构件。

越南馆由柱子结构和树木作为馆顶的庇荫遮盖，下面是一个"莲花池"，莲花池作为整座建筑的底层给馆内带来清凉的微气候环境。在天气较冷的时候，一幅可折叠的屏风展开来可以保护馆内的热空气流失；而在暖和的时候，屏风可以移开让清风吹入馆内保证清凉。设计师希望通过越南馆的建筑设计向全世界展示出越南人民对自然的热爱。

Inspired by the lotus, the pavilion features a number of bamboo clad, umbrella-like structures supporting trees above a pool of wate. "The Lotus is Vietnam's national flower, a symbol of purity, commitment and optimism for the future," say the architects.

Apart from its beauty, the lotus has a strong connection with Vietnamese cuisine; none of the plant is left for waste, with all parts of the plant considered a delicacy. As a temporary event, the architect's role in designing the pavilion is to reduce its impact." To do so, the design uses bamboo extensively, a fast-growing and low-carbon material. The pavilion is also designed to be disassembled so that its parts can be reused.

For its visitors, the pavilion will provide shade under the bamboo structures and trees, while the 'Lotus Pond' that permeates the building's floor will provide a cool microclimate inside the pavilion. A folding screen will provide protection from the elements on cooler days, however on warm days the screen can be removed, and the pavilion will be cooled by the breeze.With the pavilion, the designer hopes to demonstrate "the Vietnamese love of nature which will be shared with the whole world."

MALAYSIA PAVILION
马来西亚馆

Towards a Sustainable Food Ecosystem
可持续性发展的食品生态系统

设计单位：Hijjas Kasturi Associates / 项目面积：2 047 平方米

Design Company: Hijjas Kasturi Associates / Project Area: 2,047 m²

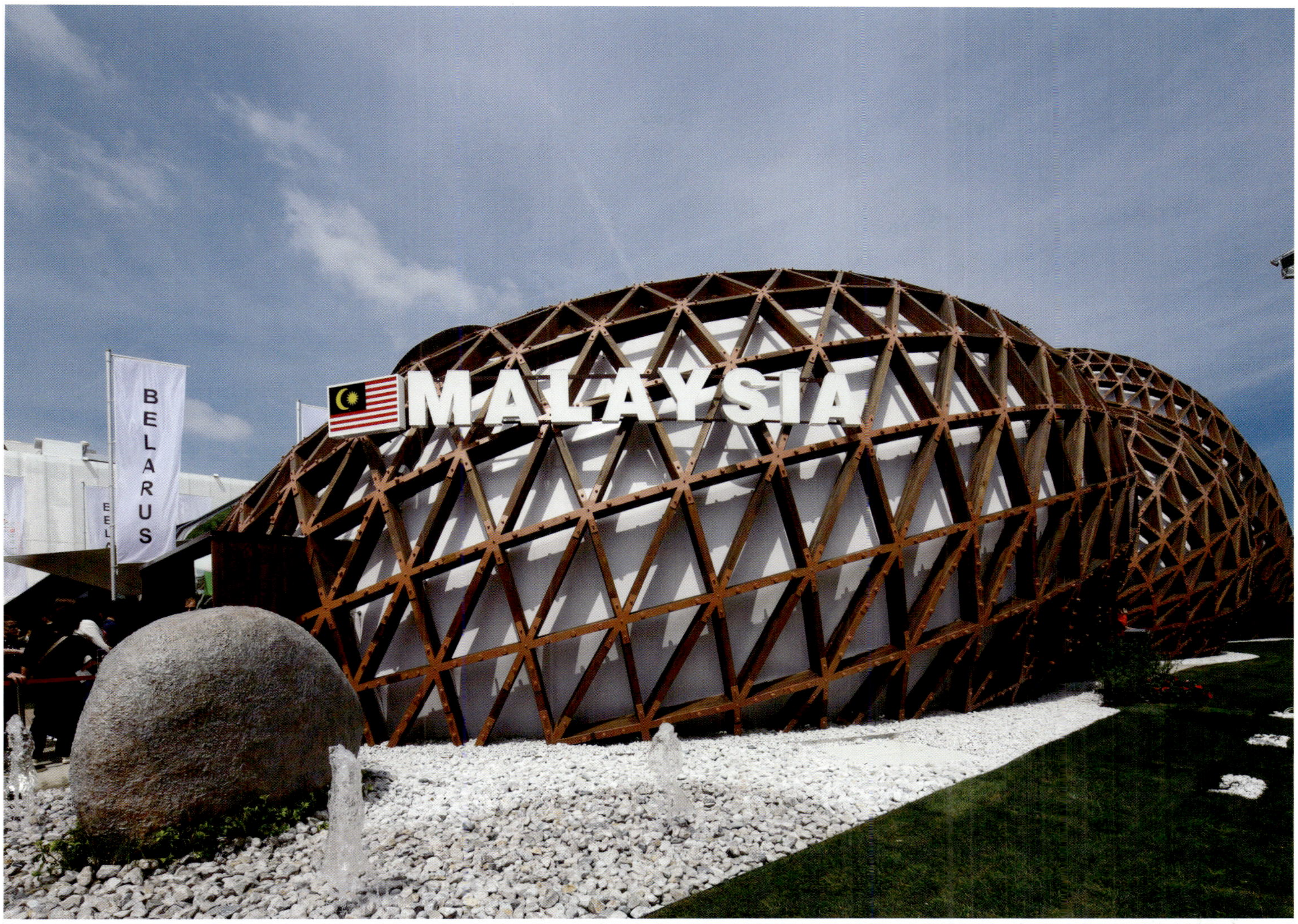
MALAYSIA
BELARUS

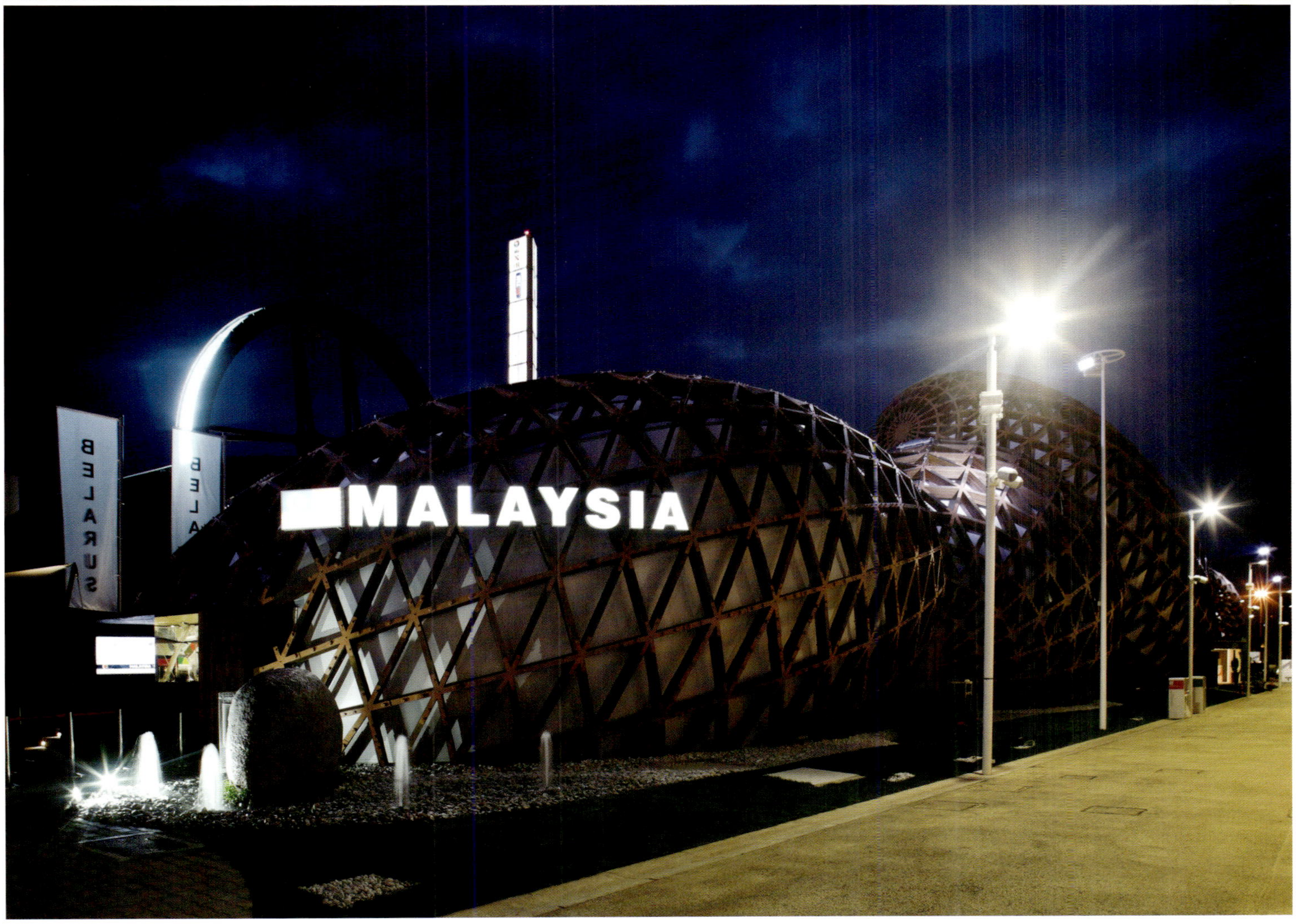
MALAYSIA
BELARUS

马来西亚作为全球17个联合国区域之一，她丰富的文化遗产和高品质的清真食品与2015米兰世博会主旨完美吻合。

马来西亚展馆面积共2 047平方米，它诠释了在建筑设计上的传统与创新，也演绎了从种子到端上餐桌食物的全过程。四颗种子的造型十分吸引眼球。曲面的设计和交织的文理体现了马来西亚的多彩与活力。展馆的设计灵感来自于雨林中不起眼的植物种子。而正是这样的种子代表着生长，代表着新旅程的开始以及自身无限发展的潜力。

建筑设计糅合了绿色和可持续发展两方面特点，符合本届世博会的主题。外部的种子造型采用了胶合木条，这种创新型结构性木材是马来西亚当地可反复利用的建筑材料。以这种轻质的木料胶合板搭建横梁，增加展馆的跨度。和钢结构的设计相比，这种木质设计更节约成本。此外，展馆周围的坡道和人行道都是用回收的稻壳铺设的。对自然材料的利用以及本届马来西亚展馆所表现的复杂建筑结构体现了马来西亚这个国家在建筑设计和创新型材料方面的先进性。

The experience of Malaysia as one of the 17 mega-diverse areas of the world, with its rich cultural heritage and high quality halal food, is made available to all visitors in perfect equilibrium with the aims of Expo Milano 2015.

The pavilion will be spread over 2,047 m^2, which is both traditional and innovative in design, it illustrates, from seed to table. The Malaysia pavilion takes the shape of four seeds. The curves of the design and the weaving patterns on the structure reflect the versatility and dynamism of the nation. The Malaysia Pavilion design drew inspiration from the humble rainforest seed. The seed, a symbol of growth, signifies a beginning of a journey, and the potential within.

The architectural design incorporates green and sustainable features in line with the sustainability theme of the Expo. The external structure of the seeds are constructed with “Glulam” or glued laminated timber, an innovative structural timber made of local sustainable material. The choice of natural materials, combined with the structurally complex form of Malaysia Pavilion at Expo Milano 2015 is a deliberate effort to showcase Malaysia’s capabilities in both design and innovative materials.

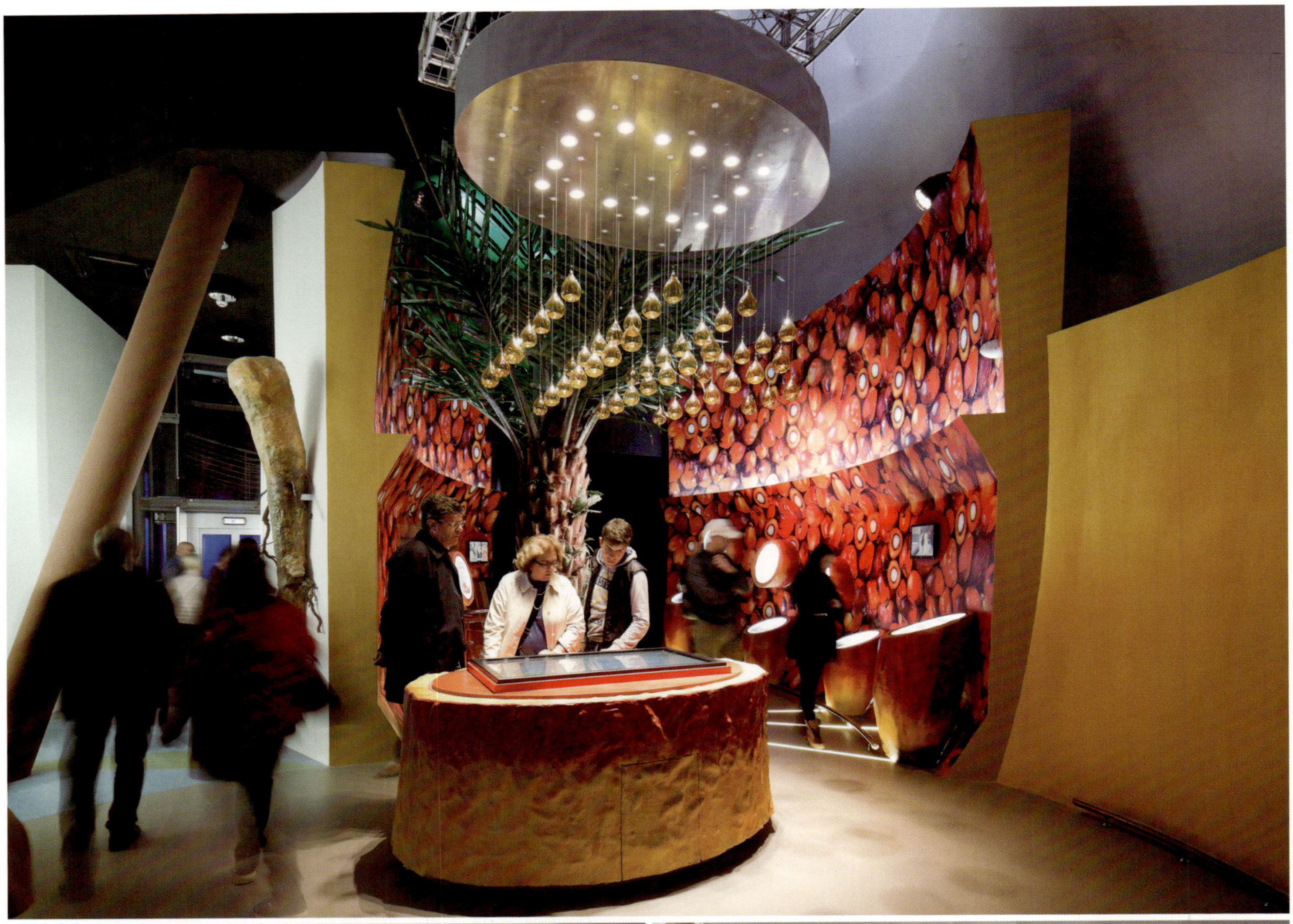

nsi...
dove si possono risvegliare i sen

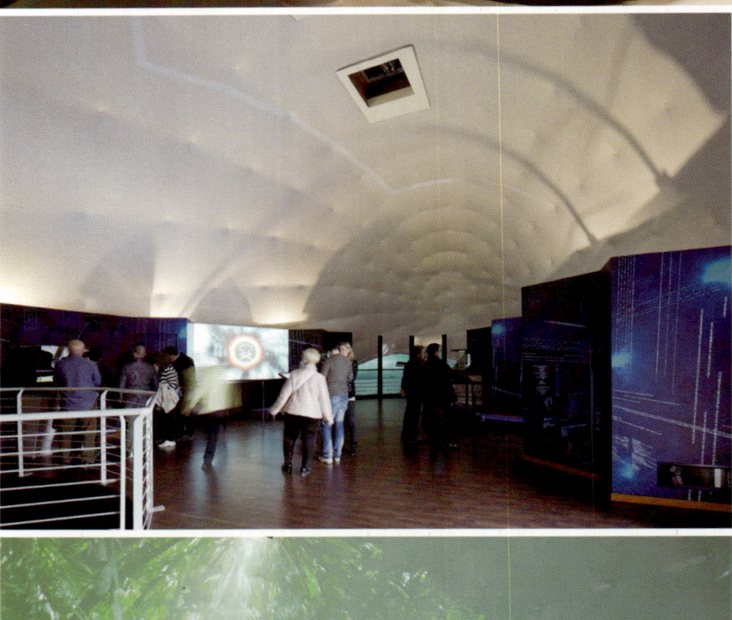

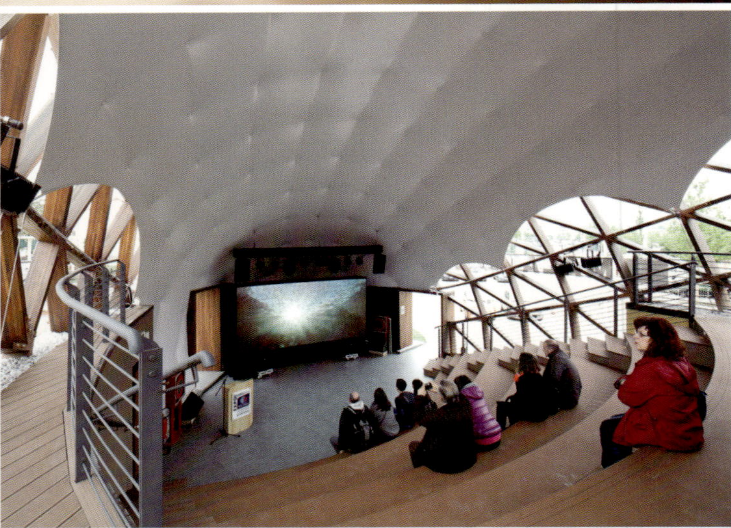

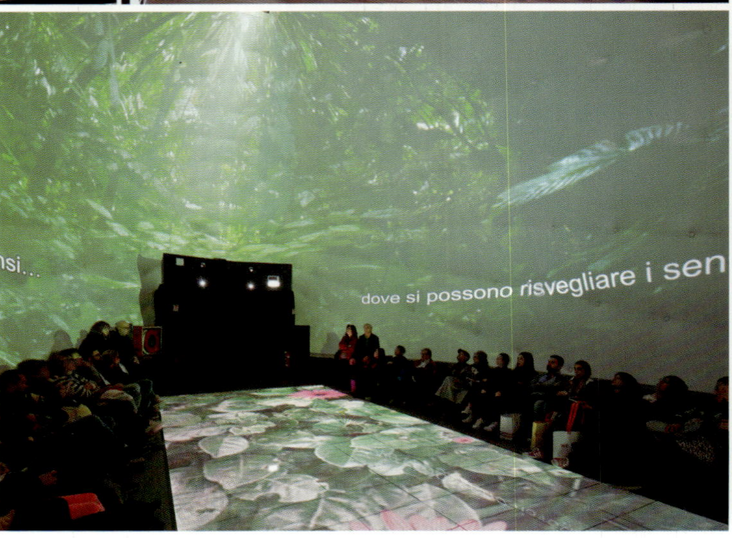

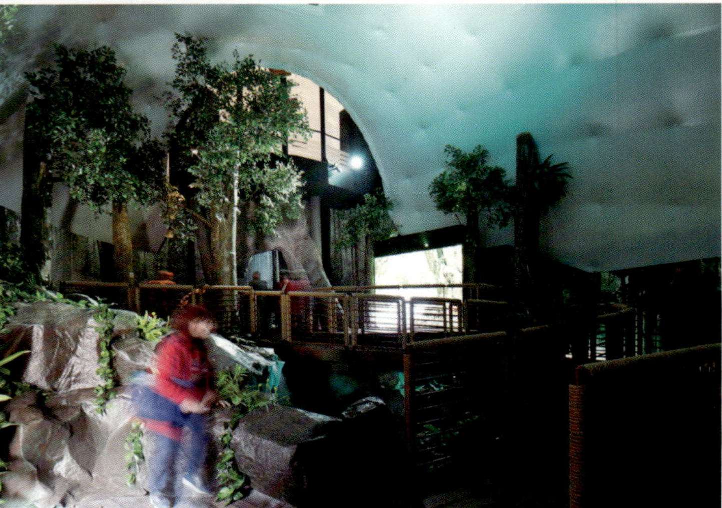

ANIMAL
SPECIES

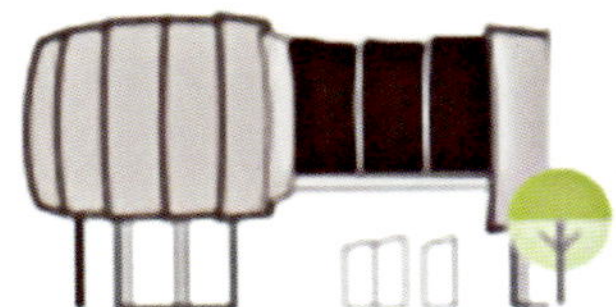

INDONESIA PAVILION
印度尼西亚馆

Tradition and Local Wisdom with a Touch of Modernity
传统与富于现代性的智慧

建筑设计：Tanah Air / 项目面积：1 175 平方米

Architectural Design: Tanah Air / Project Area: 1,175 m²

印度尼西亚馆的造型像一幢大房子，容纳着各种活动在里面进行。印尼人把它称之为家，因为这里就好像是他们生活的家园一般。印尼人管他们的家园为水的领地。因此，印尼馆的设计结合了群岛中的农场和渔场概念，设计上分别用藤制和竹制的捕鱼工具和传统的印尼农作物储藏室来象征印尼人精巧的手工艺和肥沃的土地以及富足的农业。

印尼馆采用的是钢架结构，这样有利于简单快速地完成建造。整座建筑的外立面采用100%环保的藤条仿制材料。展馆顶层的咖啡馆墙面采用植物作为遮挡，为室内提供充足的新鲜空气。

The Indonesia Pavilion represents a house that accommodates many activities inside it. A home, that is familiar to the Indonesian, just like their homeland. Using a more noble term, Indonesia people call their homeland Tanah Air. The building concept of the Indonesian Pavilion refers to the interaction of farming and fishing communities in the Nusantara (an Indonesian word for archipelago) through Bubu and Lumbung. Bubu Ikan (Fishing Tool)–handmade from rattan or bamboo by the skilled Indonesian craftsmen-represents the nation's maritime wealth, whereas Lumbung symbolizes the fertile soil of Indonesia and the nation's agricultural wealth.

The Pavilion is built using a steel structure, to simplify and expedite the construction in Italy. Almost the entire building skin is made out of imitation rattan which is 100% environment-friendly. The wall of the café is vertically covered at the top with plants to act as a filter, provide fresh air.

INDONESIA
PAVILION
Stage of The World

NEPAL PAVILION
尼泊尔馆

Food Security and Sustainable for Development
食品安全与可持续发展

建筑设计：Implementing Expert Group / 项目面积：2 717平方米

Architectural Design: Implementing Expert Group / Project Area: 2,717 m²

尼泊尔馆由IEG设计，这个设计团队曾参与尼泊尔在1988年，1990年，2000年和2010年的世博会展馆设计。本次米兰世博会，IEG为尼泊尔设计的独立国家馆让人联想起曼陀罗，即在佛教里象征了宇宙的设计。通过各种几何造型塑造出典型的圆形构架，唤起人们对具有神秘色彩的佛教徒和印度教徒生活的好奇和探究。

步入尼泊尔馆，参观者仿佛置身于加德满都的古老聚落。几百年来，不同种族、不同信仰和不同社会地位的人在这里和谐共居，形成了一个多彩世界。尼泊尔本土的房屋多用金属、石料、陶瓦并嵌以木材而建，几百年代代相传的建屋手艺让尼泊尔的工匠们敢自诩为最棒的建筑家。IEG培养的木工、石匠、工匠和艺术师一齐上阵，让世界重温美丽的尼泊尔传统房舍。

在世博会建馆期间，因尼泊尔国内发生严重地震，大部分参与建展的设计和施工人员皆回国参与灾后重建，故尼泊尔馆未完全完工。

Nepal's pavilion has been designed by the Implementing Expert Group (IEG), the same team of architects that was chosen by the Nepalese government for their pavilions at the Universal Expositions of 1988, 1990, 2000 and 2010. The pavilion at Expo Milano 2015 is reminiscent of the Mandala, a circular symbol formed by geometric shapes, that evokes the mythological circle of life for Buddhists and Hindus.

Visitors will feel as if they have stepped into an ancient settlement in the valleys of Kathmandu, where people of different ethnicities, religions, and social backgrounds have lived in harmony for centuries, and will be immersed in a world of vivid colors. The Nepalese houses have long been decorated with metal, stone, and terracotta, as well as inlaid wood, skills that have been honed through centuries of experience by the artisans who competed among themselves to be the best. The Implementing Expert Group (IEG) trained teams of carpenters, masons, craftsmen and artists to replicate the many elements of these beautiful traditional Nepalese houses.

During the construction of the pavilion, there outbursted a disastrous earthquake in Nepal, therefore, most of the designing and constructing personnel went back for post-disaster construction, and the Nepal Pavilion has not completed yet at the opening ceremony of the Expo.

AZERBAIJAN PAVILION
阿塞拜疆馆

Protection of Organic Food and Biodiversity for Future Generations
为了下一代，保护有机食物和生物多样性

设计单位：Simmetrico Network, Arassociati Architecture, AG&P / 项目建筑师：Riccardo Cigolotti
结构工程师：Ideas / 景观设计师：AG&P / 建筑公司：Simmetrico

Design Company: Simmetrico Network, Arassociati Architecture, AG&P / Architect: Riccardo Cigolotti
Structural, Mechanical and Electrical Engineer: Ideas / Landscape Design: AG&P / Architect: Simmetrico

Azerbaigian
Azerbaijan

对称的网格结构很好地展现了阿塞拜疆馆简约又不失现代感的建筑。它很好地利用了阿塞拜疆传统的建筑用料，如石材和木材，同时也创新性地融入了金属和玻璃素材。

利用高度弯曲的木料搭建的阿塞拜疆馆有887平方米。展馆背面相对开阔，引入自然风，形成微气候环境。展馆内丰富的空间造型旨在创造一个大范围的气候生态多样性，同时也展示出阿塞拜疆不同的文化侧面。馆内设置了3种不同的生态环境，一块是风景地貌环境，体现阿塞拜疆与多国接壤的特殊地理特征；一块是阿塞拜疆9种气候地域；还有一块是为阿塞拜疆的传统文化和针对下一代发展创新而设置的区域。

阿塞拜疆馆的设计遵循模数化，以在这个临时展馆中实现多种方式布局的灵活性。建筑的围合结构使用了横向而柔韧的木材，为馆内带来自然光线，减少能源消耗。游客进入馆内需经过一个大型中庭，然后通过自动扶梯进入三个不同的楼层，每个楼层分别代表不同的生物圈。第一层重点介绍阿塞拜疆的地理位置，而第二层关注该国家几种不同的气候区域，顶层布置了餐厅和屋顶平台，可俯瞰世博会展区的其他地方。在2015年10月31日世博会结束之后，该展馆会被拆除，然后在阿塞拜疆的首都巴库重建。

The Simmetrico Network project presents a very simple and modern architecture achieved with traditional materials like wood and stone, which combine innovatively with metal and glass.

The sides of the pavilion are created using highly flexible wood over an area measuring 887 m²; the north side is more open to favor air ventilation and a micro climate. Its variety of spaces and forms looks to recreate an extensive climatic biodiversity and reflect cultural aspects of Azerbaijan. Visitors can explore its different features through the way in which the pavilion is built. It has three different biospheres; the first, a biosphere of geographical landscapes, as a crossroad between countries; the second, the nine geographic climatic zones of Azerbaijan, and the third, dedicated to traditional culture and innovation for generations to come.

The project follows a modular system that allows for a greater flexibility of space and the potential to reconfigure the temporary structure in a variety of different ways. Horizontal and flexible timber bands form the structure's envelope, bringing natural light inside the pavilion and reducing required energy consumption. Guests enter through a large atrium that doubles an event space, before escalators lead to three separate levels-each representing a different biosphere. At first floor level installations highlight Azerbaijan's geographic location, with the second level focusing on the country's nine different climatic regions. the uppermost storey comprises a restaurant and terrace overlooking the rest of the expo site. after the event closes on october 31st, 2015, the pavilion will be dismantled, and reused within the Azerbaijani capital of baku.

AZERBAIJAN
PAVILION
EXPO 2015 MILANO

BAKU

CULTURAL CROSSROADS
BAKU

RABBI
RABBINO

TRADITIONAL FL
KEBAB FUSION

TURKMENISTAN PAVILION
土库曼斯坦馆

Water is Life
水即生命

建筑设计：Tilke GmbH& Co KG　建筑师：GessCon GmbH
项目面积：1 175 平方米

Architectural Design: Tilke GmbH& Co KG　Architect: GessCon GmbH
Project Area: 1,175 m²

土库曼斯坦馆将展现代表本国传统和现代的标志性符号。在这幢白色建筑的入口处是一处喷泉，装饰着世界上已知最古老的阿克哈——塔科马头雕像。经过主入口会来到一个木结构的传统土库曼的圆顶帐篷里，在LED灯的光照下，参观者可以一睹最精美的手工土库曼地毯。展馆侧面的三道水流和LED光束形成的水流面积达250平方米，它们最终形成了一道巨瀑，此处的景观将吸引无数游客在此拍照留念。建筑物内部是模仿土库曼斯坦首都阿什哈巴德建造的，共分为三层。在这里，参观者能了解到土库曼斯坦的食品生产、生态多样性、食品健康、巨型手工织毯、水幕投影、5D电影和原汁原味的圆顶帐篷屋顶。首层的餐厅和屋顶的咖啡馆都会提供传统的土库曼食物给参观者品尝。

The Pavilion displays traditional as well as modern symbols of Turkmenistan. At the entrance of the white pavilion, there is a water fountain with a horses head of the oldest known horse breed in the world, the “Ahal-Tekke horse”. Over the main entrance there is a wooden structure of a traditional Turkmen yurt and a large LED carpet which offers a glimpse of the most beautiful hand-made turkmen carpets. The three drops of water at the entrance and the large LED water drops measuring approximately 250 m² on the side of the pavilion with the long waterfall behind it are certain to invite visitors to take some memorable photos. Inside the solid construction, following the example of the white capital Ashgabat, three exciting levels are waiting to be explored. There, you will find the theme of quality food production, biodiversity and health, even huge hand made carpets, a water feature with projection, a 5D cinema and a genuine traditional yurt on the rooftop. The restaurant on the ground floor and the cafe on the rooftop will invite visitors to taste and feast on traditional Turkmen dishes.

VIP

KAZAKHSTAN PAVILION
哈萨克斯坦馆

The Land of Opportunities
希望之地

建筑设计：GTP2 Architects / 项目面积： 2 396 平方米

Architectural Design: GTP2 Architects / Project Area: 2,396 m²

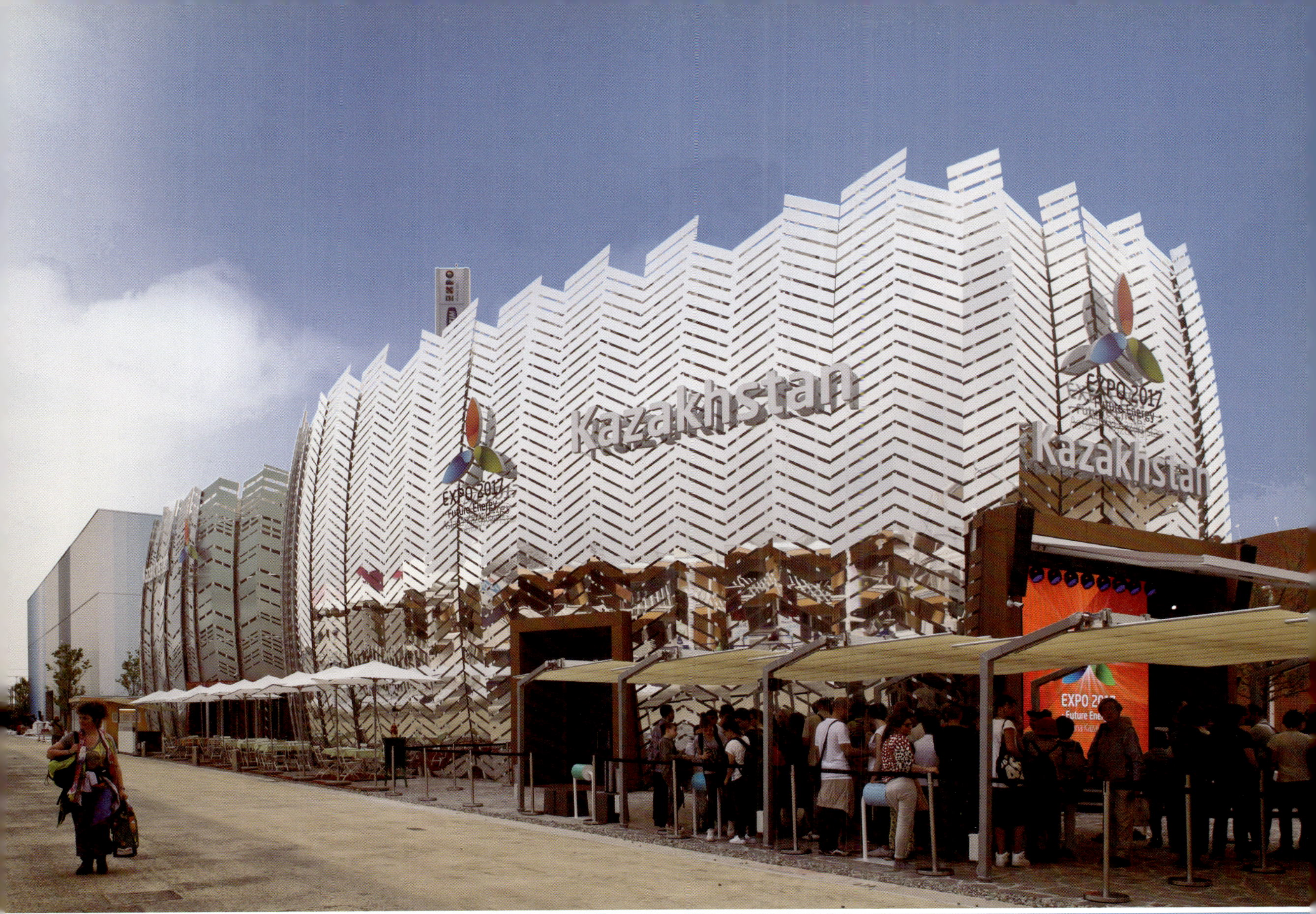
Kazakhstan
Kazakhstan
EXPO 2017
EXPO 2017
Future Energy
EXPO 2017
Future Energy

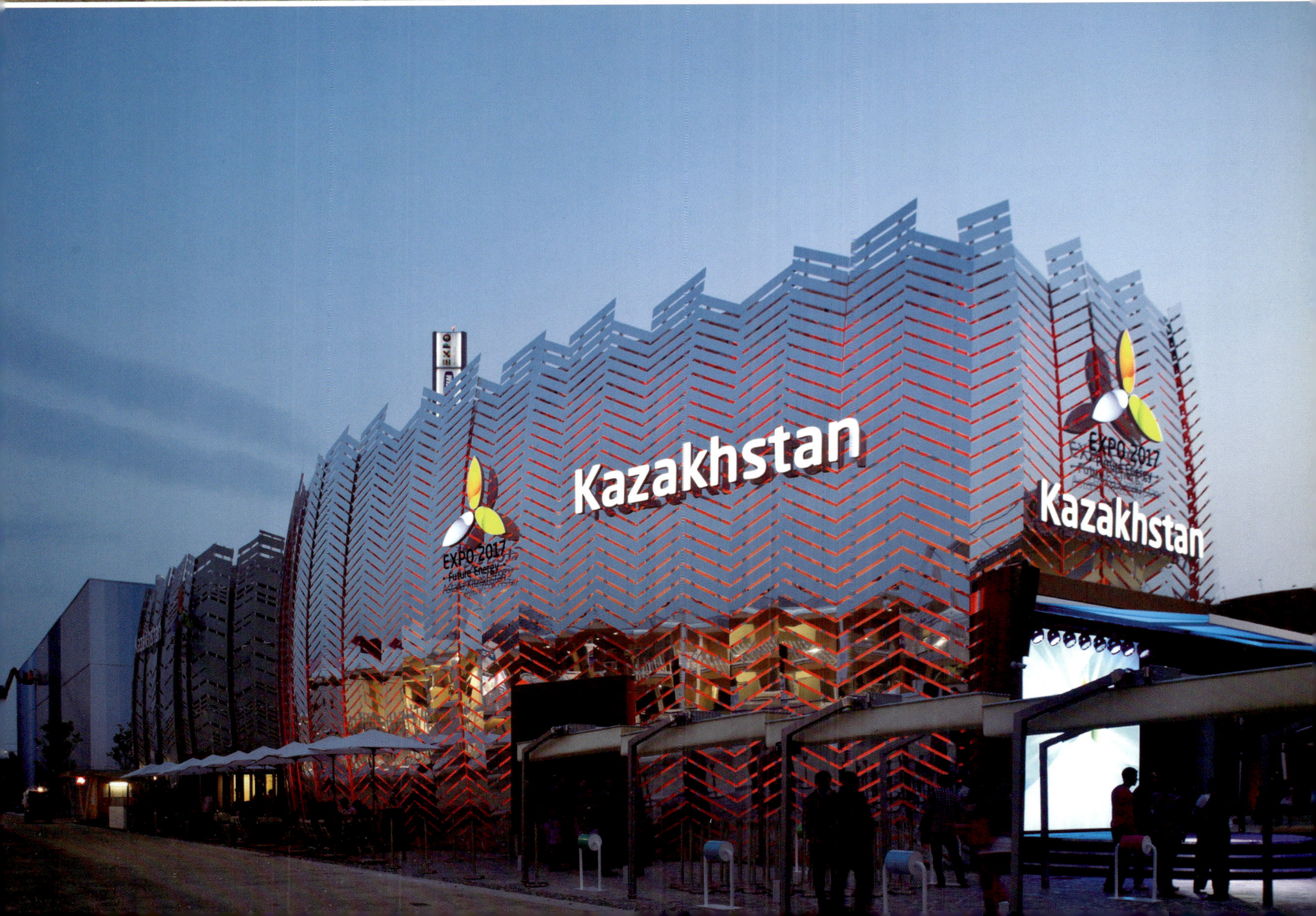
Kazakhstan
Kazakhstan
EXPO 2017
Future Energy
EXPO 2017

哈萨克斯坦的生存环境让其先人们开启了游牧文化传统，也正是因为这一历史文化背景，哈萨克斯坦展馆的设计分成了6个不同农业主题的圆形大厅来逐一展示她的历史和文化。参观者进入的首个大厅主题便是农业，这里介绍了哈萨克尖端的耕作技术，也因为此她成为世界上主要的小麦和面粉出口国。第二个展厅是关于牲畜饲养的，因为理想的畜牧环境，哈萨克3/4的农业用地可用于放牧。第三个展厅介绍了哈萨克一些不为人所知的新奇事物，比如哈萨克美味的苹果居然是产自东哈萨克的野生苹果树林。第四个展厅的主题是关于哈萨克的生态及生物多样性的，哈萨克大草原的生态区域处在世界最大的干旱大草原上，那里有很多珍稀和濒危动物，比如塞加羚羊；此展厅也介绍了哈萨克的治水专家们如何处理咸海越来越少的水资源问题。接下来的第五展厅便介绍哈萨克的水产养殖，重点介绍了他们是如何保护里海中一种特殊鱼类——欧洲鳇。第六展厅着眼于农业的未来发展以及哈萨克在对抗蝗虫侵袭中所做的各种开创性的尝试。除了6个各具特色的展厅，哈萨克斯坦馆的另一大参观点在整个展馆的中心处，在这里参观者能提前感受将在哈萨克首都阿斯塔纳举办的2017年世博会奇景——突破性的3D版太阳高能粒子之旅。哈萨克斯坦馆内设置了富于本国特色的餐馆，游客可以在这里领略哈萨克人的热情以及他们的美食。

In Kazakhstan, the ancestral connection between man and the environment is rooted in its traditional nomadic culture, because of that, the overall pavilion is divided into six rotundas to give insights into the agricultural sectors of Kazakhstan. The first rotunda highlights agriculture. Kazakhstan is one of the world's major wheat and flour exporters by using state-of-the-art techniques for soil cultivation. Rotunda 2 deals with livestock breeding which finds ideal conditions in Kazakhstan where three quarters of all agricultural land can be used for grazing. Rotunda 3 is all about the wonders of Kazakhstan and shows amazing things that are mostly unknown. For example, did you know that our eating apples come from wild apple tree forests in eastern Kazakhstan? Many more fascinating and surprising facts await the visitor here. Rotunda 4's main theme is ecology and biodiversity since the Kazakh steppe ecoregion is the world's largest dry steppe with several rare and endangered animals like the Saiga antelope. The exhibition space also deals with the desiccation of the Aral Sea and the attempts by Kazakhstan's authorities to save the lesser Aral Sea. The main motif of Rotunda 5 is aquaculture. Special attention is given to the conservation efforts to save the beluga sturgeon in the Caspian Sea. Rotunda 6 looks at the agriculture of the future by highlighting the various groundbreaking attempts to fight locust infestations.Another highlight is the main show, where visitors can join energy particles on their journey from the sun to Expo 2017 in Astana. This breathtaking 3D spectacle takes place in the huge central dome of the Pavilion. Guest can round off their visit by experiencing Kzakh hospitality and cuisine in the Pavilion's own restaurant.

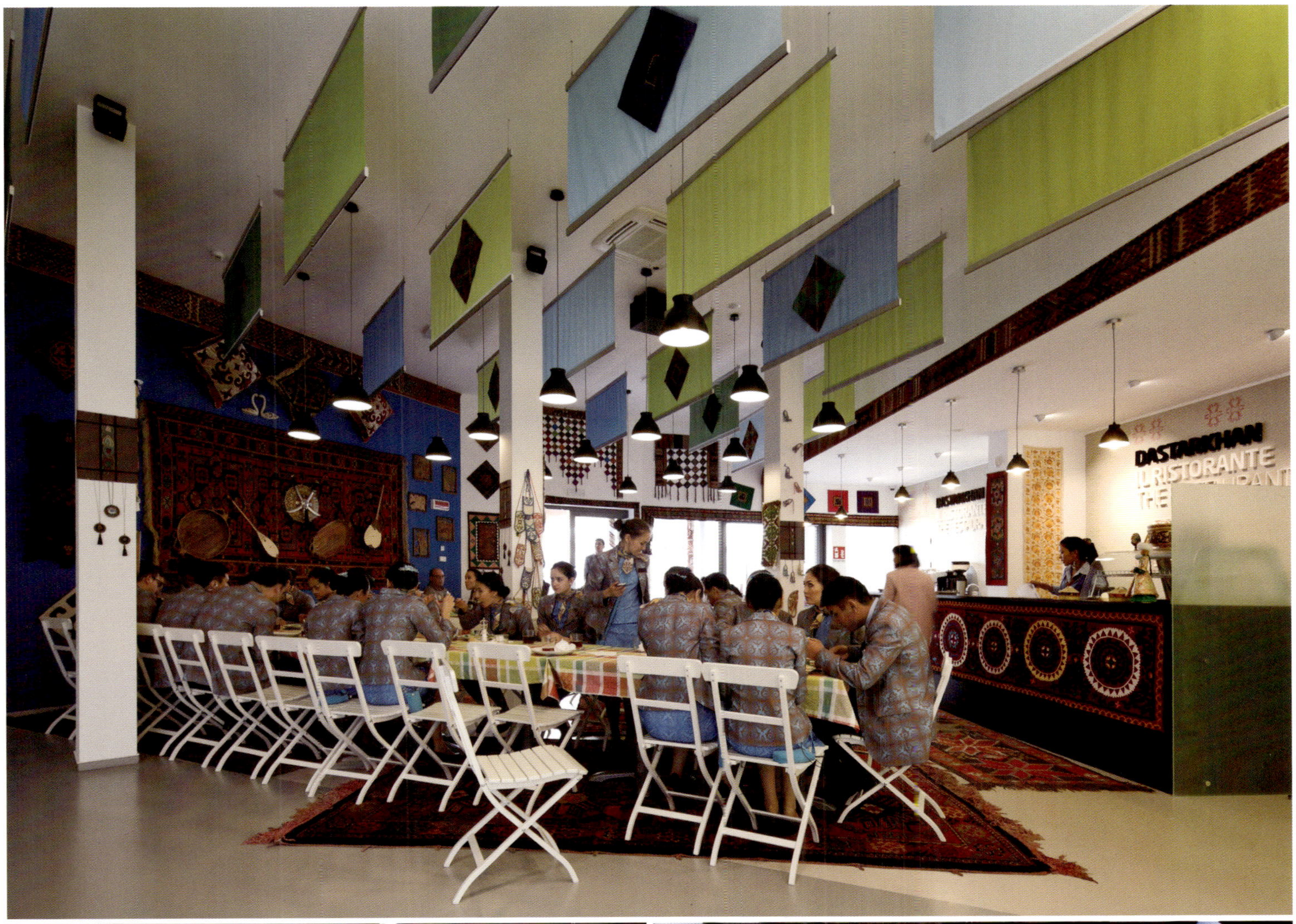
DASTARKHAN
IL RISTORANTE

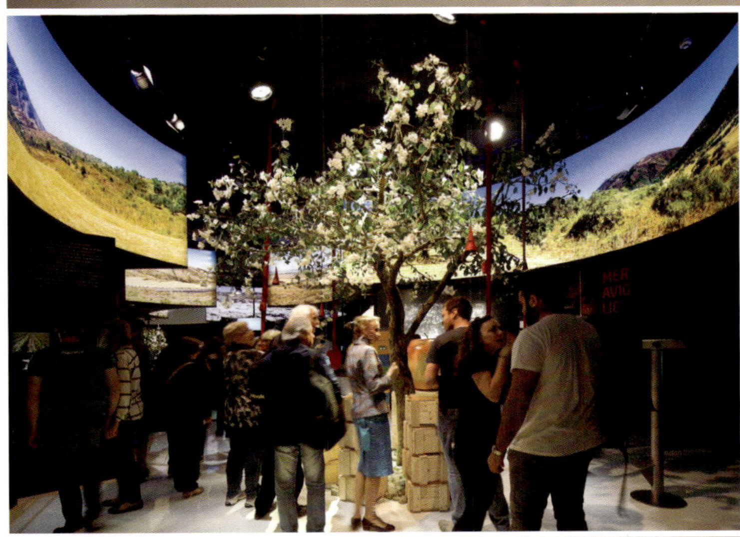

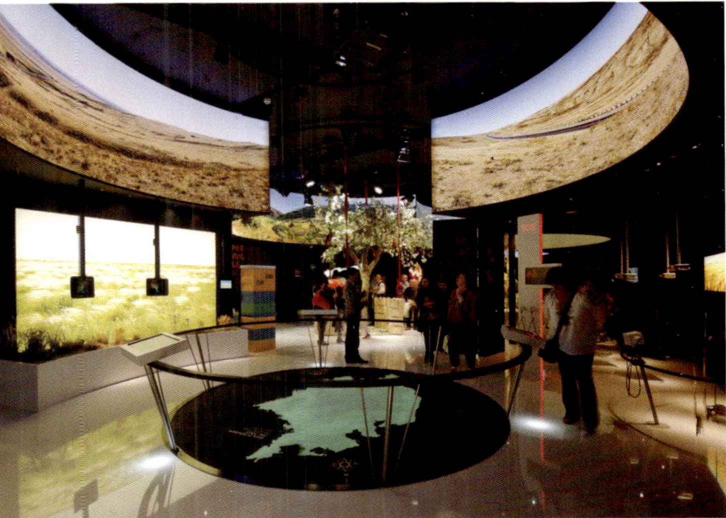

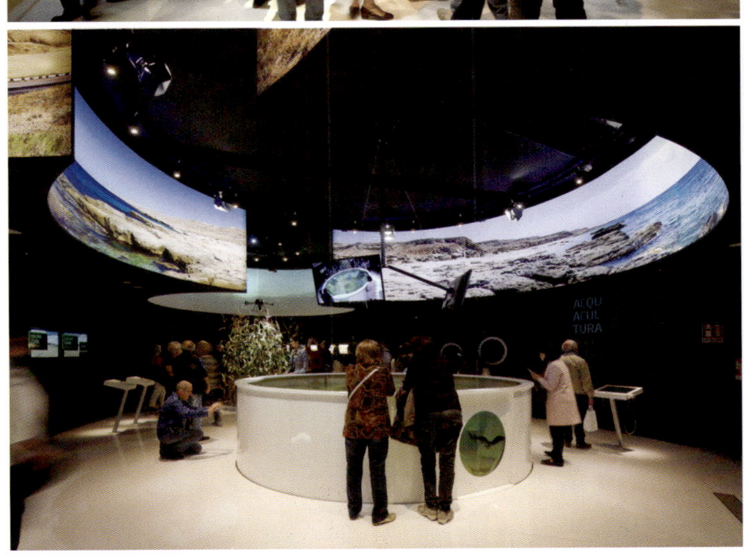

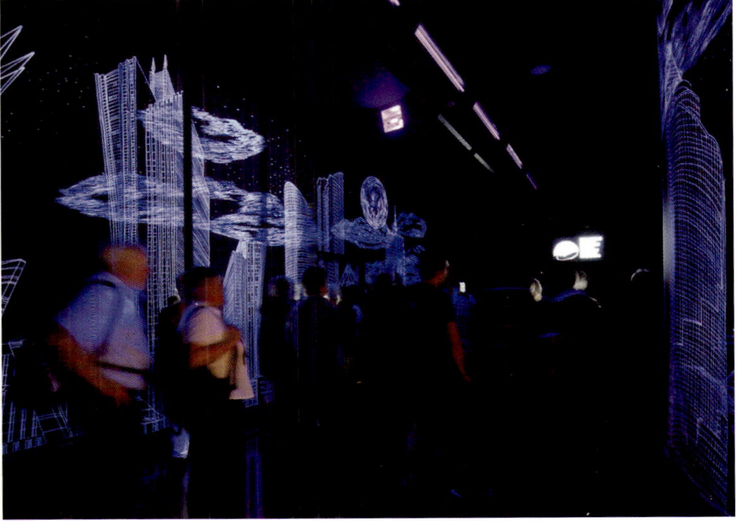

UNITED ARAB EMIRATES PAVILION
阿联酋馆

Food for Thought-Shaping and Sharing the Future
精神食粮–塑造并分享未来

建筑设计：福斯特建筑事务所
设计团队：Norman Foster, David Nelson, Spencer de Grey, Gerard Evenden, Martin Castle, John Blythe, Andre Ford, Giovanna Skylos Labini, Ronald Schuurmans, Daniel Skidmore, Andrea Soligon
项目面积：5 000平方米

Architect: Foster + Partners
Design Team: Norman Foster, David Nelson, Spencer de Grey, Gerard Evenden, Martin Castle, John Blythe, Andre Ford, Giovanna Skylos Labini, Ronald Schuurmans, Daniel Skidmore, Andrea Soligon
Project Area: 5,000 m²

阿联酋国家馆将会建在靠近世博中心的一个140米宽的基地上，通过一道“引人注目的峡谷式入口”后人们才能真正领会到其中的魅力，该入口由两面12米高的波状墙构成。这种12米高的结构墙体让人忆起阿联酋传统住宅中狭窄遮荫的街道和一座座宏伟的沙丘。“沙丘”体的表面投影出沙丘的真实质感。这些蜿蜒的波浪起伏的走道带领参观者进入展馆内去体验新奇有趣的内部空间。

内部设计中设计师继续延续了马斯达尔城“封闭式社区”的设计方法，这也是传统的沙漠化城市规划设计准则之一。场馆中央有一个大礼堂，游客进入后首先会对阿联酋的历史有个初步认知，随后依次进入其他空间区域学习到有关“沙漠绿洲”的知识，最后则来到咖啡厅和餐厅，这样的环绕式设计也恰好迎合了本次世博会的主题：给养地球。

主设计师福斯特描述：“场馆传达了该国的独特性。墙的纹理源于沙漠里的扫描，建筑会利用材料来展现阿联酋沙子的不同明暗度。玻璃纤维增强水泥板由钢结构支撑，方便拆卸用于阿联酋本国的重建。”在展示走道的尽头，游客到达一个进入地面咖啡馆的绿色舒适区。一层是正式餐厅，上面是环保的屋顶平台。场馆周围及户外公共区域的风光让人想起了阿联酋的地形和覆盖植被。

在这里，参观者将能了解到2020年将在阿联酋举办的世博会的一些构想。

The UAE Pavilion is to be built close to the Expo Center on a site of 140 m wide. Through a striking entrance like a valley contructed by 12m wavy walls at sides. These impressive 12m structures evoke both the narrow self-shaded streets of the UAE's historic settlements and the magnificent open sand dunes of its deserts. 3D scans of dune surfaces have informed the wall design to create an authentic texture. These sinuous, curving shapes guide visitors through a range of intriguing spaces and exciting, informative experiences.

Then, visitors will enter an enclosed community featured in Masdar City, which is one of construction plan standards in desert cities. In the center of the pavilion is a grand auditorium for visitor to access UAE's history, then they can follow a path to other spaces to get information about “desert oasis”. The end of the pavilion is a café and a restaurant. The spiral route design is in accordance with the theme of the Expo: Feeding the Planet.

The chief desinger Foster described that the pavilion design expresses a unique UAE. The testure of walls is from the scan of desert, and variety of materials depict different intensity of sand in UAE. Fiberglass enhances the strength of concrete slate supported by steel structure, which is also feasible for rebuild in UAE. At the end of exhibition corridor is a green area connecting to ground café. The ground floor is a restaurant while the upper level is an environmental roof terrace, here visitor can enjoy the periphery and outdoor public landscapes which evoke them of the topography and vegetation of UAE.

Visitors can also find out about the UAE's exciting plans to host the next World Expo in 2020.

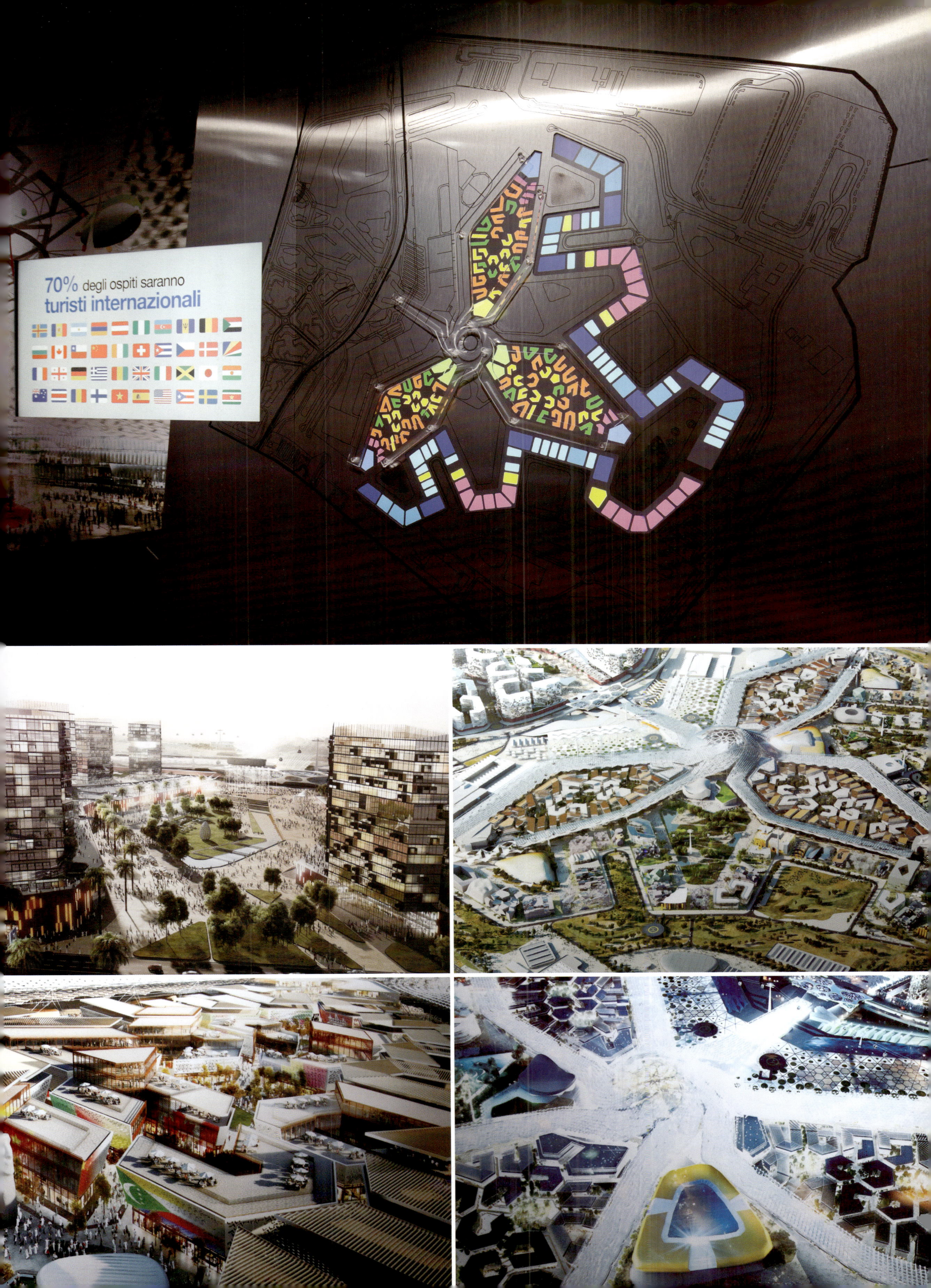

70% degli ospiti saranno
turisti internazionali

FUTURE
BUSINESS
UAE
UAE.
IL TUO BUSINESS
PARTNER
GLOBALE
Ufficialmente approvato dal
UNITED ARAB EMIRATES
MINISTRY OF ENVIRONMENT & WATER

Please take a seat. Our 8-minute
movie Family Tree will be starting shortly.

PROSSIMO
OSPITE, GRAZIE
Cosa è più
importante per te?

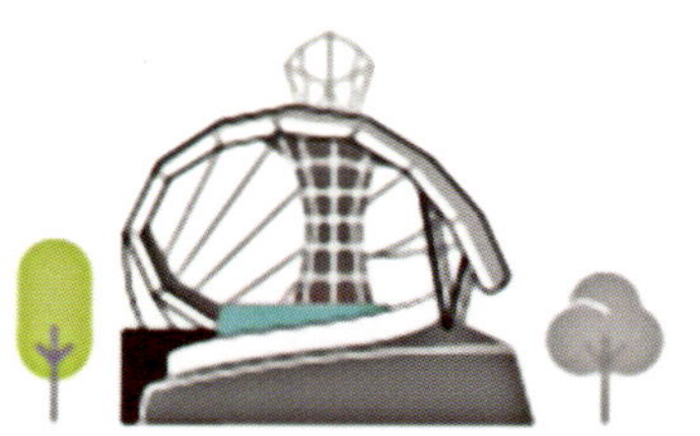

ISLAMIC REPUBLIC OF IRAN PAVILION
伊朗馆

Global Sofreh, Iranian Culture
神赐的餐桌

建筑设计师：Kamran Safamanes / 室内设计：Rahshahr International Group / 施工单位：RPA s.r.l.

Architect: Kamran Safamanes / Interior Design: Rahshahr International Group / Construction: RPA s.r.l.

This is Iran.
We would like to
welcome you.

伊朗馆是集体现传统、可持续性、开放的多样性展馆，其战略定位是要搭建供游客在东西方世界沟通的桥梁。

设计共分三个阶段完成。三个主题全部结合在一个单一的标志性物件上，它就是Sofreh。Sofreh是一块方形的布料，一块用于庆典活动的桌布，标志着一张摆设好的桌子，这是伊朗传统文化中最重要的物件之一。展馆建筑由手工艺品衍生而来，形成一个开放形的结构，类似于一个帐篷，而她的内层能使人联想到传统的Sofreh刺绣。她的编制纹样讲述了这个国家的人民、他们的食物和农业从古到今的历史。

内部表面逐渐展开成为由三角形单元格组成的弧形墙，每个单元格都在展示不同的内容。在顶部，镜子做的马赛克反射了下方正在发生的事情。这个建筑分成两层：上层是展示伊朗的七个气候区的展览空间；下层则留给当地的产品和伊朗的美食，同时还有这次世博会的接待和信息服务区。

建筑师试图让观众从南往北，根据气候划分，去体验伊朗的国土，这和展馆的南北延伸形式相协调。展览从南边的波斯湾开始到里海结束(伊朗中北部紧靠里海，南靠波斯湾和阿拉伯海)。自然、环境、文化、生活方式和旅游业，尤其是他们的饮食文化全部都得到呈现。

Tradition, sustainability and openness to diversity, all have been developed in Iran thanks to its strategic position as a bridge between East and West and serve as the three main themes of the concept of the Iranian pavilion designed for Expo Milano 2015.

The conceptual design of pavilion was prepared by the team led by local architect Kamran Safamanesh, the advanced first phase of architecture was performed by Rah Shahr Architectural Consulting Engineers and the second phase was developted by the Italian studio RPA S.r.l. The three themes are summarized by an object that conveys them all: the Sofreh, a square of fabric that identifies the set table, one of the most important objects for the culinary culture of Iran. The Pavilion's architecture is derived from this image in the form of an open structure, similar to a tent, where the inner skin is reminiscent of the traditional embroidery of the Sofreh. Its weave tells the story of the Iranian people's food and agriculture from past to present.

The surface gradually unfolds into a curved wall of triangular cells containing different objects on display. At the top, a mosaic of mirrors reflects and reproduces what happens below. The pavilion is divided into two distinct levels: the upper floor is devoted to exhibition space, divided according to the seven climatic regions of Iran, while the lower floor is reserved for local products and the cuisine of Iran, along with all other services required for the reception of visitors.

Architects try to lead visitors to experience climatic division in Iran along with south to north direction, which is also correspond to placement of the pavilion. The exhibision begins with the Persian Gulf and end in the Caspian Sea, because Iran is against the Caspian in the mid-north and adjacent to the Persian Gulf and the Arabian Sea in the south. In the progress of the exhibition, visitors can harvest the knowledge of nature, environment, culture, life style and tourism of Iran, especially their culinary culture.

This is Iran;
We would like
welcome you.
This is Iran;
We would like to
welcome you.
WELCOME YOU

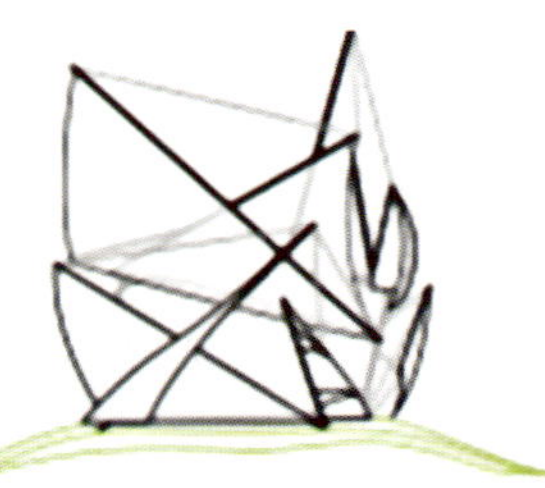

KUWAIT PAVILION
科威特馆

Challenge of Nature
自然的挑战

设计公司：Italo Rota, Nussli Italia / 项目面积： 2 790 平方米

Design Company: Italo Rota, Nussli Italia / Project Area: 2,790 m²

UNITED STATES OF AMERICA
Kuwait

水、农业和能源是科威特在追求更好生活和可持续发展中面临的三个最大的挑战。2015年米兰世博会，科威特将在2 790平方米的场馆内向全世界展示他们在水、农业和能源方面取得的成就。
科威特馆将向世界展出一个来自沙漠的国家怎样通过自己的文化、人类的劳动和有限的自然资源来创造她自身的价值，同时也带来一个备受关注的展览。世界各国的游客远道而来，科威特将展示沙漠国的热情，并通过360度投影方式来展现科威特的地域风情。
通过被水流冲刷岩石的大峡谷，游客将来到展馆正中心，一块巨大的玻璃模型会向你讲述科威特的历史，并带你走入“沙堡”（这是科威特人对自己国家特有的叫法）。馆内的景观元素体现回收和节约自然能源的方式；被无土栽培区（马铃薯、草莓和莴苣）围绕的场内最大的区域是餐饮休闲区。这个区域被装饰成阿拉伯特色市集，中心是熊熊篝火，在游客们休憩的同时也能领略到中东的特有风味。

The water, agriculture and energy are the biggest challenges that Kuwait is facing to ensure a better quality of life aligned with sustainability. Participation at Expo Milano 2015 provides an opportunity to acquaint visitors with the 2,790 m^2 pavilion, with both its big projects in these three areas and the results.

The pavilion offers a fascinating view of the territory of Kuwait, its culture, its human and natural resources in a State born from a desert where it has been able to create its own wealth. It is the desert that welcomes visitors, who after a long promenade arrive at the event area where they are immersed in landscapes recreated by 360 degree projection.

From the canyon where the water plays with the rocks, you arrive in the heart of the pavilion, a huge glass model which recounts the history of the area, taking visitors on a tour inside its "small fortress" (this is the meaning of the Arabic word from which Kuwait takes its name), from the different types of desert to the sea that washes the shores. Its highly scenic elements embody principles of recouping and saving natural energies. Surrounded by hydroponics outside (tomatoes, strawberries, salads), the largest space, used for dining and refreshment, is colored by the typical elements of the Arab souk and by a large central fire, allowing visitors to relax and enjoy the flavors of the Middle East.

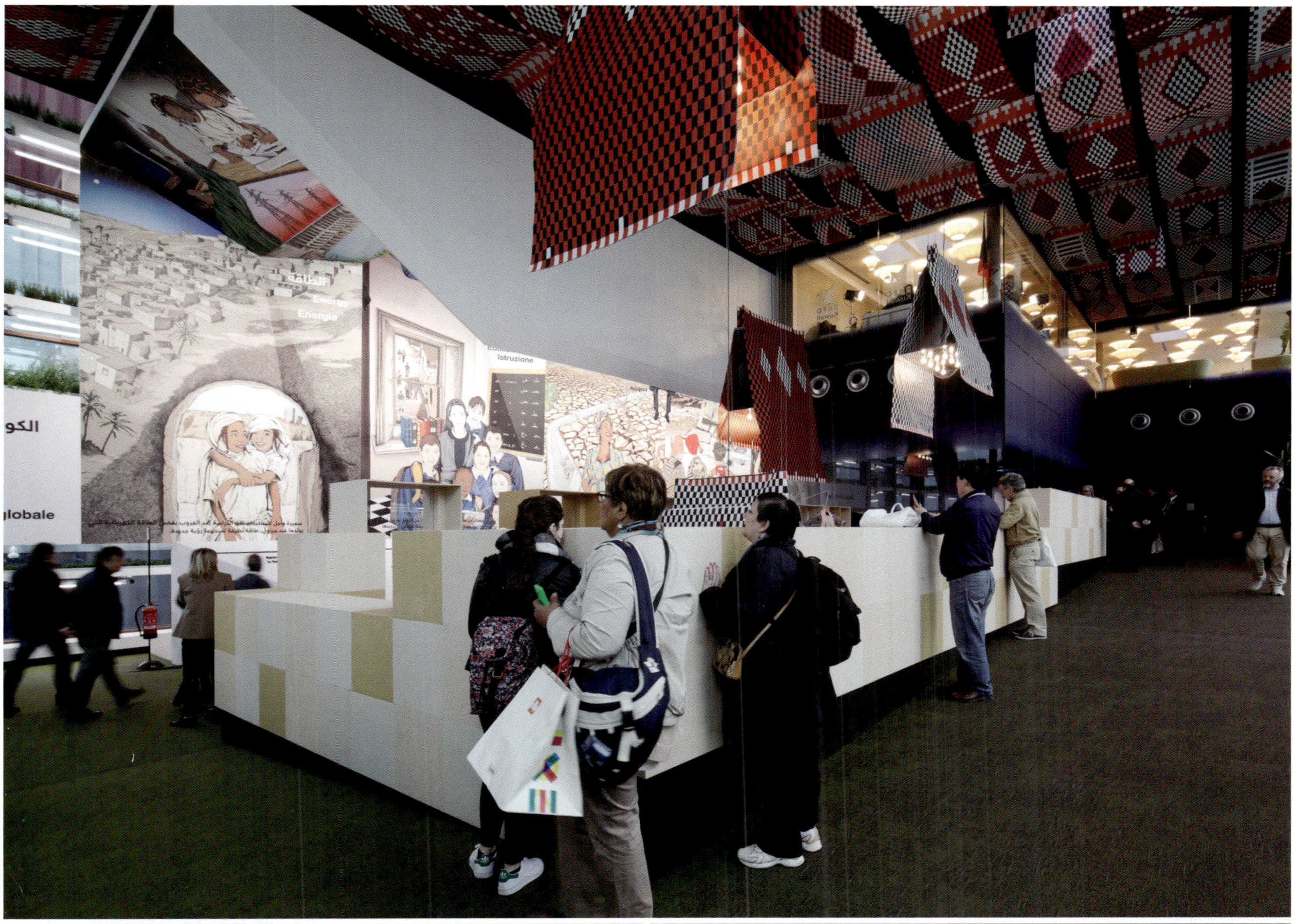

ation
ruzione
Water

Heritage in Harvest

收获文化遗产

建筑设计：Cityneon（中东），WLL / 项目面积：2 790平方米

Architectural Design: Cityneon (Middle East), WLL / Project Area: 2,790 m²

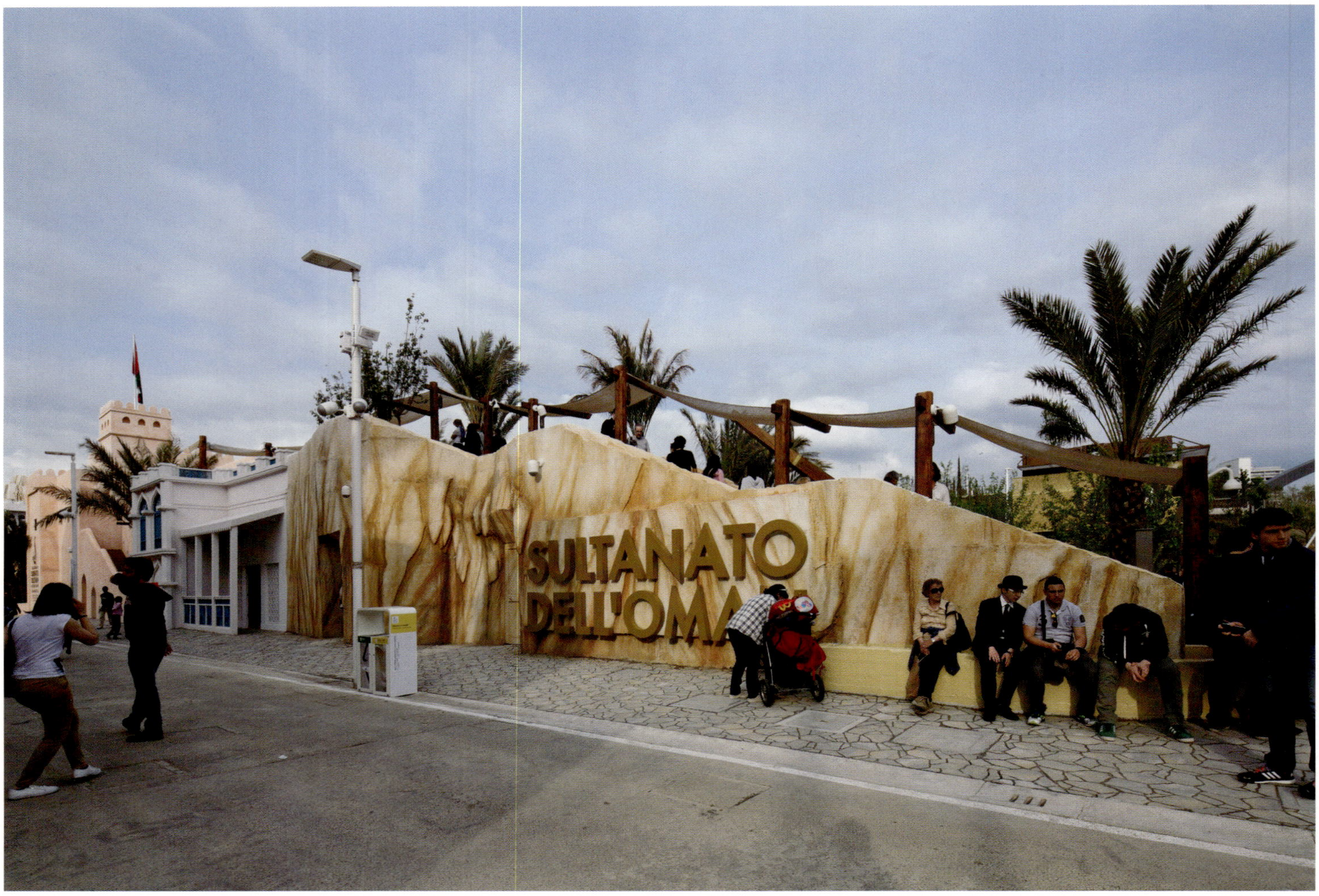

SULTANATO
DELL'OMAN

阿曼是在地球上最干旱的地区之一，拥有3 165千米的海岸线，领土由连绵的崎岖山地和沙漠覆盖。在太阳的猛烈蒸烤下，阿曼苏丹国在可持续发展和食品安全方面面临巨大挑战。面对水资源的持续匮乏，合理的管理和水资源分配是首当其冲亟待解决的问题。

阿曼馆占地超2 790平方米，建筑造型为凉亭形状，它传达了阿曼人民呼吁对水资源的管理和保护并突显了水资源是一种重要和宝贵的资源。在这里，参观者可以品尝当地特产，如蜂蜜、红枣和骆驼奶，或漫步在分别象征着阳光、沙滩和大海的不同空间里。

阿曼馆的设计分为两个截然不同的区域。西部是一个碉堡状建筑物，在这里，参观者可以通过多媒体来了解阿曼的地貌特征，在一天的不同时段有不同面貌的山地、沙漠和自然景观被一一展现出来；走过1 480多平方米的西部区域可以直接到来东部区域，这里有一座高高耸立的宏伟雅致的城堡，传统的尖头窗和镶嵌格栅让参观者想到阿拉伯之夜的神秘之境。

Oman is located in one of the driest areas on the planet. With 3,165 km of coastline, lapped by rugged and mountainous lands and deserts, whipped by the sun, the Sultanate of Oman has faced enormous challenges to ensure that a sustainable and safe food production. Faced with a constant shortage of water, proper management and distribution of water resources has become of utmost priority.

The pavilion, which is spread over an area of 2,790m^2, conveys the care with which the Omanis protect, manage and preserve water as a vital and precious resource. Visitors can taste local produce such as honey, dates and camel's milk, or stroll in the garden that is divided into three spaces, symbolizing the sun, the sand, the sea.

The pavilion built for Expo 2015 is split into two distinctive areas: the western part, a fortress is recreated where inside the visitor can watch a multimedia show based on visual representations of the characteristic landscapes of Oman. In this section of the pavilion, mountains, deserts and natural resources of the Sultanate are shown in various stages of the day. The tour inside Oman's pavilion continues for the visitor at Expo 2015 through a walkway of 16,000 ft^2 leading directly in the eastern area of the building, where a majestic and elegant castle stands tall, built in the traditional local architecture with lancet windows and inlaid grilles, providing the visitor with an evocative atmosphere of Arabian Nights.

SULTANATO
DELL'OMAN
SULTANATE OF OMAN
EXPO MILANO 2015
OMAN AIR

MIELE DELL'OMAN,
UN DONO DELLA NATURA
JEBEL AKHDAR
LA MONTAGNA
VERDE
الجبل الأخضر

ISRAEL PAVILION
以色列馆

Fields of Tomorrow
未来田地

建筑设计：AVS / 设计师：Knafo Klimor / 项目面积：2 369平方米

Architectural Design: AVS / Designer: Knafo Klimor / Project Area: 2,369 m²

Fields of Tomorrow
JOIN US FOR A 10 MINUTES UNIQUE EXPERIENCE

以色列展馆将以“未来田地”为主题参加2015年米兰世博会。展馆设计长70米，高12米。全方位立体化地展现了以色列有史以来在农业现代化方面所取得的巨大成就。

以色列农业是农业的实验室，在世界范围内拥有最先进的案例研究，并向全球输出农业知识、经验以及技术。在石化土地上耕种，在沙漠中种植蔬菜，发明新的灌溉方法以及提高种子的品质，这些都是当今社会公认的具有创造力、勇气和成就的行为。 2015年米兰世博会的主题是“滋养地球，生命能源”，该主题为展示以色列农业的先进特性提供了平台。

该展馆的结构创造了一种直接且富有冲击力的农业和工程视觉效果。主要特点是一块垂直的田地，以一个新鲜的角度，演示了食物的生长和供应过程。垂直田地的表面是由模块化的瓷砖构成，用来在钢架上培育产品。通过电脑控制每一块瓷砖区域的供水让垂直田地得以实现。此外，由多种谷物和其他基本食物构成的马赛克纹理、香味和颜色，提升了展馆的整体美感。

Knafo Klimor Architects have been chosen to represent Israel at the 2015 Milan Expo with their “Fields of Tomorrow” pavilion. The elongated pavilion, stretching 70 m across and rising 12 m high, will act as a “living” billboard revealing Israel's past and present successes in modern agriculture.

Israel is an agricultural laboratory and a worldwide case study that exports knowledge, experience, and technology to the entire globe. The cultivation of rocky land, the growth of vegetables in the desert, the invention of new irrigation methods, and the upgrading of seed quality are part of the present-day society marked by creativity, dare, and achievements. The theme of expo milan 2015 – 'Feeding the Planet, Energy for Life' provides a unique opportunity to present these characteristics.

The structure creates an immediate and powerful visual atmosphere of agricultural and engineering performance. The main feature is a vertical field, which provides a fresh perspective on how food is grown and supplied. Its surface is comprised of modular tiles utilized for optimally cultivating products on a steel frame elevated above ground. This is possible through the insertion of a computer-controlled drip watering system into each panel. In addition, cereal varieties and other basic foodstuffs will enhance the overall aesthetic with a mosaic of textures, smells, and colors.

Turkey

SEED SHARING HANDS
SHARECONTAINPRESERVESUSTAINRECYCLE

DIGGING INTO
HISTORY FOR
FUTURE FOOD
Turkey
EXPO MILANO 2015

土耳其馆由室内，半室外和室外三个主要分区组成，包含七处独立的半室外空间。其中五处作为展览和活动空间，剩下的两处是土耳其餐厅和纪念品精品店。展馆的主入口在室外区域，镂空的顶棚采用现代钢艺塑造星罗棋布的网格造型。建筑设计上通过喷泉、石艺、传统土耳其屋舍和玻璃工艺品来体现土耳其特有的图形艺术和文化。

土耳其馆的建筑设计和整体构架设计灵感来源于石榴丰富的内在特质。参观者将沿着独特的情境设计路线依次了解土耳其的饮食文化历史，传统农业工具，数字时代的饮食和艺术，以及未来的食品技术。

The Turkish Pavilion consists of three major divisions of indoor, semi-outdoor and outdoor venues, including seven separate semi-outdoor sections. Five of these are designed for theme related events and the remaining two as a Turkish restaurant and a souvenir boutique. The main entrance is in the outdoor area, where an openwork roof is crowned with a modern interpretation of the Seljuki Star made of steel. The architectural design as a whole reflects the country's values through fountains, stones, the traditional Turkish dwelling known throughout the world glassware and motifs peculiar to the Turkish culture.

The theme, inspired by the pomegranate's opulent and abundant attributes, is embedded and displayed in the entire architectural and contextual design and structure of the Turkish Pavilion. Visitors can enjoy exhibits Culinary History, Historic Agricultural Tools, Digital Food & Arts and Future Food Technology.

QATAR PAVILION
卡塔尔馆

Sowing Sustainability, Innovative Solutions for Food Security

推行可持续发展
用创新保证食品安全

建筑设计：Andrea Maffei Architects / 项目面积：2 450 平方米

Architectural Design: Andrea Maffei Architects / Project Area: 2,450 m²

在卡塔尔馆的设计中，建筑师想要创建一种流动的参观方式。一般展馆会设置大型的横向空间，将展品陈列出来。然而建筑师想要创建一个慢慢参观、渐渐了解卡塔尔的食品文化的参观过程。展馆共3层，通过一个逐渐上升的大斜坡（坡度为5%），游客最终可通往屋顶的全景观景平台。这将是一次独特的体验，游客可以慢慢体会卡塔尔的魅力。

卡塔尔馆的造型让人联想到卡塔尔的传统集市——苏克，集市里有阿拉伯式走道连通内部。展馆占地面积达2 450平方米，伫立中央的是一幢圆形食品篮形状建筑，它代表着卡塔尔人的生活与全球创新的多元化交融。

展厅区域由一条又长又宽的螺旋状走道串连一直引领参观者到达天台。这个走道宽10米，一直延伸到展馆外部，像是要迎接参观者进来再一步步带大家步上天空。这条长长的螺旋走道内侧能观赏到一片大的绿洲，而外侧则是一面纯白的墙壁，墙面有一个个的大孔，自然光线可以通过大孔自由地穿透进馆内。

In the design of the Qatar Pavilion we wanted to create a new fluid way of visiting the Pavilion. Usually a pavilion consists of a single large horizontal space in which everything is exposed. However, we wanted to create the theme of a long process in which the visitor turns out, little by little, the food and culture of Qatar. It will be a long process of training in which the visitors will be started to the charm of this beautiful country. This will be done through a large inclined plane which rises gradually with a gentle slope of 5% to the three floors of the pavilion and then continue on a panoramic terrace on the roof.

The architecture of the Qatar Pavilion recalls the traditional market – the souq - with internal paths in Arabian forms. It covers an area of 2,450 m² and it consists of a large central space with a circular structure at the center that is reminiscent of the form of the traditional food basket - the jefeer - symbolizing the interweaving of local dimensions and global innovation which characterizes Qatar.

The exhibition space is composed of a long and wide spiral floor that climbs slowly up to the roof terrace.The ramp is designed 10 m wide and represents a continuation of the external land of the visitor, who will enter the hall and slowly start to climb towards the sky. The long spiral path will have a glazed side all around to look out in a large oasis inside and the outer side will be composed of a white wall with big holes that will leave enter small rays of natural light.

Qatar

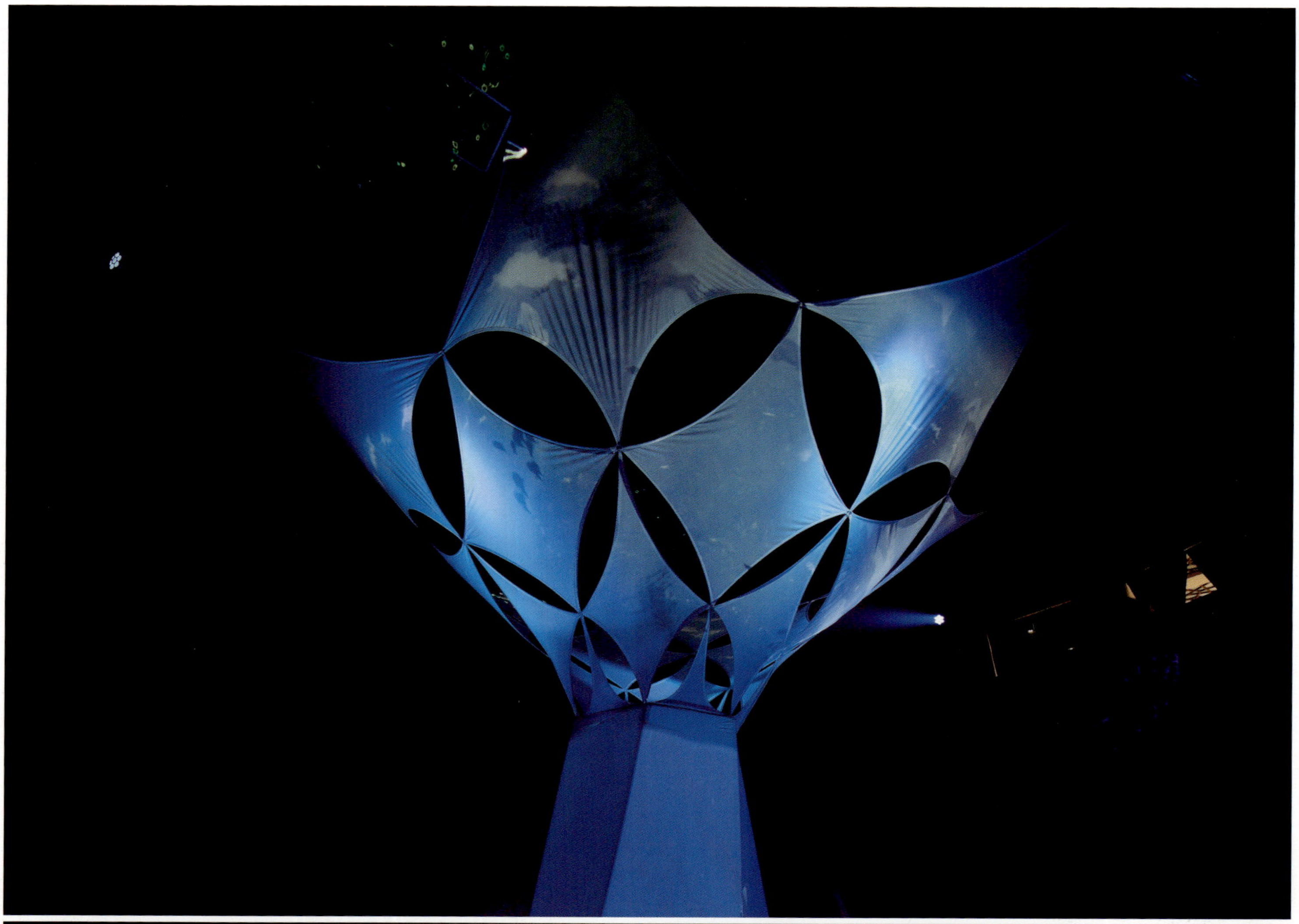

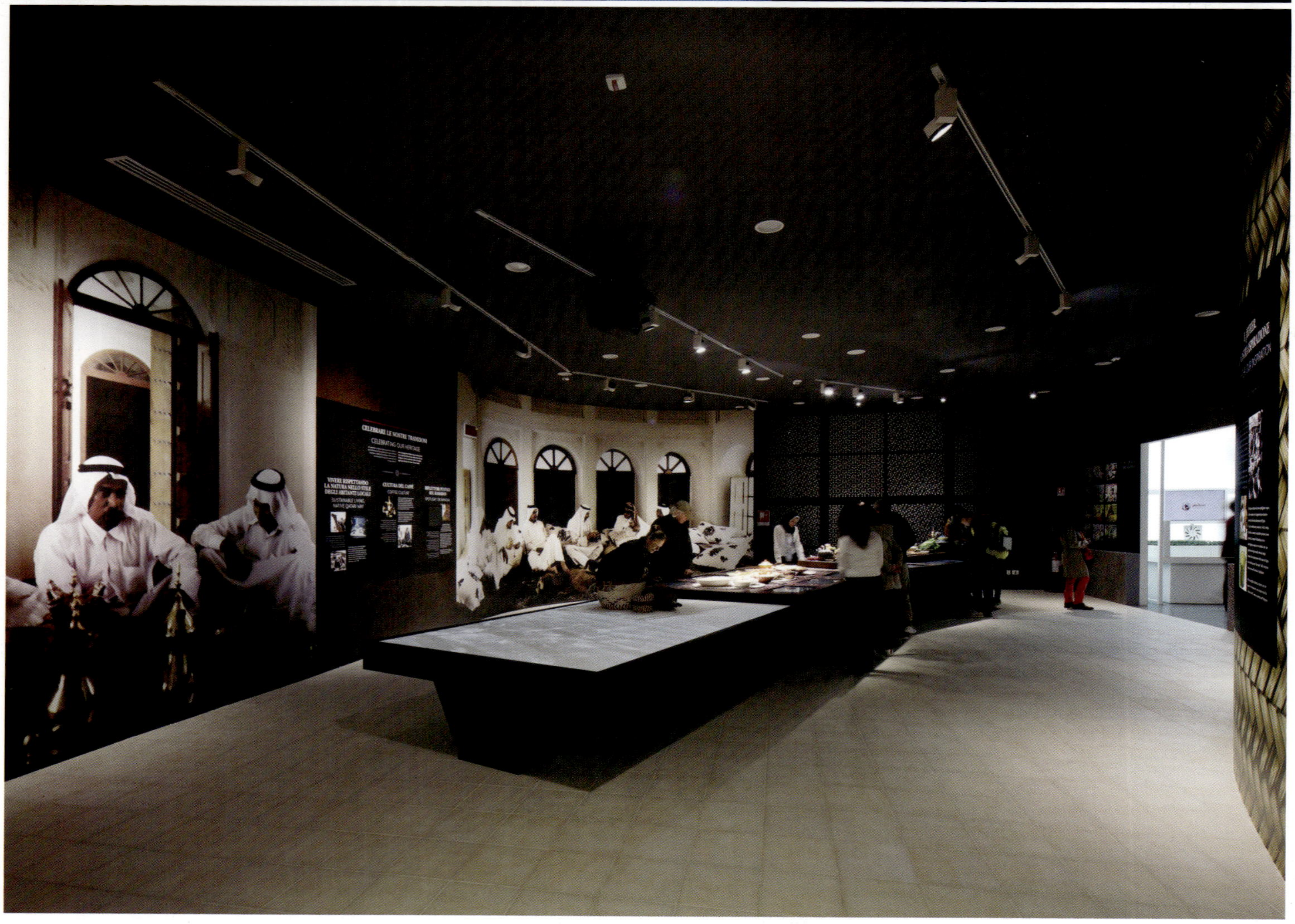

ANGOLA PAVILION
安哥拉馆

Food and Culture: Educate to Innovate
饮食和文化：教育与创新

建筑设计：Studio di Progettazione Padiglione Angola / 项目面积：2 010平方米

Architectural Design: Studio di Progettazione Padiglione Angola / Project Area: 2,010 m²

ANGOLA
ANGOLA

安哥拉馆的整体设计是想为参观者创造一次领略安哥拉生活方式的体验之旅，利用现代技术让参观者对自然材料形成感官上和触觉上的切身体验。为了迎合本次米兰世博会“滋养地球，生命能源”的主题，馆内的装饰采用了非洲历史文化中的传统元素，并把它们自然地体现在展馆的整体构建风格中，同时也传达了安哥拉在食物生产和食品消费方面的理性处理。

安哥拉馆室内分为三层加上顶层的平台共四层，展馆的构架极具简约之美。采用环保可续用材料构建的展馆也有利于展后拆卸和再利用。

安哥拉馆的设计灵感来源于安哥拉文化中的非洲圣树猴面包树。随着对猴面包树的了解，参观者也将开启真正的安哥拉文化和美食之旅，并逐渐理解安哥拉馆的主题“饮食和文化：教育与创新”。安哥拉文化，安哥拉人的精神和这个国家对文化，自然资源以及可持续发展的重视都体现出他们最为看重也是最全面的因素——教育，以及妇女在社会发展中的核心地位和对传统的守护。

The intention of Angola is to create an unforgettable experience, inviting visitors to live the lifestyle of Angola, using technology and augmented reality that ensure physical and tactile experiences through interaction with natural materials. Angola responds to the theme of the Expo, Feeding the Planet, Energy for Life, imagining an exhibition that starts from the traditional elements of African history (represented in a stylized manner in the structure of the Pavilion) to address the delicate issue of production and conscious food consumption.

The Pavilion of Angola is divided into three floors plus a terrace. The structure, made with sustainable materials, is very simple and can be easily disassembled and reused.

The Pavilion of Angola has an architectural concept inspired by a representation of the "Iimbondeiro", the sacred African baobab tree in the Angolan culture. The tree will also be the starting point from which visitors start a cultural and gastronomic journey inside the Pavilion through which they become acquainted with the content of the Angola Theme Statement: "Food and culture: Educate to Innovate."
The Pavilion offers visitors a reflection based on the culture, the soul and the expression of a country focusing on food culture and its resources, as well as the importance of sustainable development. The most important and all-encompassing elements are education and the central role of women as promoters of development and guardians of tradition.

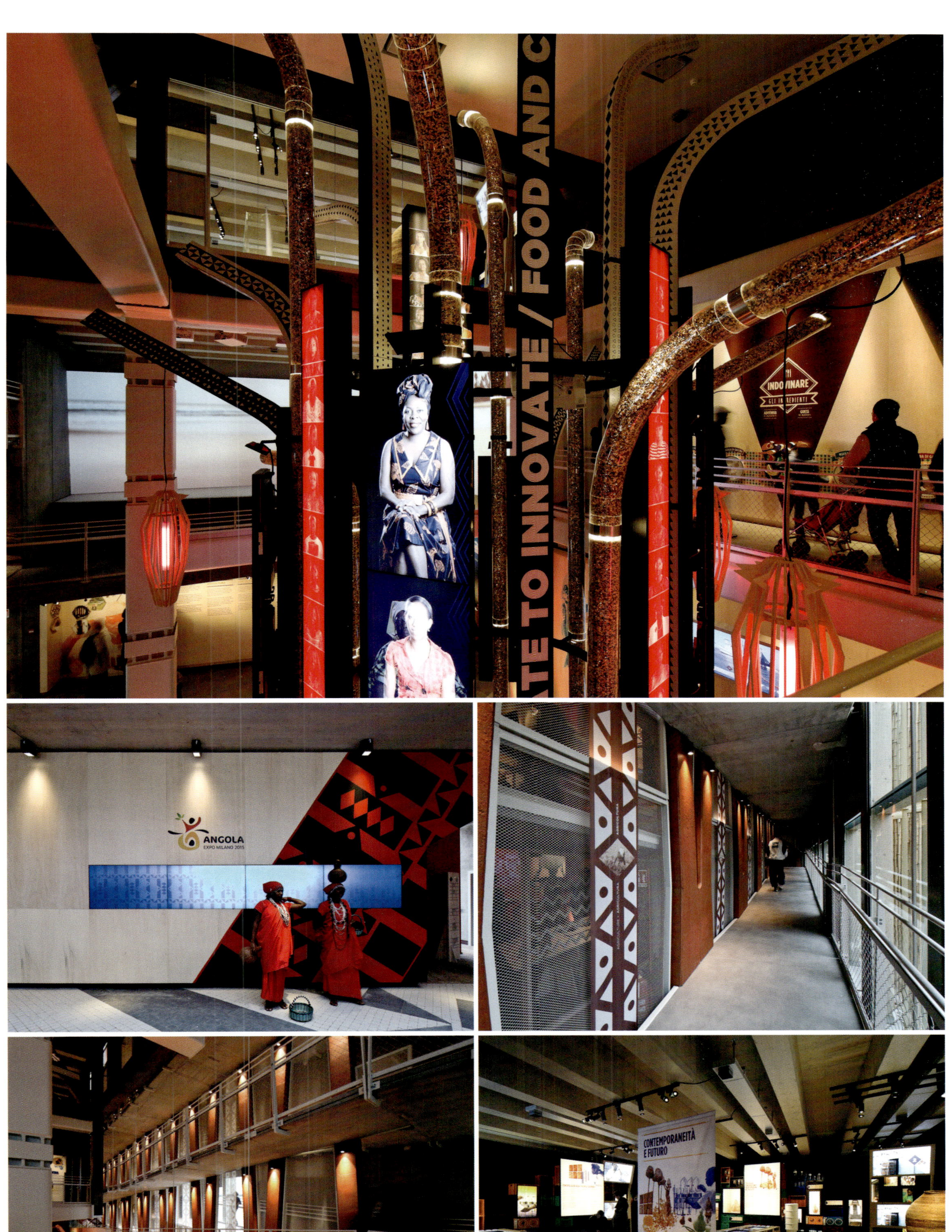
TE TO INNOVATE / FOOD AND C
INDOVINARE
GLI INGREDIENTI
ANGOLA
EXPO MILANO 2015
CONTEMPORANEITÀ
E FUTURO

MOROCCO PAVILION
摩洛哥馆

Morocco, a Journey of Flavours
摩洛哥，一趟味道之旅

建筑设计：KILO Architecture / 项目面积：2 900平方米

Architectural Design: KILO Architecture / Project Area: 2,900 m²

摩洛哥馆的设计简单又独具本土特色。设计上围绕感官的探索，通过食物的呈现展示摩洛哥的丰富多样性，也让参观者能亲历一次摩洛哥之旅，了解其不同地区的农业特色和地域文化传统。

摩洛哥馆采用卡斯巴原著民的土木建筑结构，展示了摩洛哥南部柏柏尔人的建筑风格，这种建筑不但与环境融合良好，也非常适合当地人的生活方式。

进入馆内，参观者将由南向北依次饱览摩洛哥的迷人风光。摩洛哥北部各省濒临地中海，这里一直延伸至中部的肥沃平原地区；穿过富有且工业发达的滨海城区就到了摩洛哥的腹地阿特拉斯山脉，这里富有原始气息；最后到达南部的沙漠地区。参观者可以探索到根植于不同区域的农业特色。

最后，参观者可以在馆内的餐馆里享受到世界级大厨Moha的厨艺，购买到精美的摩洛哥特色产品，也可以在展馆外的摩洛哥草坪里观赏美丽的橙子、橄榄和棕榈树。

With its simple yet distinctive theme Morocco's Pavilion is built around sensorial discovery, food and gastronomy, and represents all the diversity of the Country, showing the richness of its food and visitors can discover the architectural expression of a trip through Morocco, with all the variety of its "terroirs", its agronomical features and the different cultural traditions from one region to another.

The pavilion is a Kasbah built of wood and clay. It is a reflection of this Berber architectural style that characterizes southern Morocco, and exists in perfect harmony with the environment and lifestyle of its communities.

On entering the pavilion, visitors travel from north to south, and discover the variety of local products and agronomic tastes inherent to each region. From the northern provinces of the Mediterranean and the fertile plains of the center, they pass through the rich, urban and industrial coastal areas and the Atlas Mountains that lie at the heart of the Moroccan rural idenity before finishing in the magnificent desert provinces of the south.

Last but not least, the visit ends with the Treasures of Morocco concept store offers typical local products and restaurant where visitors can taste Moroccan fine cuisine, created by the famous chef Moha. Finally, they can relax in the typical outdoor Moroccan gardens southern orange, olive and palm trees.

l'Oud

COPORATE PAVILIONS
企业馆

企业馆是本次米兰世博会能够取得成功的一个重要的参与群体。世博会认为通过技术创新来作为未来发展的基础，不能脱离企业的支持，因为企业是新技术研究和发展的重要推动力。参与到世博会中的企业馆都是在技术、创新研究或产品上符合世博主题“滋养地球，生命能源”的全球尖端企业。

参与世博会的企业馆需要提交自己建馆的主题，其主题需要与世博的主题相呼应。展馆的设计要符合世博会的环保节能标准，并在展期结束时能够拆除再利用。

世博会是一个极佳的国际交流平台，在这个独一无二的平台上，企业品牌和形象将得到来自世界各地成千上万人的关注，因此，拥有竞争力的国际企业都不会错失这样的好机会。参与了本次世博会并自建了独立展馆的有：中国企业联合馆、万科馆、可口可乐馆、纽荷兰馆及意大利本土的航空、电力、银行等展馆。

The involvement of the corporate with Expo Milano 2015 is of major importance for the event's success. A Universal Exposition looking towards the future and towards technological innovation would not be effective without the active involvement of business, which is the driving force behind much research and development. Companies that are involved in the development of technology, innovative research, or products that align with the theme: Feeding the Planet, Energy for Life.

To become a Corporate Participant, the Company must, as part of the Request for Proposal (RFP), submit a Theme Statement and sign a Participation Agreement with Expo 2015 S.p.A to build, equip, operate and dismantle their Pavilion, highlighting one or more aspects of the Expo Milano 2015 theme.

The Universal Exposition is in fact an outstanding international communications platform and a unique stage upon which businesses can boost their brand image with the millions of visitors expected to attend Expo. In this Expo, we can visit the following independent coporate pavilions: China Corporate United Pavilion, Vanke Pavilion, Coca-Cola Pavilion, New Holland Agriculture's Pavilion and Italian local corporate pavilions such as Alitalia, Enel and Bank (Intesa), etc.

COCA-COLA PAVILION
可口可乐馆

The King of Soft Drink
软饮之王

设计师：Giampiero Peia (Peia Associati)

Architect: Giampiero Peia (Peia Associati)

Coca-Cola
Coca-Cola
Coca-Cola
Coca-Cola

Coca-Cola

Coca-Cola
Coca-Cola
Coca-Cola

可口可乐馆靠近湖景区，场馆高12米，立面面积达1 000平方米。采用木材、玻璃和水等环保可再利用的建筑材料，此馆将创造一个既具现代性又充满创新的标志性空间。外墙采用玻璃和木材再现可口可乐的商标和可口可乐经典的玻璃瓶造型，这样的外墙装饰恰好迎合了2015年可口可乐100周年纪念。

场馆的出入口采用水帘来代替门，这样有助于自然通风。屋顶种植了适宜米兰气候的植物作为覆盖。植物作为屋顶不仅不需要人为的料理，并且只需要一定的浇灌就能帮助室内空间降低温度，减少了对能源的消耗。

进入可口可乐馆的参观者将有机会参与一系列互动活动来探索可口可乐的点点滴滴，可口可乐公司的企业核心价值也会通过三个部分一一展示：可口可乐在不同地方的作为，能源保护与均衡以及环境保护。

场馆内还规划了一个篮球场场地，在米兰世博展结束后，这个展馆将变成一个全新的体育运动场所，供当地人使用。

The Coca-Cola Corporate Pavilion is located near Lake Arena and Padiglione Italia.

The building, 12-meter high and 1,000 square meters of surface area, is made of environmentally sustainable materials: wood, glass and water will create an iconic space that is simultaneously contemporary and innovative. The outer walls - made of glass and wood - recreate the Coca-Cola logo and the Contour silhouette of the historic glass Coca-Cola bottle, which will celebrate its 100th anniversary in 2015.

The entrance and exit of the pavilion will be marked with water cascades and will not have doors to allow natural ventilation. Even the roof of the pavilion will be covered with plants suited to the climate in Milan, being maintenance-free and require limited irrigation, plus it will reduce overheating in the interior spaces and decrease the energy required for cooling.

Visitors to the pavilion will be led along an interactive journey where they participate in the discovery of the Coca-Cola world, learning about the company's values in three different sections: local presence, energy balance and protecting the environment.

The building outlines the dimensions of a basketball court and, at the end of the exposition, the pavilion will a new covered space that the local community can use for physical activities.

Coca-Cola

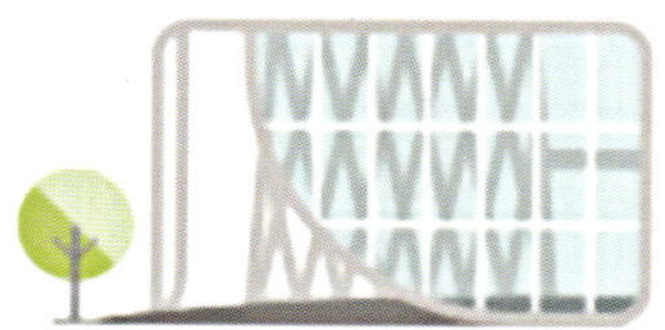

CHINA CORPORATE UNITED PAVILION
中国企业联合馆

Seeds of China
中国种子

建筑设计方：同济大学建筑设计研究院（集团）有限公司 / 主创建筑师：任力之（总裁、总建筑师）
设计团队：吴杰、李楚婧、邹昊阳、许文杰 / 用地面积：1 270平方米 / 建筑面积：约2 000平方米

Architectural Design: Tongji Architectural Design (Group) Co., Ltd. / Principal Architect: Ren Lizhi, Vice President & Chief Architect of TJAD
Design Team: Wu Jie, Li Jingchu, Zou Haoyang, Xu Wenjie / Site Area: 1,270 m² / Building Area: about 2, 000 m²

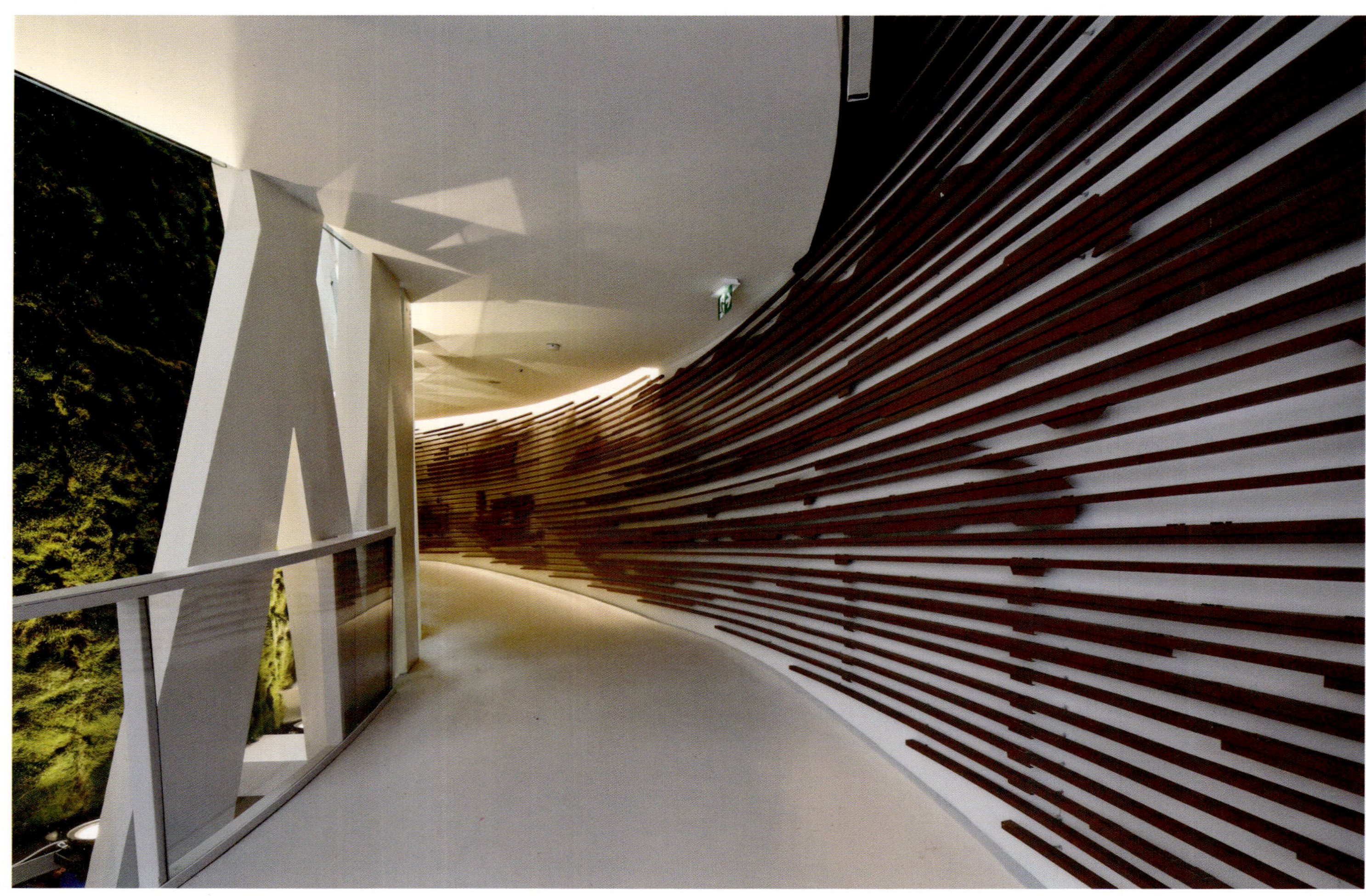

中国企业联合馆的主题是“中国种子”，设计上充分利用种子的象征意义，诠释一群中国公司的梦想——寻找并实现保护自然资源和食品安全的价值。中国企业家的精神充满了历史意义、坚持和创新，并通过种子的本质集中地体现出来。这是中国公司首次联合起来以独立展馆的形式参加世博会。

展示空间分为“生命原点”“成长力量”“种子梦想”“生命之光”“重生之路”和“食之艺术”等几个展区，展示了在中国快速发展环境之中，商界的成长之路以及扮演的角色。

中国企业联合馆的设计源于萌芽的种子破土而出彰显的力量。孕于绿色礼堂的生命转换成DNA螺旋结构，成为缓缓向上的参观坡道，将参观者引入一个椭圆形的敞开空间——花园和露台。简单的长方形几何立面因为采用透气薄膜和玻璃幕墙，使得整个展馆看起来很轻盈，而且具有很强的可呼吸性。内部空间线条同样弯曲，表现了中国企业的活力。

展馆将会被打造成一个温和的自然环境。在白天，展馆中心的环提供光线和空气；绿色圆柱形墙体将自然引入室内，创造了一种独一无二的感官体验。展馆内提供了4条参观路线。经过二层的展览大厅和礼堂，参观者可以到达一层和地下层。在这里，他们可以亲身感受准备食物，然后到达餐厅和礼物店。

With the name “Seeds of China,” and drawing on the symbolism of the seed, the China Corporate United Pavilion interprets the dream of a group of Chinese companies that seek to live the values of conservation of natural resources and food security. The entrepreneurial spirit of China, imbued with heritage, perseverance and innovation, is truly epitomized by the living essence of seeds. It is the first time that Chinese companies unite to take part in a Universal Exposition with their own pavilion.

In the exhibition spaces, the themes on display are “The Origin of Life,” “The Power of Growth,” “The Dream of the Seeds,” “Light of Life,” “Cycle of Life,” “The Culinary Arts,” and others, showing the path of growth and the role of the business community within the rapid development that China has enjoyed.

The image of power that arises from the breaking of ground to the sprouting of seeds has inspired the design of the China Corporate United Pavilion. The life that comes from the green heart, that contains the auditorium space, transforms into the spiral of a DNA chain tracing an upward path, to then take on an elliptical form: the ramp gently accompanies visitors upwards towards the open spaces of the Italian-Chinese garden and the terrace. Its simple geometric shape of an outer rectangle – aesthetically lightweight and breathable thanks to the breathable membrane and glass walls – covers the harmonious inner curves that represent the vitality of Chinese enterprises.

The goal is to create a gentle and natural environment: during the day the exhibition gallery uses the center ring for light and air; the heart of the pavilion is wrapped in a cylinder of green walls allowing nature to murmur within its interior, creating a sensory experience that is both natural and unique. The pavilion offers four different itineraries. From the first floor in the exhibition hall and in the auditorium, visitors proceed down to the ground floor and basement where they can enjoy the direct experience of food preparation, and then towards the restaurant and beyond, to the gift shop.

SHIMAO GROUP
上海纺织
SHANGTEX
五粮液
WULIANGYE
BAOSTEEL
China Seeds Change the World

VANKE PAVILION
万科馆

Shitang
食堂

建筑师：Studio Daniel Libeskind / 室内展示：Ralph Appelbaum / 平面设计：韩家英
面积：1 000平方米 / 摄影：Vingtsix, Courtesy of Studio Daniel Libeskind

Architects: Studio Daniel Libeskind / Interior Exhibition: Ralph Appelbaum / Graphic Design: Han Jiaying
Area: 1, 000m² / Photographs: Vingtsix, Courtesy of Studio Daniel Libeskind

继2010年成功参展上海世博会后，万科将再度亮相米兰世博会，成为世博163年历史上首家以海外独立建馆形式参展的中国企业。万科馆将会通过重塑中国传统的食堂，探索与世博会主题“滋养地球”相关的关键问题。

“食堂”作为中国传统的社会结构，以各种形式存在于当代社会，代表了在一个健康、宁静的环境中社交的可能性。展馆的设计概念源于中国传统山水画——岩石、稻田和远古的岩层，旨在讲诉文明、科技和21世纪的故事，以及为不同文化提供反思和庆祝的空间。

万科馆位于湖心公园的边缘，看起来像是一个从东边突起的动态垂直景观。建筑上，场馆的外形和材质完美联结了文艺复兴气息与现代性。其内外部间的音乐比例、流动感创造出一段时间和空间的旅程。展馆内外均采用弯曲有致的几何形状，红色的蛇纹岩雕刻出一个开口，沿着白色马赛克瓷砖铺设而成的楼梯直达中部。展馆顶部的观景台提供了极好的视野，湖心公园和意大利馆一览无遗。整个展馆由立体的红色金属瓷砖包裹着，几何形状的陶瓷板不仅具有较强的表达性，而且具有较强的自我清洁和空气净化性能。

进入馆内将看到的是由无数根柱子上挂着一簇簇电子屏组成的五彩森林。这些柱子隐喻树的根与枝干。穿过这条长长的多媒体展示通道，不同的内容在一个个独立食堂内展现，有的展现生活中用餐、庆祝和交谈的场景；有的展现中国的土地和城市风貌。这些生动的电子屏幕将把游客带入画面，使其犹如身临其境。一些当地的传说也将转换到更大的全球化的主题和活动中。

Following the success participation of 2010 Shanghai Expo, Vanke will unveil in 2015 Milan Expo, to become the first Chinese enterprise in the Expo 163-year history as the overseas self-built pavilion. The pavilion will explore key issues related to the Expo theme of “Feeding the Planet” by reimagining a traditional Chinese Shitang (dining hall).

“Shitang”, as a traditional Chinese social structure, lives on today in contemporary society under various forms, representing a possibility to socialize in a healthy, tranquil environment. The concept for the pavilion was inspired by traditional Chinese landscape painting—rock formations, rice fields, and prehistoric outcrops. The pavilion aims to tell the story of civilization, technology and the 21st Century as well as offer a space for reflection and celebration of different cultures.

Situated on the edge of the Lake Arena, the pavilion appears to rise from the east forming a dynamic vertical landscape. The construction shape and material boast a renaissance breath and modernity. Musical proportion and fluid sense on inner and outer spaces create a journey in the regard of time and space. The design features a sinuous geometrical pattern that flows between inside and outside. The red serpentine form carves an opening up the middle to a grand staircase clad in a white mosaic tile. A roof-top observation desk will provide stunning views of the lake and near-by Italian pavilion. The pavilion is clad in an innovative three-dimensional red metalized tile, and the geometric ceramic panels not only create an expressive pattern, but they possess highly sustainable self-cleaning and air purification properties.

Entering the Vanke Pavilion, visitors will see a colorful forest that consists of myriad pillars,symbolizing roots and branches of tree, filled with multimedia screens. Through the long media exhibition passage, various film stories telling Chinese people’s dining, celebration and consersation scenarios,as well as stories of the local conditions and customs Chinese cities. The lively electronic screen will bring visitors immersively into pictures. Chinese local legends will also be displayed on gobalized themes and activities.

Vanke Pavilion
食堂
Costruire una comunità
attraverso il cibo
以食物构建社区
Building community
through food
vanke

GIFT SHOP

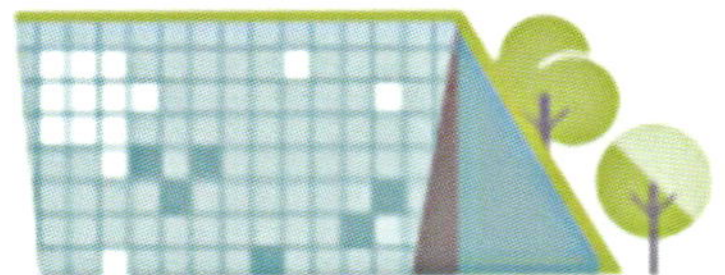

NEW HOLLAND AGRICULTURE'S PAVILION
纽荷兰馆

Respect the land and grow the future
尊重土地，发展未来

组长和项目经理：Recchi Engineering / 项目设计: Carlo Ratti Associati / 可行性和建造管理: NUSSLI
可持续性顾问: Manens–Tifs Ingegneria / 结构工程: M. Durbano Ingegnere / 面积：1 579平方米

Group Leader and Project Manager: Recchi Engineering / Project Designer: Carlo Ratti Associati / Feasibility and Construction Management: NUSSLI
Sustainability Consultants: Manens-Tifs Ingegneria / Structural Engineering: M. Durbano Ingegnere / Area: 1, 579 m²

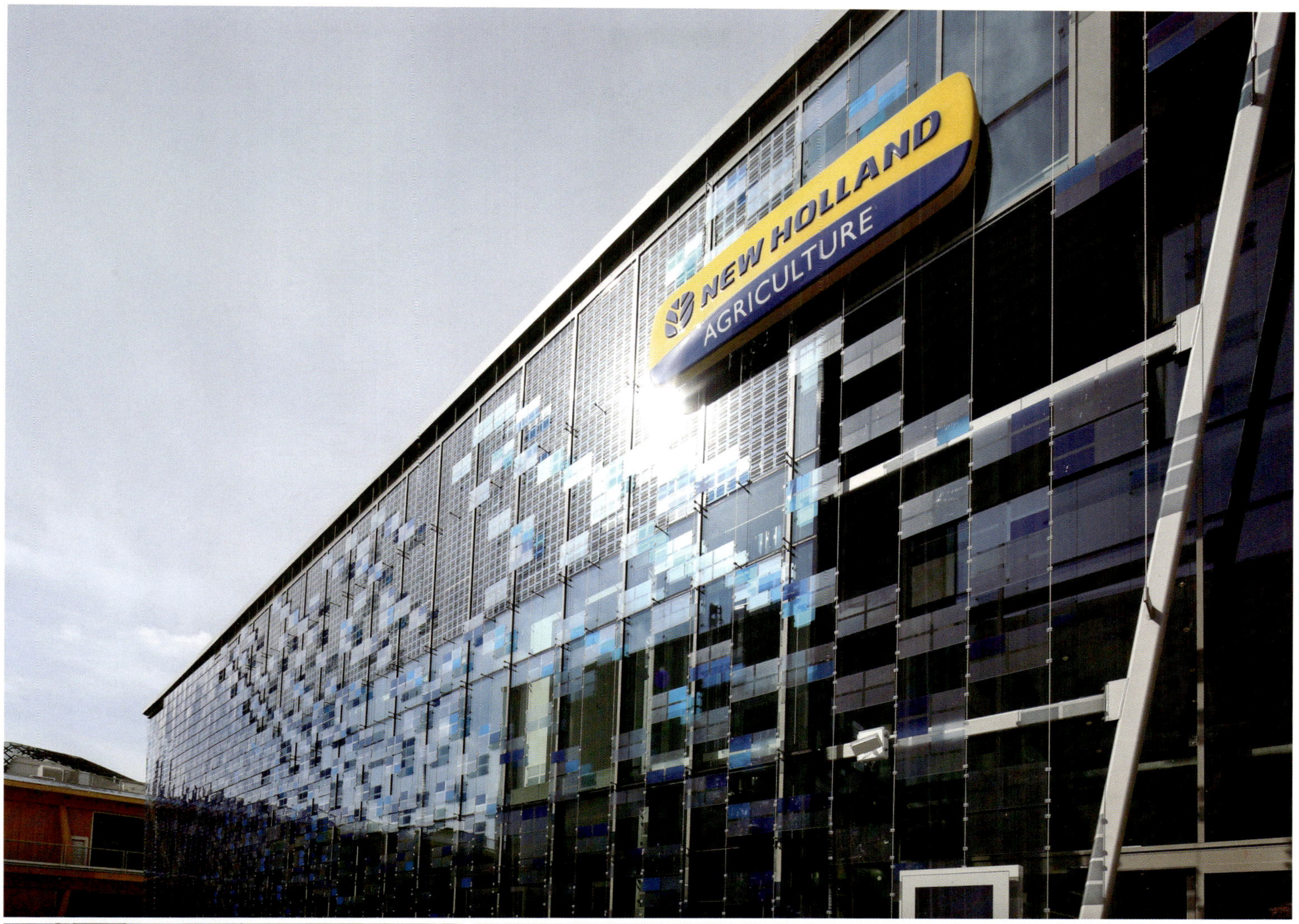
NEW HOLLAND
AGRICULTURE

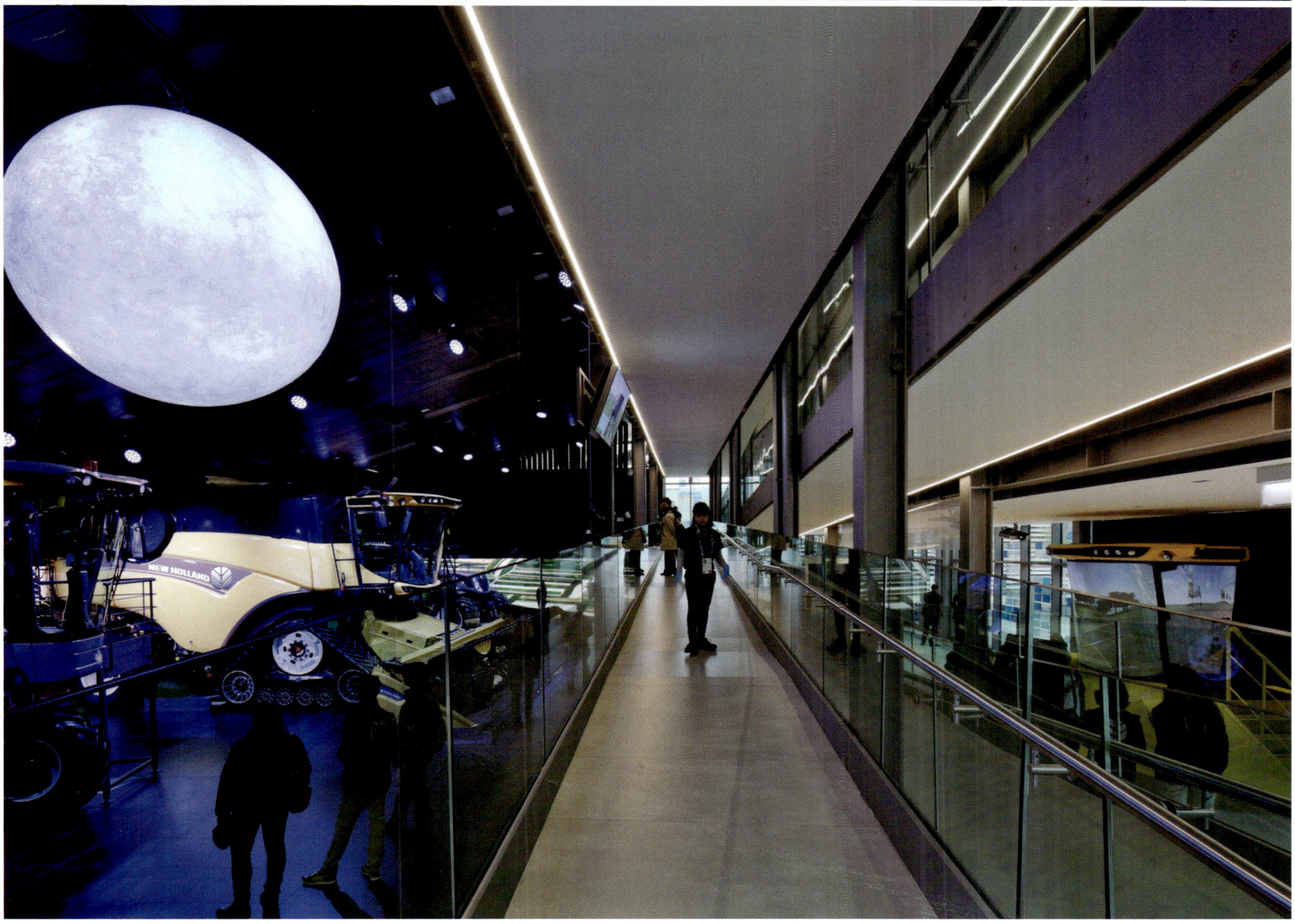
NEW HOLLAND

纽荷兰展馆看起来就像是一台巨大的3D打印机。屋顶上是一大片农田，两辆全自动、零排放、以自生能源为动力的拖拉机在农田上不停地耕作。但是，项目的设计理念不单单是建筑屋顶上自动驾驶的拖拉机，它还展示了在有角度的土地上耕作的可能性。这预示着未来农田可以进行农业复制，还有利于生物多样化和资源保护。

在展馆内部，参观者们可以通过物理和数码的方式，与纽荷兰公司在关于可持续性农业最新的研究、产品和创新的问题上进行互动。通过巨大的屏幕，参观者们可以观看到在世界各地拍摄的农田情况，近距离了解可持续性农业的季节和栽培周期。整个展馆所需要的能源，包括屋顶上无人驾驶的拖拉机，都是就地产生的。米兰世博会闭幕后，这个可拆卸展馆将被拆除并在另一个地方重新组装成一个创新教育农庄。

New Holland Pavilion features a large agricultural field on its roof, similar to a giant 3D printer thanks to the constant activity of two zero-emission, robotized, self-driving tractors, which will constantly move over the roof, "writing" and working the land. However, the idea of EARTH SCREENING is not just about self-driving tractors, which can draw patterns on the roof of the building. It is about how we can sense and respond to the conditions of the soil to a degree that was impossible before. This points to a future where an agricultural field could be considered as a giant base for "agricultural printing", with major advantages foreseen in terms of plant biodiversity and resource preservation.

While the roof uses real moving tractors, inside the pavilion visitors can interact with the latest research, products and innovations in sustainable agriculture developed by New Holland, in both a physical and digital way. Using a sort of "augmented rurality", made of large screens featuring dynamic footage collected from fields across the world as the backdrop for static agricultural equipment, visitors are taken on a journey that closely mirrors the seasons and cultivation cycles and taught about energy and sustainable farming. The aim is that the energy for the pavilion - including that for the self-driving tractors on the roof - will be generated on site. After the Expo, the New Holland pavilion will be dismantled and reconstructed in a second location as an innovative didactic farm, embodying the very idea of recycling and sustainability.

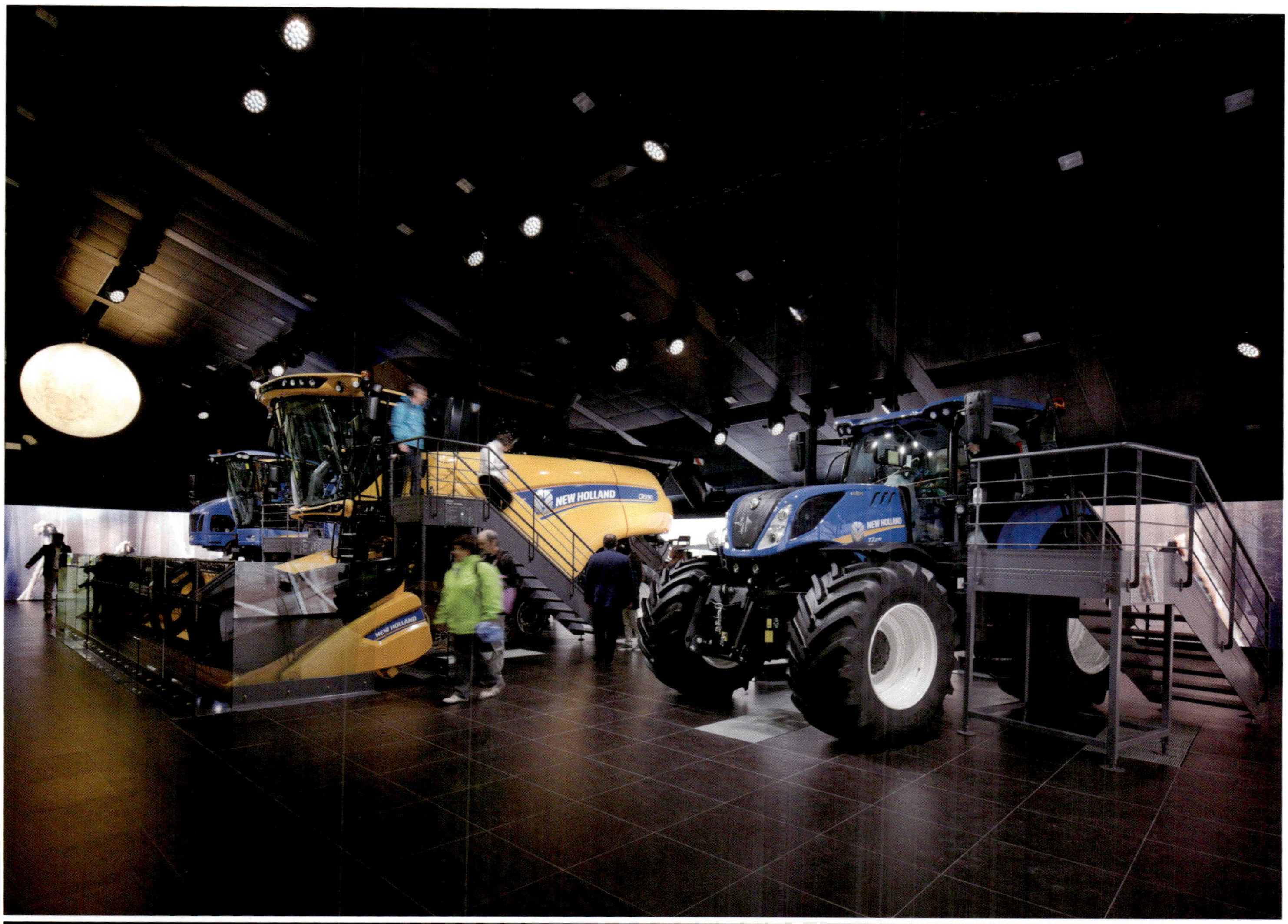
NEW HOLLAND
NEW HOLLAND

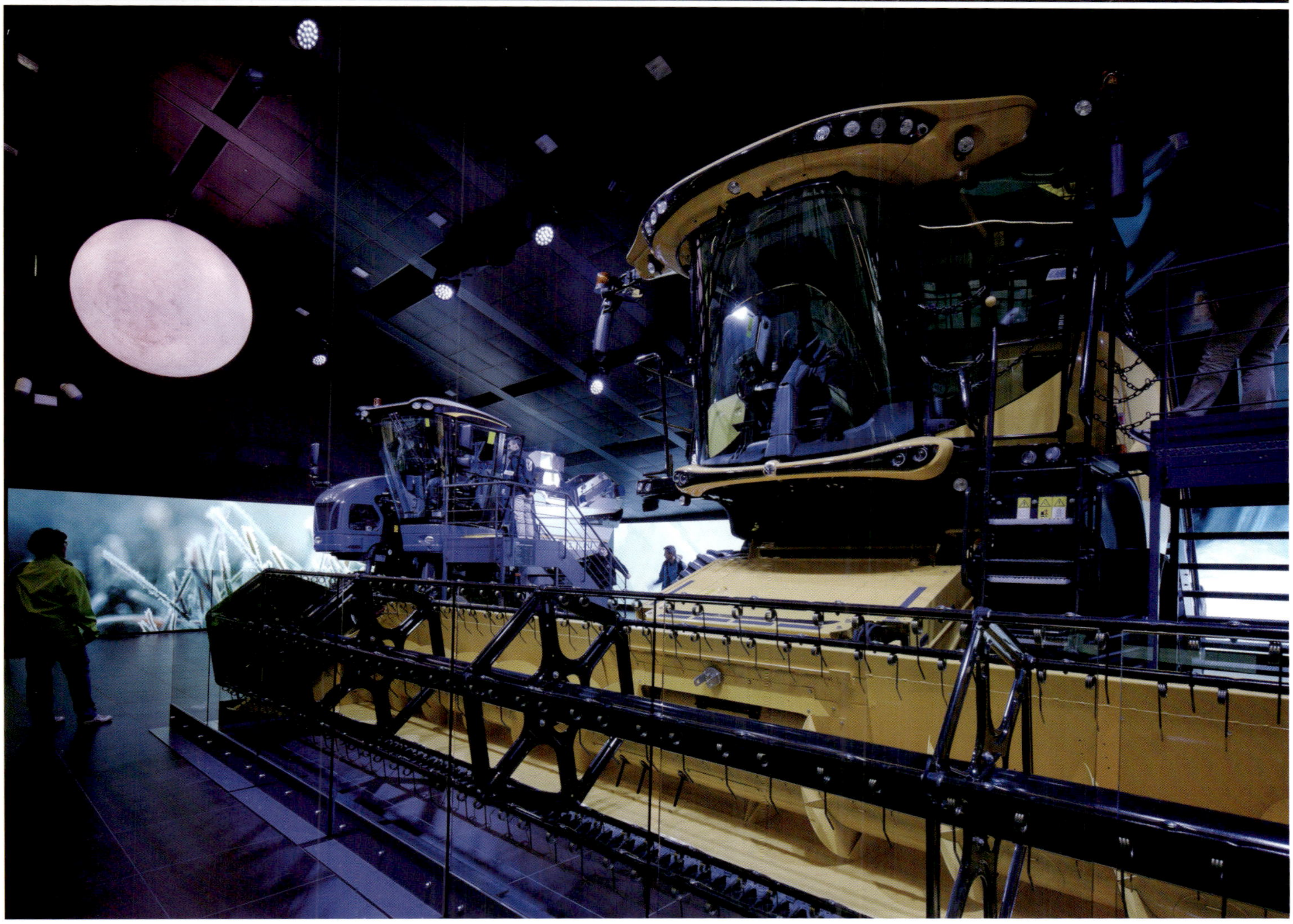

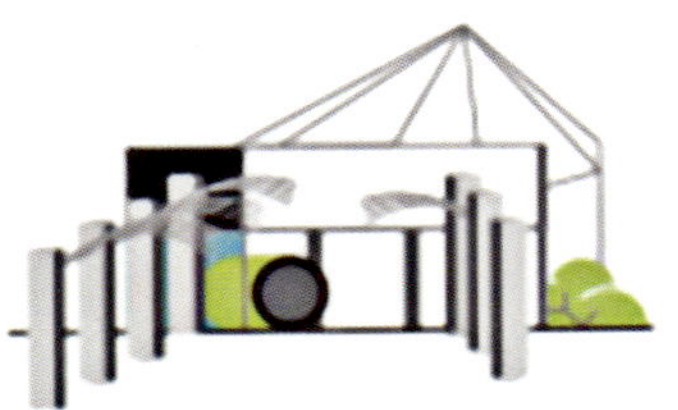

FERRERO PAVILION
费力罗馆

The Future Belongs to the Children of Today
孩子是我们的未来

建筑设计：Paolo Maldotti
项目面积：3 640 平方米

Architect: Paolo Maldotti
Project Area: 3 640 m²

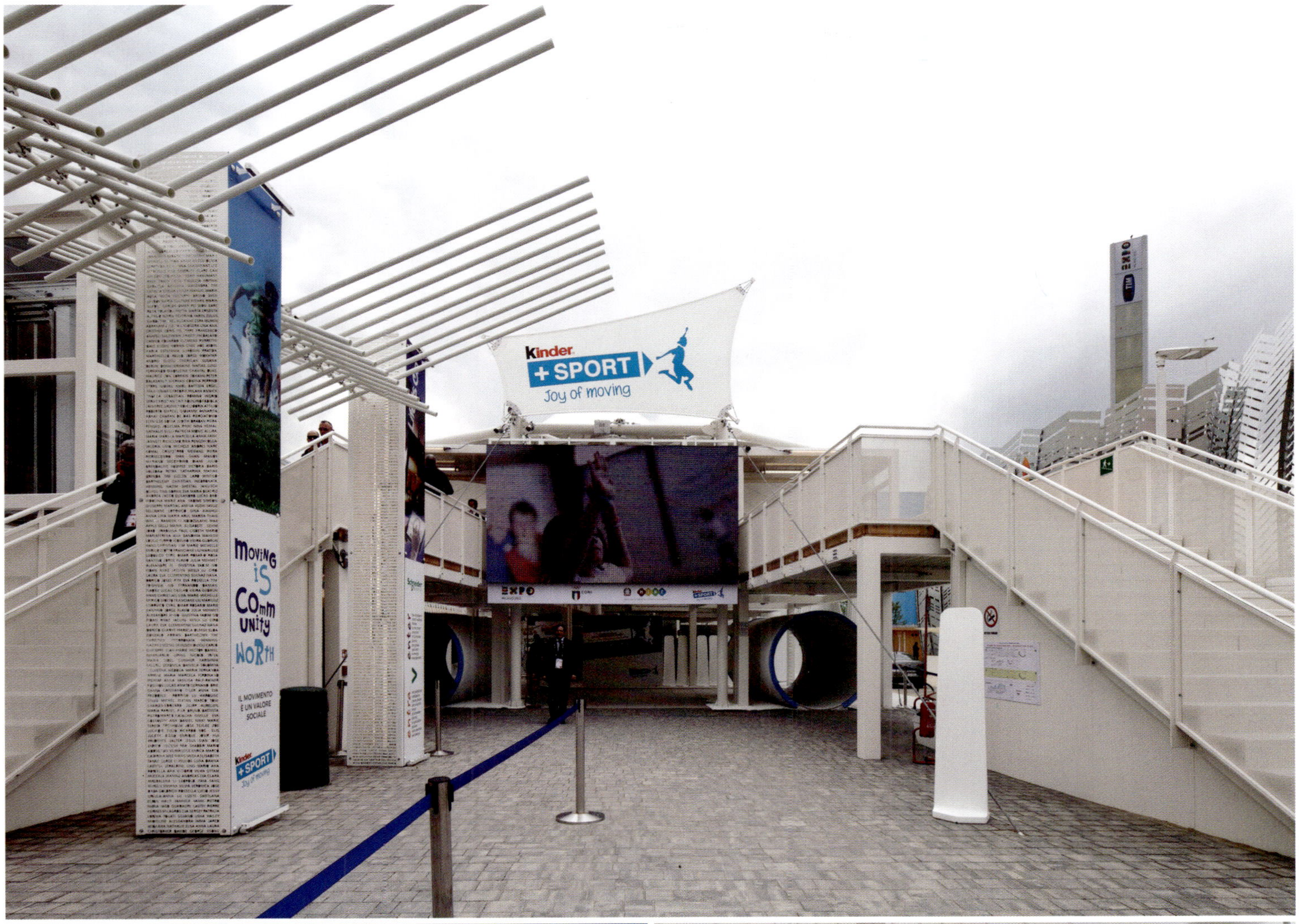
Kinder
+SPORT
Joy of moving
MOVING IS COMMUNITY WORTH
IL MOVIMENTO È UN VALORE SOCIALE

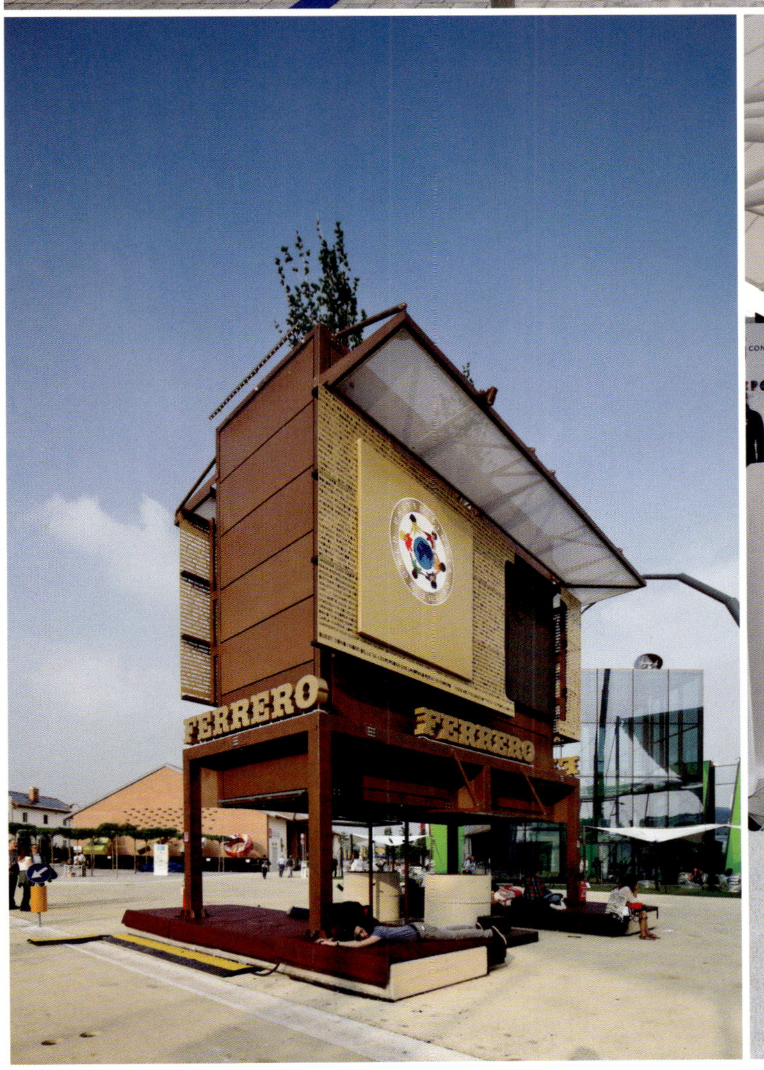

FERRERO
FERRERO

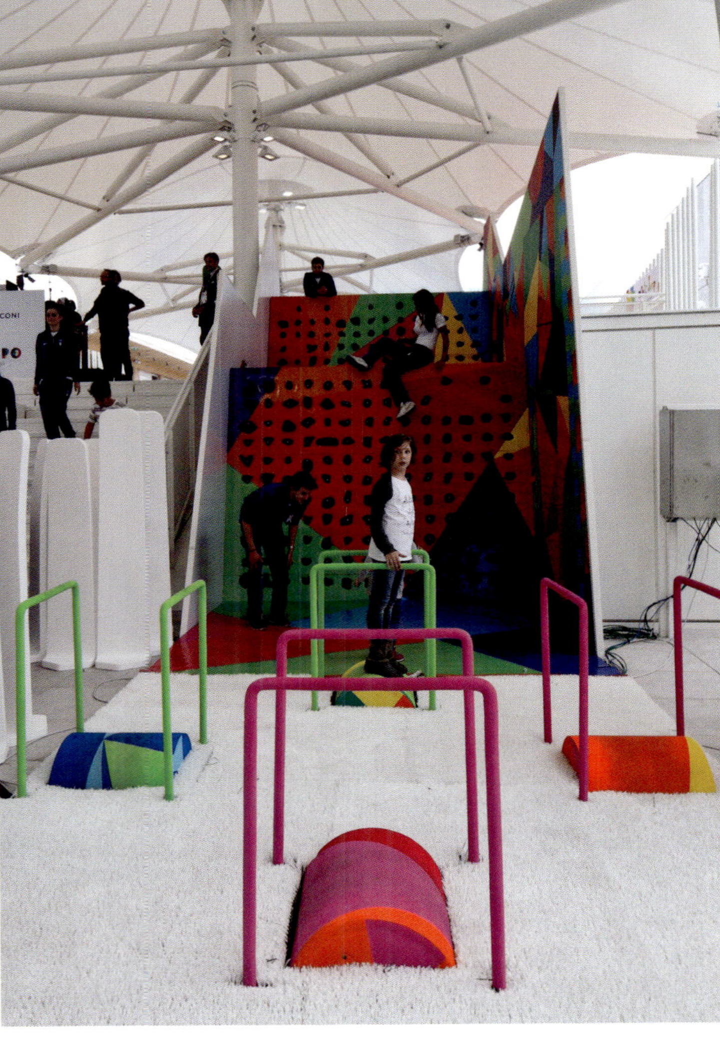

费力罗馆的标志性特点便是它修长轻盈的整体拉伸结构。柔和的曲线屋盖一路沿儿童游乐区和公共竞技区而建。这一连续的空间里人造的芦苇一路环绕，随风摆动。

费力罗展馆梦幻般的入口处设计了各种造型的树木围绕着展馆的金属构架，为吸引眼球，它们都被涂成白色，而互动和游乐项目区域则采用绚丽的色彩作为装点。

展馆后面有座绿草油油的小山。静坐在这里，随着时间的推移，那梦幻般的世界仿佛就是真实存在的。

The Ferrero Pavilion's hallmark feature is its long, lightweight tensile structure. The soft curves of its white covering provide a roof over communicative pathways, games for children and arenas for the public, in a succession of spaces delineated by an artificial reed bed sculpted by the movement of the wind.

The entrance is evocative of a dream in which stylized trees encompass the pavilion's metallic structures, absorbing them into a magic wood painted pure white; inside, all communication and play-related items are picked out in bright colors.

A grassy green knoll at the back of the pavilion is dotted with dozens of trees: here the dreamworld becomes a reality, a metaphor for a design project that moves and evolves with time.

Joy of moving

INTESA SAN PAOLO PAVILION
意大利联合圣保罗银行馆

Innovative Protagonist
创意主角

建筑设计：Michele De Lucchi
展览面积：100 平方米

Architect: Michele De Lucchi
Exhibition Area: 100 m²

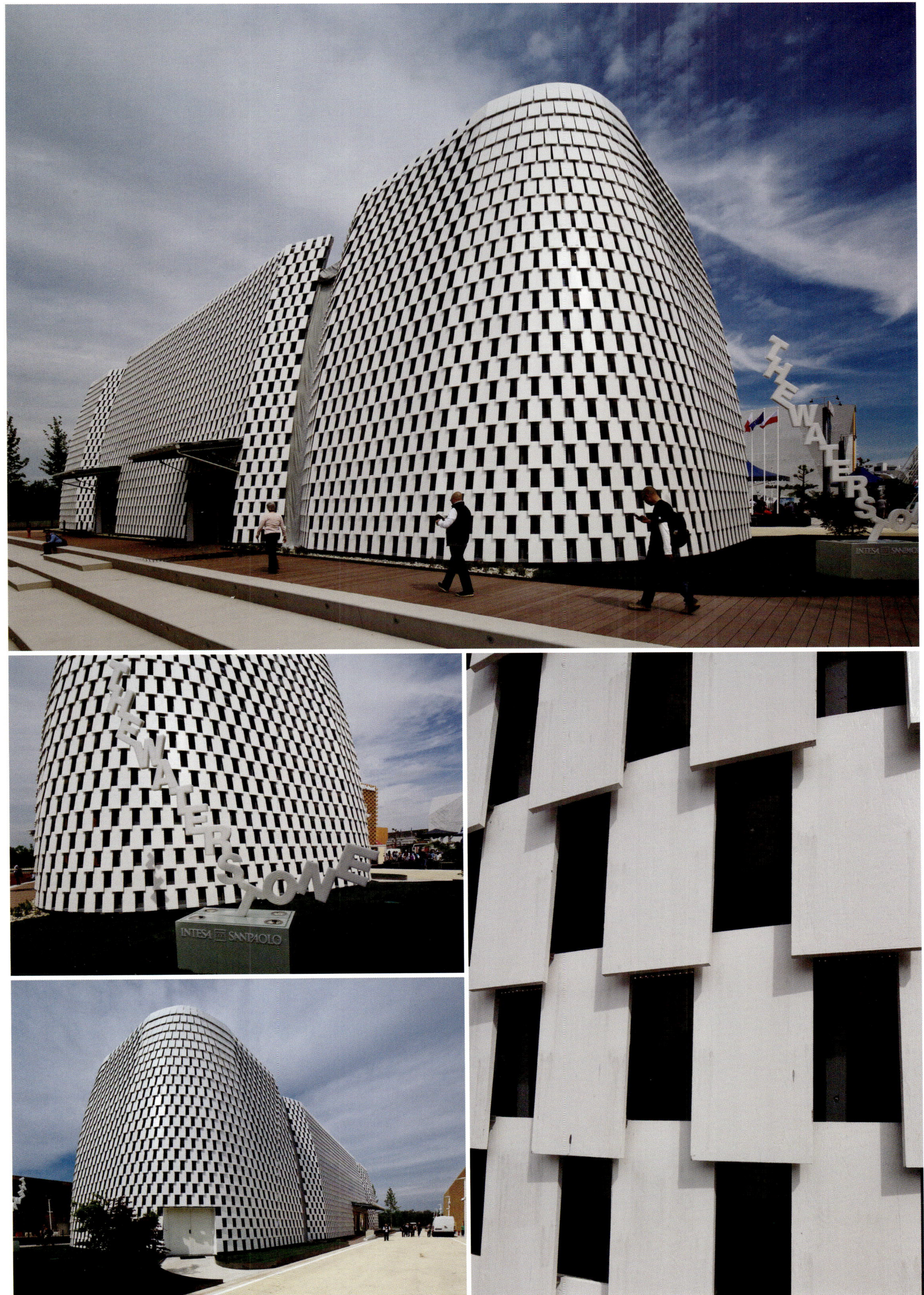
THEWATERSTONE
INTESA SANPAOLO

意大利联合圣保罗银行馆位于米兰世博展主干道中心，展馆造型似四条湍急的瀑布挂在三块平滑的大卵石中间，十分吸引眼球。胶合木板构成的双重幕墙同时作为承重结构，其内墙能够起到防风挡雨的作用，而外墙则构建出整个展馆的外部形态。

展馆外壳由6 363块白色木块有序地重叠拼接而成，形成状似山岭的屋顶结构。空气可以通过里外层墙面的空档进入馆内，这样也起到了很好的隔热效果。到了晚上，LED灯会在这鳞鳞的木块中制造出绚烂的灯影效果。

展馆内部设计成两层。首层是公共空间，精致的艺术装饰体现出意大利联合圣保罗银行的文化和品位。二层则留作活动空间和会议区。

Standing in a strategic, central location on the Decumanus, the Intesa San Paolo Pavilion is an intriguing construction that recalls three smooth boulders with four waterfalls. The load-bearing structure is of plywood with two walls, one internal of wood that affords protection from water and wind, and one external that provides shade and gives shape to the building.

The outer shell is made up of 6,363 white shingles laid out in orderly rows that overlap slightly as on the roofs of houses in the mountains. Air rises through natural induction in the empty space between the walls so as to prevent heat from penetrating. A LED lighting system creates an evocative luminous effect between the shingles at night.

The interior is on two levels. The lower floor is designed for the general public with refined artistic installation featuring the bank's cultural and social commitment. The upper floor has spaces for reserved events and meetings with firms.

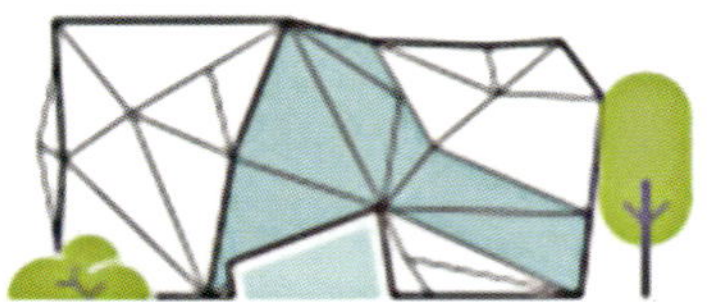

ALITALIA AIRWAYS PAVILION
意大利航空公司馆

Connecting the World
连接世界

建筑设计：阿提哈德航公司视觉传播部
项目面积：959 平方米

Architectural Design: Visual Communications Departmant-Etihad Airways
Project Area: 959 m²

意大利航空公司馆处于米兰世博会的正中心。两层结构的展馆矗立中央，像一个未来感的社交中心。展馆首层被设计成为空中飞人和股东们精心准备的贵宾休息区。

进入展馆，参观者将有幸观摩和体验生动的旅行故事和真实的环球旅行，参观者也可以利用由先进的交互式屏幕创造的互动体验真正领略什么叫“连接世界”。

除了丰富的航空飞行故事和环球体验，参观者还可以在幻想主题活动区观看不同主题的表演秀，同时，品尝世界级星厨为大家带来的全球五大洲不同的风味美食。幻想展厅还可以让参观者从天空的角度来观察这个世界，飞行模拟器让每个人都有机会感受在天空中驾机翱翔的奇妙体验。

The Alitalia Pavilion is at the very centre of the Expo Milano 2015 site. The two-storey structure features a futuristic Social Hub on the ground floor, and an exclusive first-floor space for the company's fregquent flyers and stakeholders on the first floor: the Premium Lounge.

Visitors embark on a multimedia voyage of discovery around the planet via advanced technologies and interactive screens that present true stories and real experience of trips made; visitors get the chance to actively take part and experience the true meaning of "Connecting the World".

There's more than just sharing and learning to the entertainment programme: the Imagination Lounge events arena hosts daily special events, offering performances by star chefs from all over the globe along with shows and events that will take visitors on taste-led tour of the world's five continents. The Imagination Lounge also offers a real opportunity to connect with the entire world, as seen from the skies! Real flight simulators allow everyone to experience the thrill of piloting one of the giants of the skies.

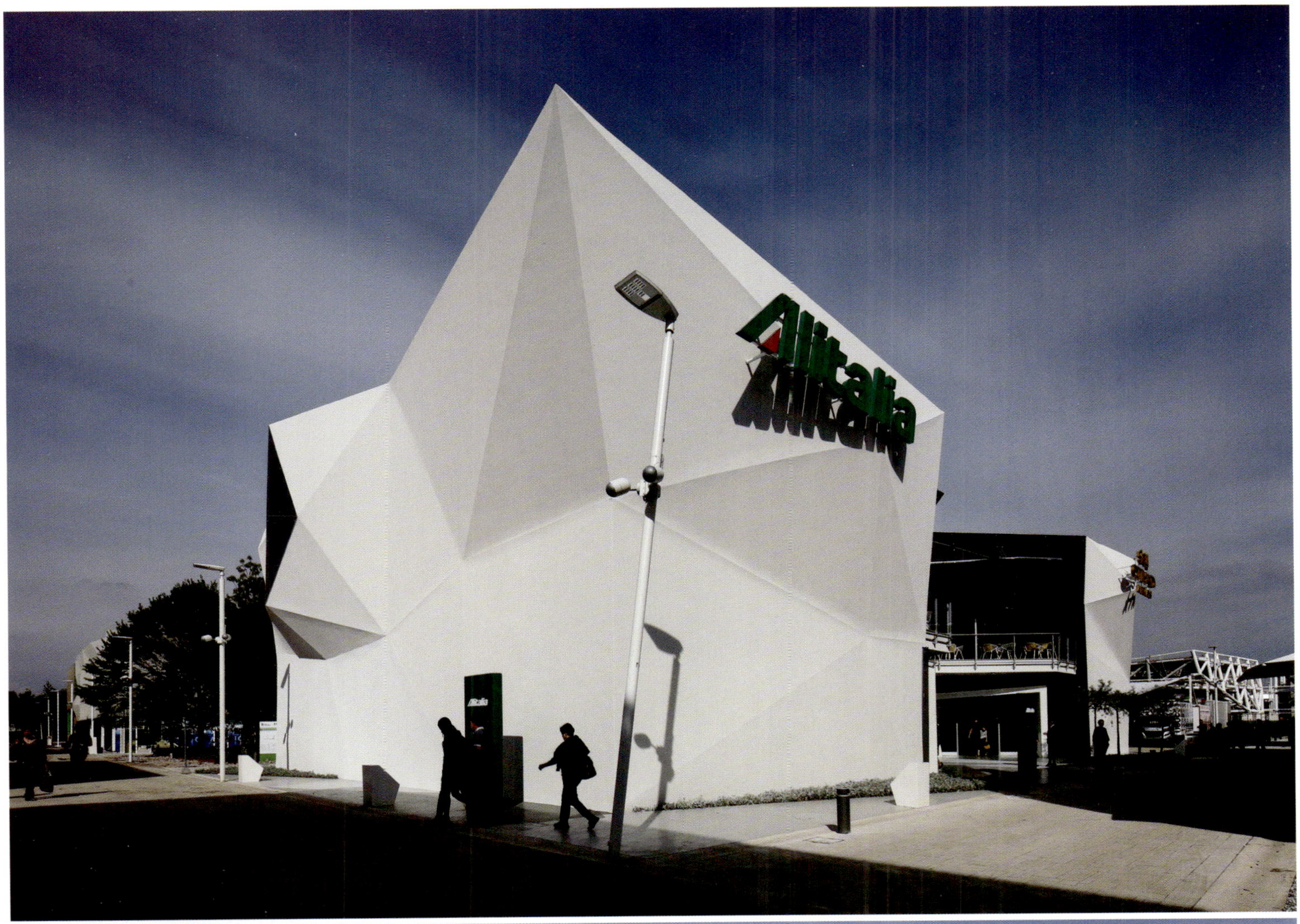
Alitalia

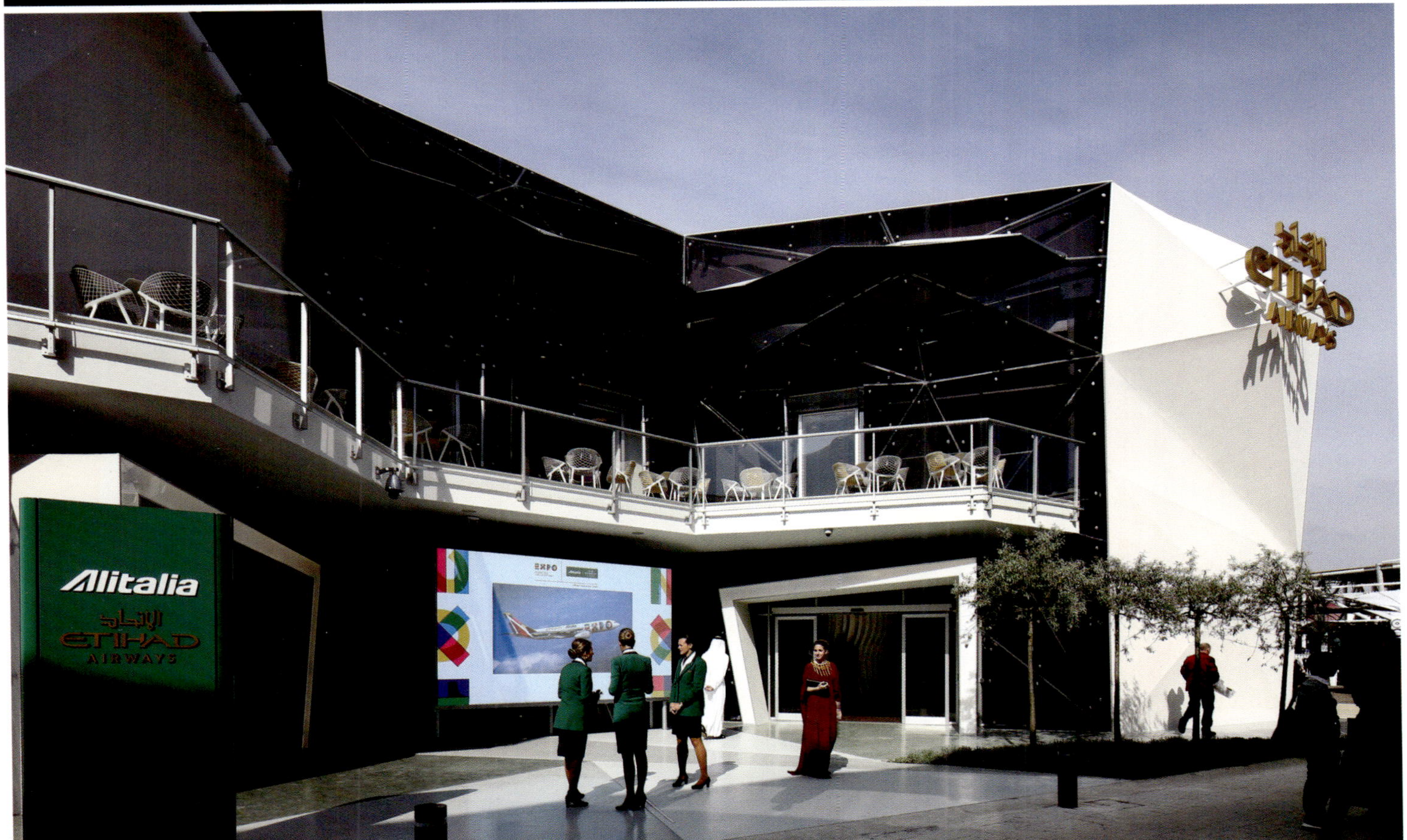
Alitalia
ETIHAD
AIRWAYS
EXPO

ENEL PAVILION
意大利国家电力公司馆

Cultivating Smart Energy
开发智能能源

建筑设计：Piuarch
项目面积：890 平方米

Architect: Piuarch
Project Area: 890 m²

意大利国家电力公司馆用一条长107米的开放式步道带领游客观赏一片交互式的发光柱构造的森林。在这里，游客将了解到未来我们急剧增长的能源需求是如何通过技术创新和进步而被满足的。

在电力馆的展示厅里，三块连接的电网控制着电站和电动交通控制区。参观者将了解本次世博会的智能电网如何操控能量流，他们也将慢慢了解复杂的电流如何跟我们的活动相交互，从而探求出人们最合理的能源消费方式。

The Enel Pavilion is an open space crossed by a walkway of 107 m that takes visitors into a virtual forest of interactive luminous panels telling the fascinating tale of how the world of energy has changed and will evolve in future with technological progress and new solutions to respond with ever-greater attention to customer requirement.

In the showroom designed by Enel, connected with three electric grid control posts and an e-mobility control area, visitors will understand how energy flows move within the Smart Grid Expo Milano 2015. They will be involved in order to understand the complexity of energy flows and the possibilities that arise from the interaction between customers and the energy market, in order to figure out how to consume the available energy in the best possible way, and in order to become aware about their consumption profile and economic advantages.

除了建有独立展馆的公司和机构，来自世界各地的其他企业和机构同样参与了本次米兰世博会，并在有限的空间里尽情发挥了他们的创意建筑设计。

特拉萨马提尼酒馆（MARTINI），作为一家提供开胃酒品的公司，他们采用了让人“开胃”的苹果绿伞盖作为馆外品酒区的顶棚。

Such as L'APERITIVO ITALIANO TERRAZZA MARTINI is an appetizer wine company who adorns apple green shade in umbrella shape in wine tasting area outdoors.

圣培露矿泉水(S.PELLEGRINO)则打出“活在意大利”的标语来吸引游客。

S.PELLEGRINO is streaming “Live in Italian” to attract visitors and promote their mineral water.

TIM (Telecom Italia Mobile)是意大利的老牌通信公司，他们通过展示过去几十年的通信工具来让参观者了解通信技术是如何随着时代进步而改进创新的。

TIM (Telecom Italia Mobile) is a time-renowned communication common carrier in Italy, and it lays out communication tools in past decades to illustrates how communication technologies improve and innovate as time progress.

Except for those have independent pavilion as exhibition site, many corporations from the globe create their special spaces to demonstrate their products and concepts in limited spaces.

麦当劳仍旧保持着快餐行业领军者的姿态，为参观游览世博会的游客提供为大家所熟识的饮料和汉堡。

McDonald's continues to be a leader in fast food industry and offer hospitble service for everyone in the site of the Expo Milano 2015.

作为全球闻名的莫雷蒂啤酒（BIRRA MORETTI），他们用麦褐色的巨大啤酒桶把啤酒爱好者召集过来，游客可以一边品尝美味的啤酒一边欣赏展墙上用莫雷蒂啤酒瓶拼出的繁复图案。

The world famous Birra Moretti builds a big brown beer barrel to attract beer lovers who can enjoy delicious beer and complicated patterns formed by Birra Moretti bottle simutaneously.

雀巢（NESTLÉ）展馆的布置很有科技感，它通过图文和视频解读饮食和健康的密切关系。雀巢150年孜孜以求的就是为人类提供更健康的饮食。

The Nestlé pavilion is full of scientific feelings, which interprets the intimate relationship between human health and diet through images and videos. Nestlé has been researched healty diet for human benings for more than 150 years.

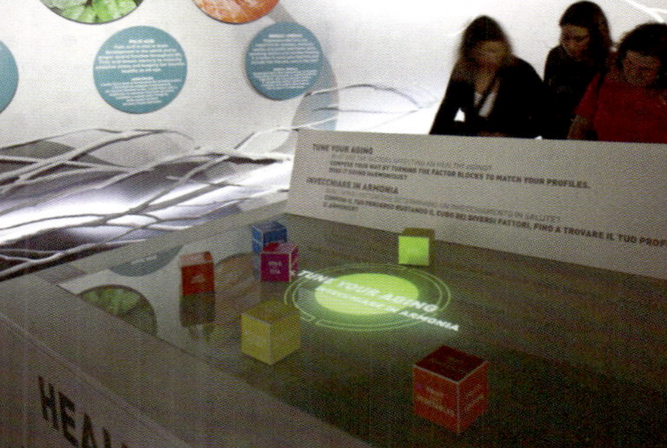

CIVIL SOCIETY PAVILIONS
民间组织馆

民间组织馆基本都采用简约风格设计，馆内设计比较注重各种活动的展示和互动空间。我们选取了部分有独立展馆的民间组织馆来着重介绍，让大家一睹国际上的民间团体在布展和策展上的精心设计。

本届民间组织馆在米兰世博会主题的宣传推广中起到了很强的主导作用。参与本届世博会的民间组织拥有专门的展馆用来举办与世博会主题相关的活动。而所有民间组织馆的参与者将把他们过往的宝贵知识和经验分享出来，并通过各种活动来宣传世博主题。可以说，民间组织的参与使得世博会更包容，更广泛，内容更丰富。

像圣·鲍思高协会提出要把对年轻一代的教育纳入到世博会的主题中来，而且他们相信：通过多方的努力协作，提供足够的食物是解决贫困，维护基本人权和追求整体发展的有效办法。

KIP国际学校馆提出“美丽土地，永恒世界”的主题。他们倡导政府、企业和机构都要联合起来促进当地各方面的均衡发展，从而为人类创造一个美丽的世界。

Civil Society Organizations Pavilions are in minimal style on exterior, while its interior spaces emphasize exhibition and interactive functions. In this chapter, we pick out those that have independent pavilions to introduce their elaborated exhibition arrangement and curatorial ways.

The Civil Society Organizations are set to play a leading role at Expo Milano 2015. Civil Society will have a dedicated pavilion to be the venue for events and initiatives related to the Expo's theme. All the Civil Society Participants will be contributing their knowledge and experience to Expo, via activities focused on developing education and awareness of the Universal Exposition's themes. The presence of Civil Societies at Expo Milano 2015 will, therefore, be inclusive, wide-ranging, and rich in content.

For the Don Bosco Network (DBN), Expo Milano 2015 represents an outstanding opportunity to encourage young people to become involved in the theme of the Universal Expo. DBN's theme statement states that it is working towards "The right to adequate food in the framework of multi-sector responses to poverty eradication, and human rights-based holistic development."

The KIP International School's pavilion is entitled "Attractive territories for a sustainable world". Which means that, to feed the planet, governments, businesses and associations need to invest, above all, in local development.

DON BOSCO PAVILION
圣·鲍思高馆

Educating the Young, Energy for Life
教育年轻一代，为生命提供能源

建筑设计：Laboratorio Archigiano
建筑面积：747 平方米

Architectural Design: Laboratorio Archigiano
Project Area: 747 m²

来到圣·鲍思高馆的参观者可能会觉得奇怪，因为它是2015米兰世博会里唯一以个人命名的展馆。圣·鲍思高是一位圣人，她不代表任何国家、机构、公司，她是一个活跃于全球130多个国家的大家庭组织。

圣·鲍思高协会成立于2010年，是由全球8个幼慈会（非政府组织）构成。幼慈会在133个国家建立了机构，从1870年开始在全球108个国家建学办校，培育了多达121.5万学生。

圣·鲍思高协会认为饥饿和营养不良远不是粮食生产和产量不足造成的，它们关乎人权，关乎教育水平，关乎水和健康以及公平的经济条件。

Surprise and great curisoty are aroused by the presence at Expo Milano 2015 of the Don Bosco Pavilion, the only one that bears the name of a person, and indeed a saint, and the only one that represents not a country, organization or firm but a religious family, and one of the few active in over 130 countries throughout the world.

The Don Bosco Network (DBN) is a worldwide federation of 8 Salesian NGOs founded in 2010. The Salesian institutions, based in 133 countries, have been active since 1870 and run schools and educational centers in 108 countries catering for over 1,215,000 young people.

According to the DBN, hunger and malnutrition are far from being just a matter of food production or the availability of food, but directly concern the right to life, access to a good level of education, to water and health, and to equitable economic conditions.

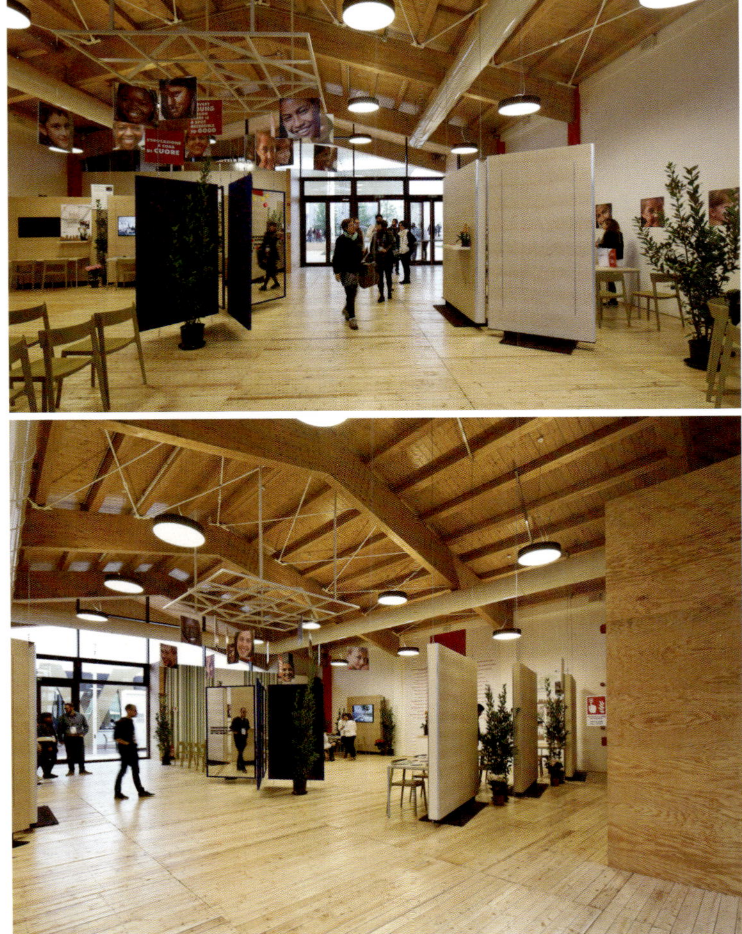

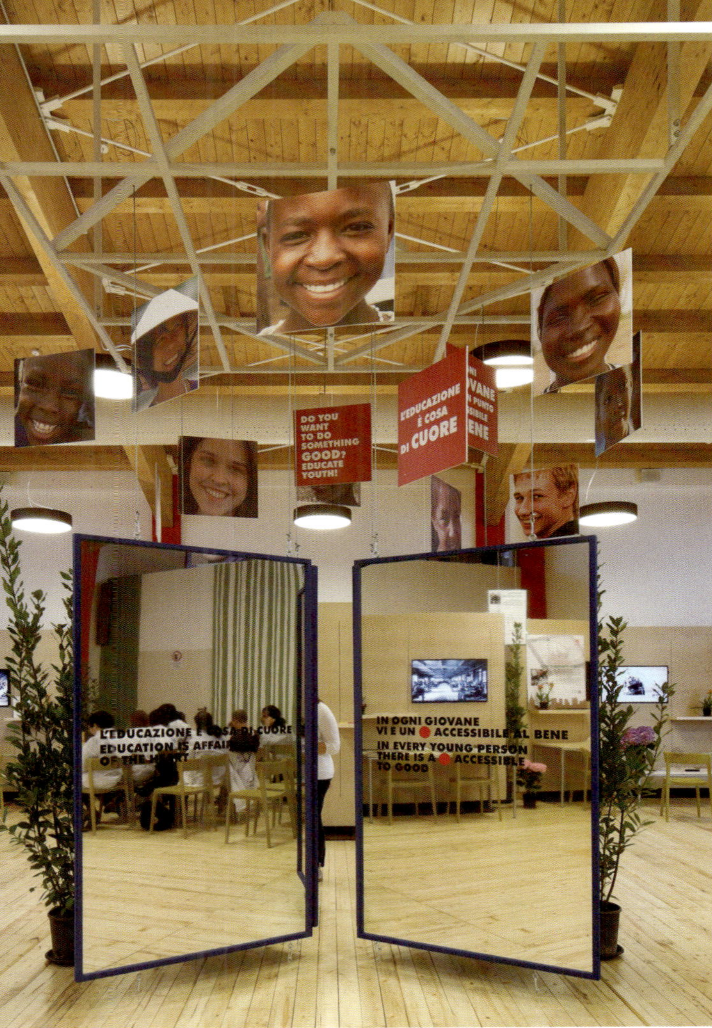

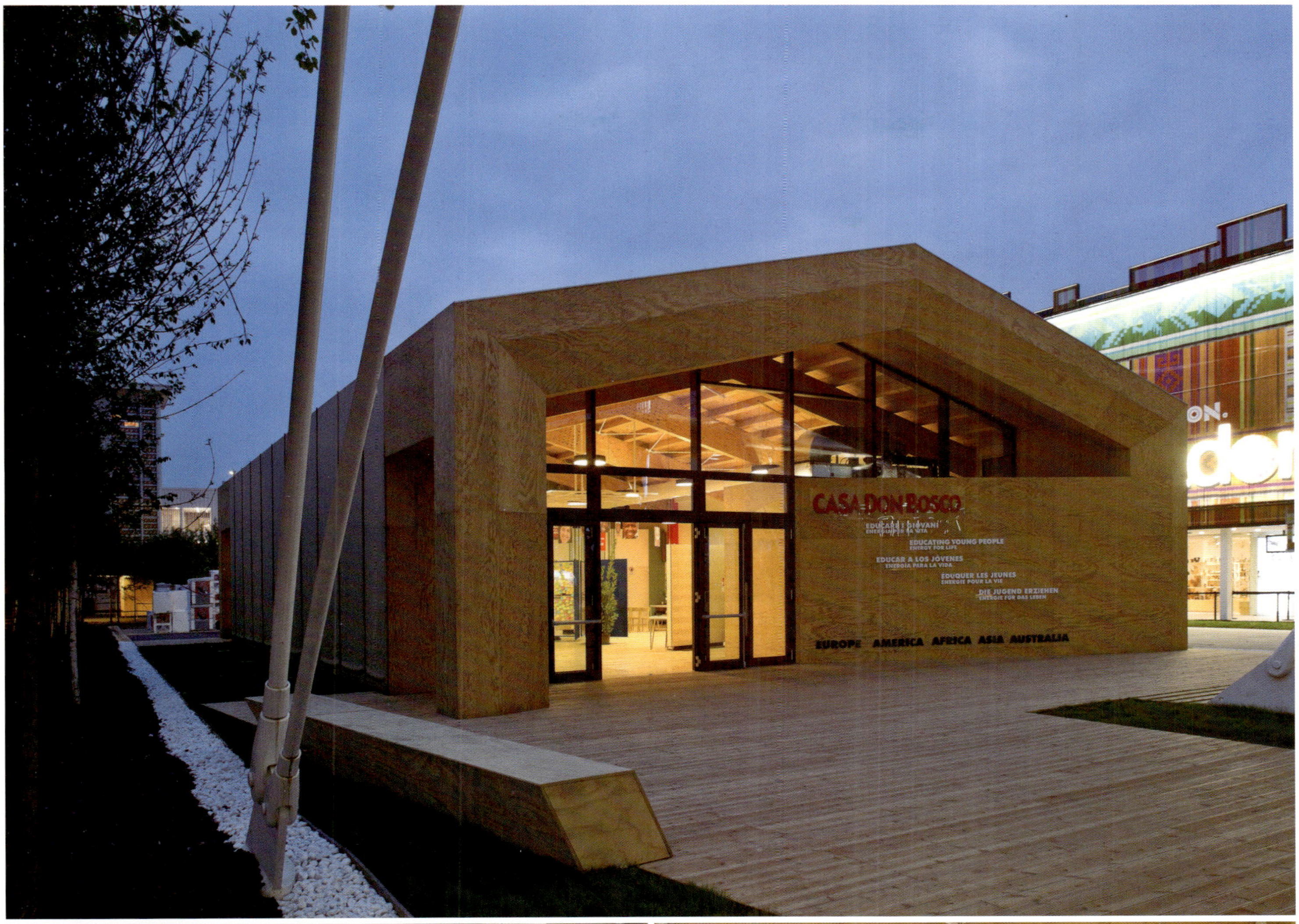
CASA DON BOSCO
EDUCATING YOUNG PEOPLE
EDUCAR A LOS JÓVENES
ÉDUQUER LES JEUNES
DIE JUGEND ERZIEHEN
EUROPE AMERICA AFRICA ASIA AUSTRALIA

L'EDUCAZIONE È COSA DI CUORE
DO YOU WANT TO DO SOMETHING GOOD? EDUCATE YOUTH!
IN OGNI GIOVANE VI È UN ACCESSIBILE AL BENE
IN EVERY YOUNG PERSON THERE IS A ACCESSIBLE TO GOOD

FOUDAZIONE TRIULZA PAVILION
Triulza协会馆

EXPIOding Energies to Change The World
发掘能源，改变世界

项目面积：8 000 平方米

Project Area: about 8,000 m²

意大利Triulza协会在2015年米兰世博会期间的任务是协助管理民间组织馆——Triulza庄园（Cascina Triulza）。此协会成立的初衷是支持和管理民间组织的各项社会活动，从国际合作到社会经济活动不一而足。目前，Triulza协会吸引了全球60个民间组织机构加入。

本届米兰世博展，Triulza协会及其中的民间组织机构将在Triulza农庄里举行展览，Triulza农庄是伦巴蒂农业系统中的一种典型老式农舍。作为唯一会在世博展之后留在原址的场馆，它将成为2015米兰世博会的物质遗产。因为它极具象征意义且与本届世博展主题非常贴切，经世博组织机构Expo 2015 S.p.A.修整后，这座场馆将成为伦巴蒂田园建筑和农业生产的模型。

Cascina是这个场馆里最大的展览区，面积近8 000平方米，户外空间有5 000平方米。整个区域分三部分建筑：老房子，谷仓和仓棚。老房子体现了一种主要的历史性建筑，作为展厅它包含多功能厅、办公室和会议室；仓棚区将作为接待区，供大型会议，餐饮以及大型展览和研讨会使用。Triulza协会还计划开辟一个专门区域供有各种需求的顾客使用。

Fondazione Triulza was established specifically to manage the Cascina Triulza - Civil Society Pavilion and is based on the initiative of organizations operating in different areas of the Civil Society, from international cooperation to social economy. To date, the Fondazione Triulza network has 60 Civil Society Organizations.

Participation of Fondazione Triulza and the Civil Society Organizations takes place inside the Cascina Triulza, a typical old farmhouse of the Lombard agricultural system. As the only remaining structure of the Exhibition Site, it will continue as one of the physical legacies of Expo Milano 2015. Restored by Expo 2015 S.p.A. it is an example of rural Lombardy architecture and a model of agricultural production, lending it great symbolic importance, through its affinity with the Theme of Expo Milano 2015.

The Cascina is one of the largest exposition areas within the Site: an architectural complex of nearly 8,000 square meters covering over 5,000 square meters of open space. It is arranged as three buildings: the former residence, the old granary and the old barn. The former residence is the main historic building, offering multi-purpose spaces, offices and meeting rooms. The old barn, which has been enlarged, will comprise the reception area, the conference room, and the dining area, and offers a large and unique exhibition and workshop space. The project of Fondazione Triulza also plans to create an area dedicated to the informed consumer.

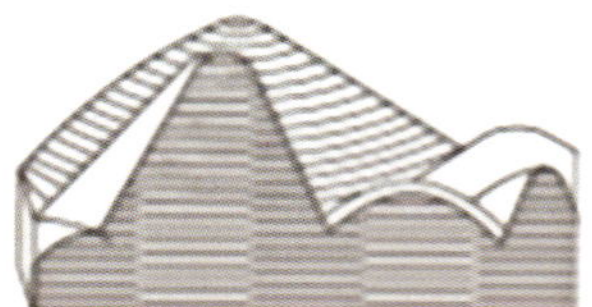

PAVILION ZERO
零展馆

The Beginning of All Stories
故事的起源

建筑设计：Michele De Lucchi
室内设计：Giancarlo Basili

Architectural Project: Michele De Lucchi
Interior Design: Giancarlo Basili

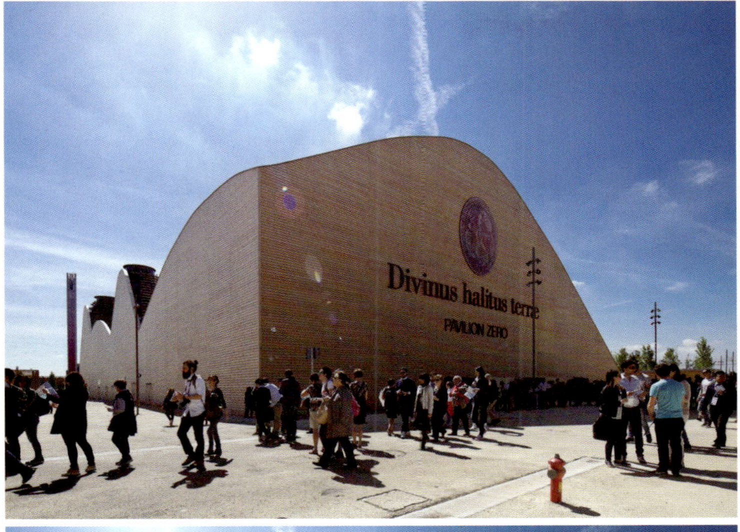

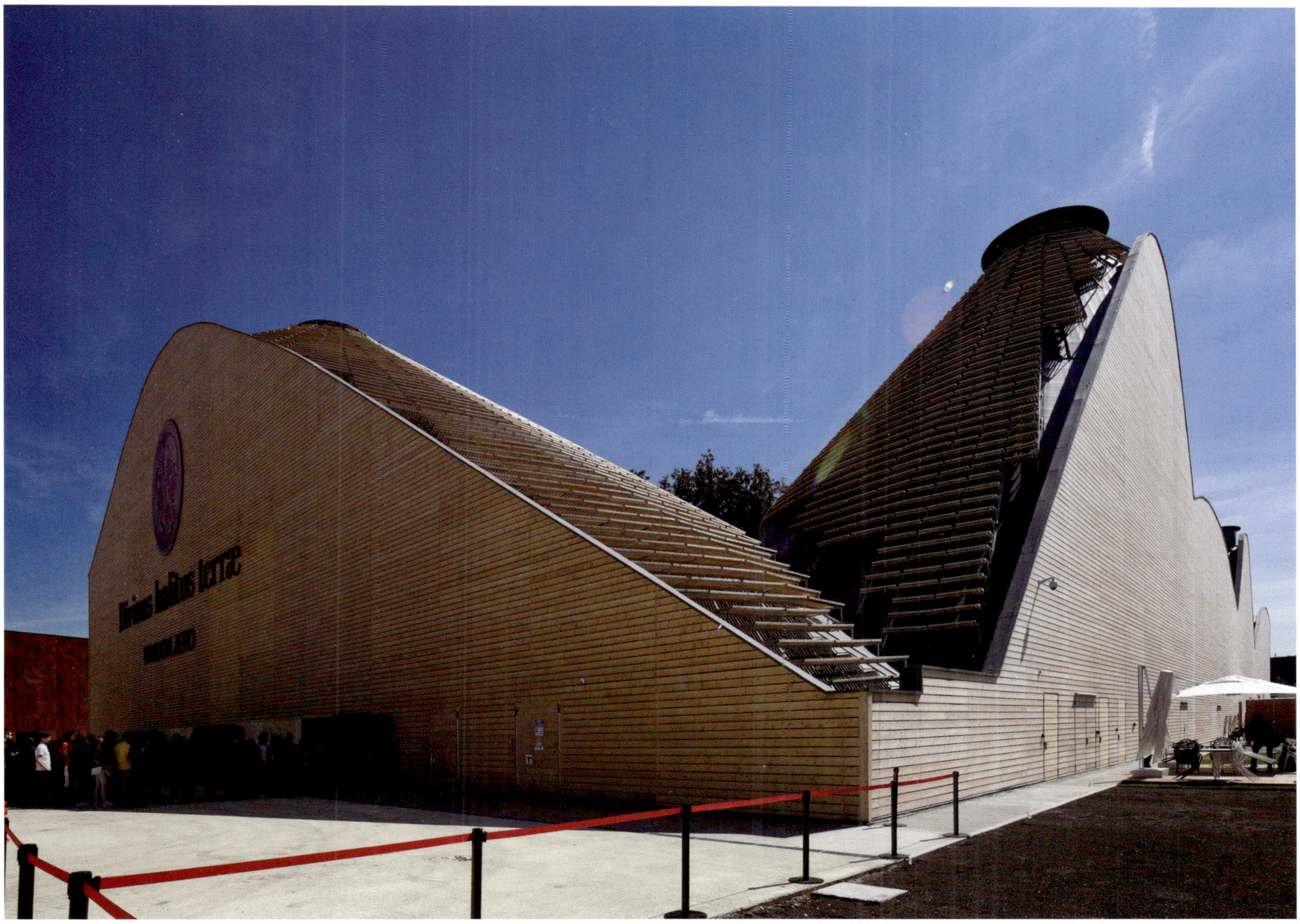
Divinus halitus terrae
PAVILION ZERO

Divinus halitus terrae
PAVILION ZERO

Divinus halitus terrae
PAVILION ZERO

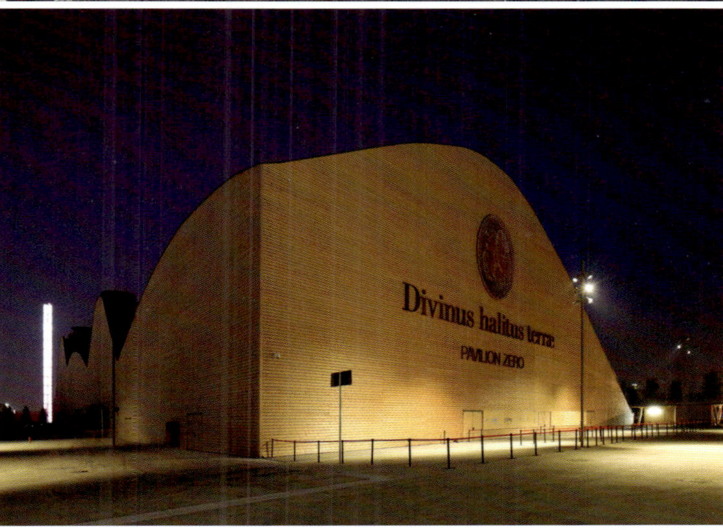

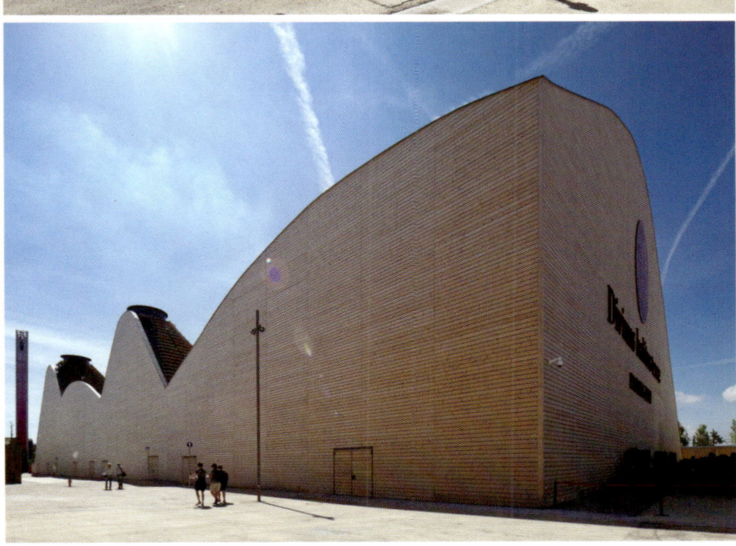

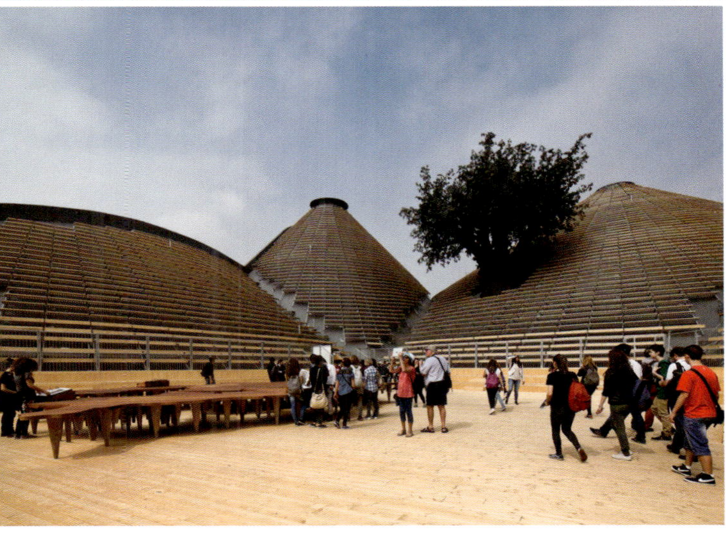

零展馆，就像它的命名一样，零代表着一切故事的开始。而其中最重要的开始是我们人类在这个地球上与食物和自然之间开启的探索之旅。

零展馆位于世博会场的入口处，它将通过引人入胜的故事和一趟戏剧化的旅程带领参观者了解世博会的展览理念。

设计师Michele De Lucchi 设计开发了零展馆的建筑造型，他构造的这个建筑结构再现了地球上地壳的一部分，而这种建筑构想的灵感来源于尤根尼恩群山，连绵起伏的群山通过一个个火山锥建筑体来表示，它们彼此相连便构成了让人印象深刻的一幢木质建筑。

零展馆戏剧化的建筑设计可以有两种解读：建筑外部是一个和谐统一的整体，而建筑内部每一处向内凹陷的幽深洞穴才是真正讲述故事的地方。室内设计师Giancarlo Basili 通过戏剧化的建筑语言不但很好地诠释了策展方的办展理念，同时征集了意大利的顶尖建筑工匠为零展馆打造了一个个各有特色的展示空间。

Pavilion Zero, like the number that represent it, marks the beginning of all stories. The first, and most important one, is the journey that man has made on this Earth in his relationship with food and nature.

Located at the entrance to the site, Pavilion Zero serves the purpose of encapsulating the philosophy of the Universal Exhibition through a striking narrative and theatrical itinerary.

Michele De Lucchi has developed the architectural project, by envisaging a structure reproducing a section of the Earth's crust. Inspiration was provided by the Euganean Hills: the idea is for the Exhibition to open with the view of a hilly landscape in the form of volcanic cones that, as they come into focus, create the framework of an impressive wooden architecture.

The theatricality of the building is open to a double reading: on the exterior it constitutes an harmonious, unbrokenform but below each concavity dark caves open up – the real settings of the narrative. The interior design has been conceived and developed by Giancarlo Basili, a set designer who has not only translated the curator's ideas into a theatrical language, but has recruited skilled craftsman from across Italy to create the various rooms.

KIP PAVILION
KIP 国际馆

Attractive Territories for a Sustainable World
美丽土地，永恒世界

建筑设计：RIMOND Group / 设计师：Tony Marincola
建筑面积：2 717 平方米

Architects: RIMOND Group / Designer: Tony Marincola
Project Area: 2,717 m²

KIP国际馆位于西主入口的1号地，毗邻世博园主干道，主体馆占地面积2 717平方米，主体馆外绿化面积包含占地1 000平方米的“联合国花园”。

KIP国际馆分为A，B，C，D馆和中心花园以及联合国花园。A馆为国际展示厅，高9米，可同时容纳100人左右的展览、会议及国际培训课程。B馆为主体会场，高12米，可容纳200人左右举行会议、展示等活动。C馆高12米，分3层，一层是企业文化及产品展示区；二、三层是VIP接待室，每个房间可容纳15人左右，用于接待各国元首和重要嘉宾，也可用于小型会议。D馆为国际餐饮区，高9米，分3层，一层是餐饮区，可同时容纳150人就餐，有各国食品秀活动；二层为交流、展示、会议空间；三层为露天花园，日间可用于咖啡休闲区，晚间可举行商务酒会派对。中心广场位于户外，处于四个展馆中央，建筑面积150平方米，高度不超过2.4米，可作为企业宣传活动户外场地（但不可出现企业LOGO）。

KIP国际馆以“魅力土地，永恒世界”为主题，其涵义为：要滋养地球，泽被政府、企业和其他组织机构，首先必须要发展地方水土，赋予一个地域正确的价值，使这片土地成为人们可以一起工作、生活、获取所需健康食物的地方。“魅力”还意味着宜居性和吸引力，每个地区有其独特的经济活力、服务质量、自然风光和文化历史，政府和地方机构要保护人们参与发展的权利。

KIP馆所有的活动将按照两条主线进行：一为食品的生产、销售和消费之间的关系，更广泛地说，是关于地方发展的主题；另一个是创新，不仅指实用科技创新，还包括新的组织形式、工作方式、新的企业和机构类型、新的投资类型等。

KIP Pavilion locates near the west entrance of the Expo Park, adjacent to the Decumano. The pavilion is of 2,717 m², and there is a UN Garden of 1,000 m² out of the pavilion.

KIP Pavilion has four sub-pavilions marked A,B,C, D and a UN Garden in addition. Pavilion A is an international exhibition hall of 9 m high for 100 visitors to participate exhibition, conference or international training courses. Pavilion B is a major assembly hall of 12 m high for 200 participants to engage meetings and presentations. Pavilion C is of 12 m high and devided into three levels; the first level is corporate culture and products displaying area; the second and third levels are VIP rooms, accommodateion of 15 people, which is for receptions for all heads of states and VIP guests holding small-scale meetings. Pavilion D is an international catering area of 9 m high and devided into three levels; the first level is a dining area, accomodation of 150 people simutaneously, offering global cuisine; the second level is for conmunication, exhibition and conference; the third level is an open air garden, and it is a coffee catering area in daytime and a commercial party area at night. There is a central plaza of 150 m² area in the middle of the four pavilions, with height less than 2.4 m. The central plaza is an ideal place for corporate campaigns ourdoors although under a confine of no corporate logos.

Attractive territories for a sustainable world is the title of the KIP International School Pavilion. It means that to feed the planet, governments, businesses and associations need to invest, above all, in local development. They must invest in and give value to the territory where people live and work together so they can produce the healthy and appropriate food they need. The pavilion's title also signifies that territories must be attractive, so that people will choose to live there because of the dynamism of the economy, the quality of services, the beauty of the natural environment, the richness of culture and history and, especially, because people can participate in choosing their development priorities, thanks to governments and local institutions that work effectively.

Two principal themes link all the activities of the Pavilion. One is the relationship between production, distribution and consumption of food and the more general question of territorial development. The other is innovation, not just technological innovation, but also organizational and social innovation, new working methods, innovative business models and forms of financing and so on.

PUBLIC AREA AND CLUSTERS
公共与集群区

2015米兰世博会展区设计模仿了古罗马的城市规制，沿两条相互垂直的通路铺展开来。东西向是较长的主干道，南北向是副干道。白色的华盖一路铺盖为游客遮阳挡雨，并带领游客直达世博会四处标志性建筑：世博中心、湖景区、露天剧场和地中海山景公园，它们是举办大型活动和表演的场所。

其中，被称为“生命之树”的瞭望塔就矗立在湖心广场的中央，通过无人机的拍摄可以实时观测各展馆的热闹情景和举办的活动。

在公共区域范围内，世博会组织者要求各展馆至少保留三分之一的场地用于绿化和举办室外活动，其目标是使整个世博园保证有不低于一半的场地作为绿化和室外用地。

绿植规划根据公共区域中不同主题和各自的特色共建有8个设置了座椅和花架的花园供游人休憩，3个主要广场在入口等重要公共区及25个小广场邻近休闲区和服务区。考虑到世博的环保主旨，展区中的植物、公共服务设施及地铺等都会在展后拆卸并再利用。

其中特别值得一提的是两个主题活动区“未来食物区”和“慢食运动区”，参观者可以亲身参与其中的活动从而学习到各种新颖又富于教育意义的健康饮食知识。

“集群区”是本届米兰世博会特别提出的一种新型参展形式。园区内共有九大主题集群区，每个集群区均有各自的建筑风格。在主题集群区，各个国家都有自己的展馆，进行代表性的主题展览，相互交流和分享最佳案例。它们可以在各自的公共区域进行相关主题活动或商业活动，提供食物，为游客提供参与度更高的体验。

The site of Expo Milano 2015 is based on two perpendicular thoroughfares of great symbolic impact, the east-west decumanus and north-south cardo if tge Roman city. Marquees set up along the streets with provide the visitors with shelter from rain and sun. The primary iconic elements of the Expo are located at the four cardinal points: the Expo Center, the Lake Arena, the Open Air Theatre and the Mediterranean Hill, which are for large-scale activities and performances.

Innovatively, “Belvedere in città” is a project created by Expo Milano 2015 and Telecom Italia that allows you to follow, through the use of drones, the progress of work on the site of the Universal Exhibition. The Tree of Life is the star of this episode of Belvedere in città.

The organizer of Expo Milano 2015 asks for no less than 30% exhibition area for greening and outdoor activity so that the whole greening and outdoor activity area hold at least 56% exhibition area.

The green space of the Expo site is laid out in different areas with different characteristics and themes of their own. The whole site contains 8 gardens with seats and pergolas for visitors to relax, 3 major piazzas, open spaces located at the strategic points of entrance to the site and 25 minor piazzas, spaces of different shapes located in the vicinity of the refreshment and service areas. Designed with a view to reversibility, the green works and related structures and paving will be dismantled for reuse at the end of the Expo.

Among many events in the Expo, the activities in Future Food district and Slow Food area are two won’t be missed. Visitors can take part in them and learn innovative and instructive knowledge on healthy diet.

Cluster is a new exhibition form in this Expo, and there are nine kinds of clusters in respective architectural styles. In different thematic clusters, every country has its own pavilion to present their products and cultures, meanwhile it is a hard-won opportunity for them to communicate and share exhibition experiences with one another. The public area is also a good platform for country pavilions to hold relative thematic activities and commercial promotions, meanwhile visitors will have chance to taste the featured food offered here and participate interactive activities.

The Expo Center
世博中心

世博中心位于主轴的最西端，由三个功能区组成：大礼堂、开放式表演区和会议区。
该建筑灵活的结构能适应音乐会、戏剧、舞蹈等多种需求，在大型演出的间隔可以进行小型表演。

Inside the Expo Center there are three independent blocks:

Auditorium: a space for conferences and workshops with a purpose-built concert hall with seating for 1,500 people.

Open Plaza: the central space for all shows and performances during the six mounths of Expo Milano 2015.

Meeting Area: made up of conference rooms, this area is located in the south part of the Expo Center.

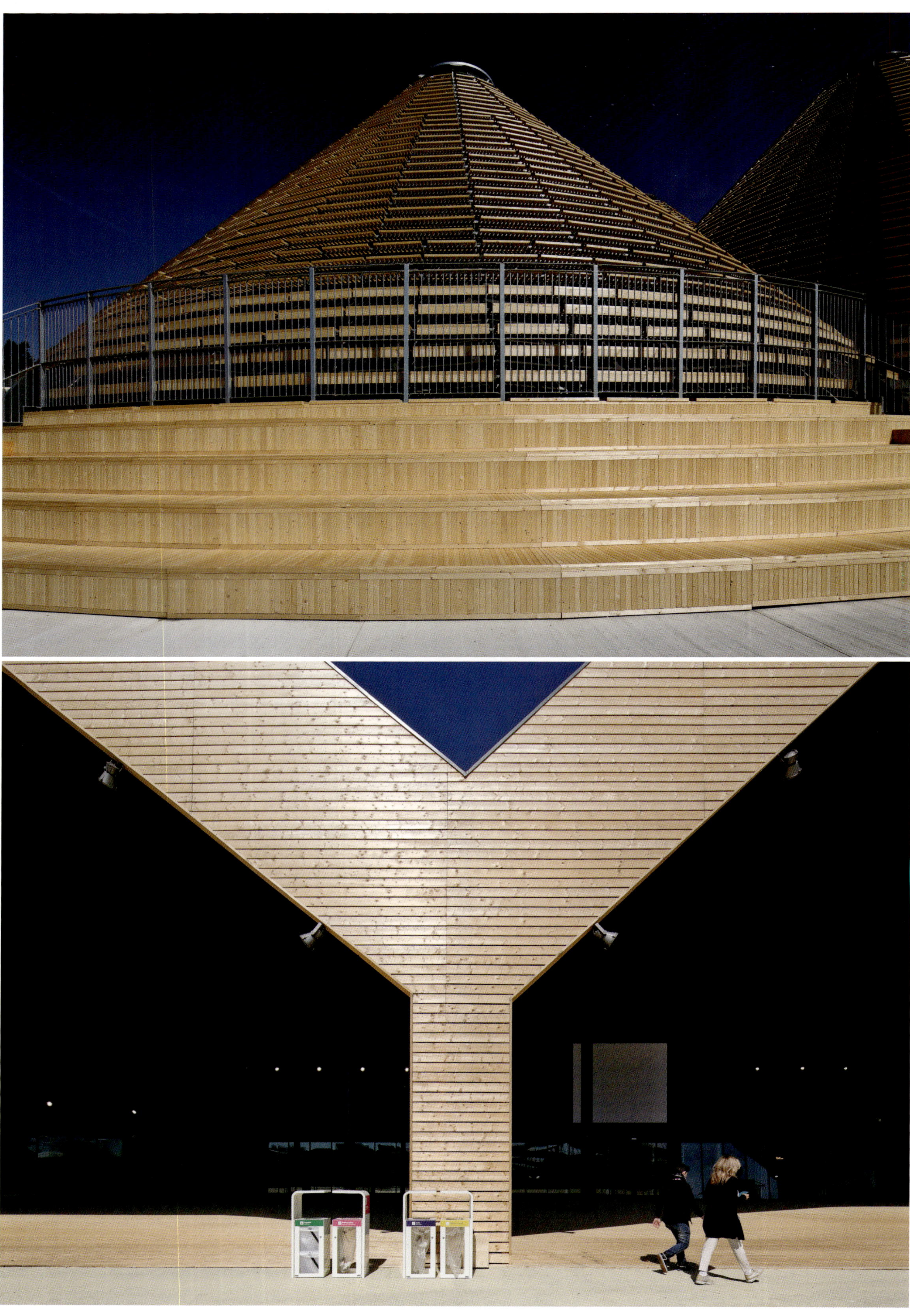

Slow Food's Space
慢食运动区

慢食运动的活动主旨是围绕生物多样性而展开的。这场活动实际上解说了滋养地球的首要任务就是要保证生物多样性，并且保证各个物种的可持续性发展。要维持生物多样性需要采取全方位的措施，用可持续发展的农业生产体系提供优良、干净又均衡的食物。慢食运动剧场是一个露天结构，有40个座位，可供举办会议、小型音乐会、图书推广等活动。慢食运动的主题围绕生物多样性、农业可持续发展、合理消费和反对浪费。在意大利的伦巴蒂大区，慢食运动组委会开垦了一个约250 平方米的植物园。这个植物园里种植着这个地区的传统蔬菜，另有园圃种植香草和草药。植物园包括一个永久对外开放的蔬菜种植学习区，参观者可以来学习生态农业的种植方法，这种方法是保护环境，保证生物多样性的关键所在。

Slow Food's space at Expo Milano 2015 is structured precisely to focus on the issue of biodiversity. In fact it illustrates how Feeding the planet is only possible by starting from biodiversity, and preserving it for future generations. To speak of biodiversity, means to adopt a holistic approach, in talking about sustainable agriculture and access to food that is good, clean and fair for all.Scheduled as part of the open-air Slow Food Theater, which seats 40 people, will be meetings, screenings, concerts, book presentations, and much more. The themes are those that Slow Food holds dear: biodiversity, sustainable agriculture, responsible consumption, and the fight against waste.Within their Exhibition Site, Slow Food will create a vegetable garden covering approximately 250 square meters that shines the spotlight on the plants of Lombardy.The garden will feature traditional vegetable varieties from the region; there will be beds featuring aromatic and medicinal herbs. The vegetable garden offers a permanent learning zone where visitors can discover how to create a vegetable garden based on the agro-ecological approach, which is keyed on farming that respects the environment and biodiversity.

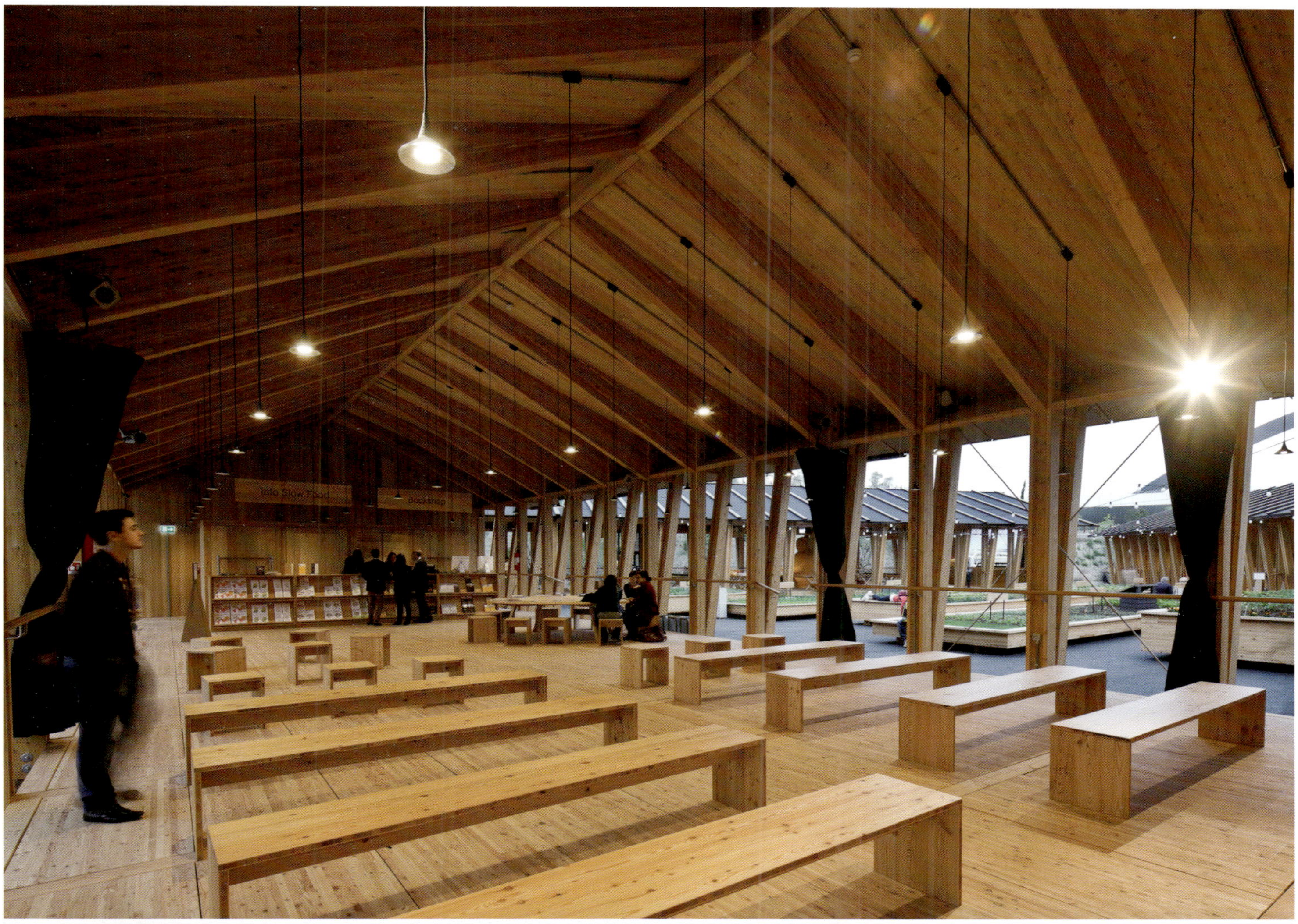
Info Slow Food
Bookshop

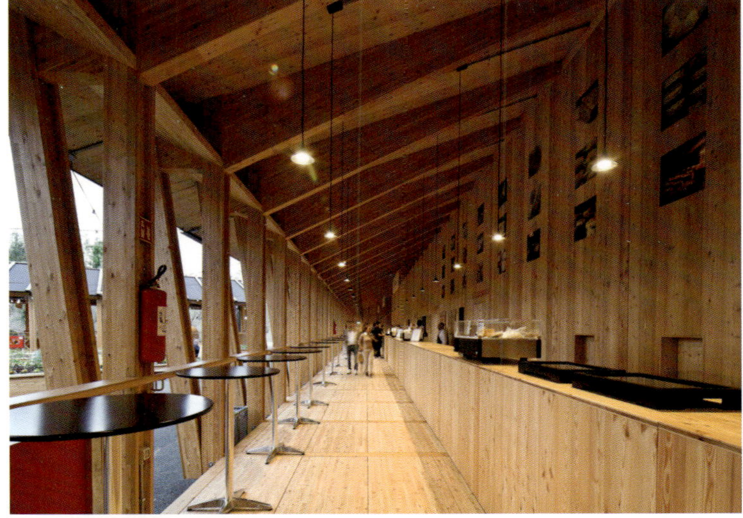

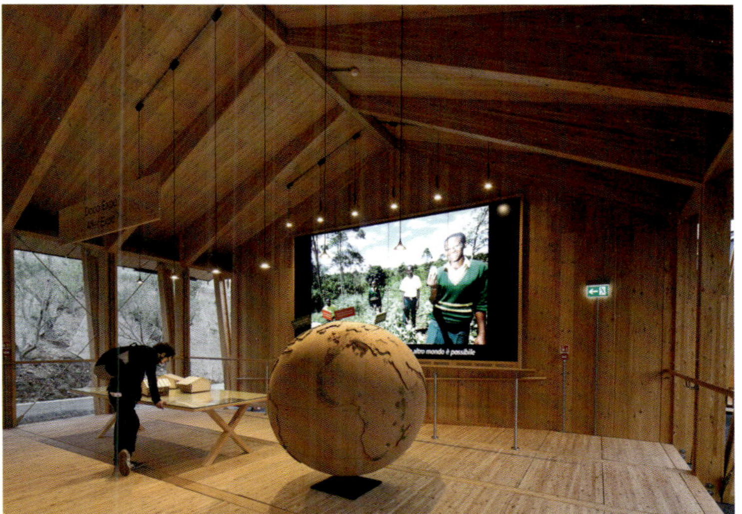

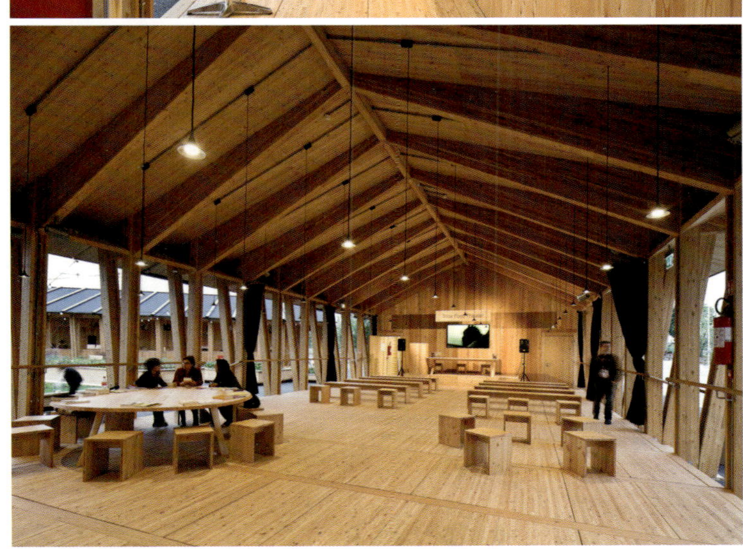

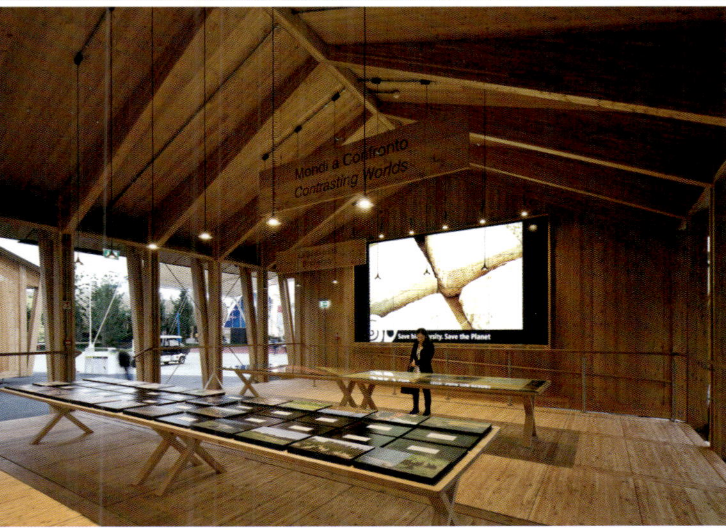

Mondi a Confronto
Contrasting Worlds

I Sensi del Cibo
Food Senses
L'Albero del Cibo
The Tree of Food
Save biodiversity. Save the Planet
A World of Corn

The Future Food District
未来食物区

未来食物区坐落在世博园区的南部，靠近露天剧院。这里展现了新科技应用于食物供应链的无数可能，把“物联网”这个概念用高科技的手段具体呈现了出来。

未来食物区展示了在食物生产中每个环节所运用的新技术。这里被分成三个空间，参观之旅由主广场开始，主广场这片小天地被一层浅浅的水面覆盖，并起到展馆间的连接作用，水中还种植了水藻与其他植物。超市共分两层。在一层，游客们将通过一个走廊进入仓库，机械系统在这里下指令并准备好产品，再运到二层展示。食物生产环节被完整地展示出来。在未来食物区，观众将穿越到未来的食物仓库、物流、超市和餐馆等场景中，亲身体验未来食物供应链中的高科技。这是一个分享和交流的绝佳平台，它包含两个展馆和一个中央广场：“超市”馆，“厨房”馆以及连接两馆的“中央广场”。

The Future Food District is located on the south side of the Expo site where there is also the Open Air Theater. Future Food District is a micro universe that explores new ways for people and food to interact. This interaction is possible thanks to the use of new technologies and by applying the Internet of Things concept.The Future Food District presents possible scenarios for the application of new technologies at each step of the food chain. This district is devided into three spaces, and every visitor will start from a plaza which is covered by a shallow layer of water with algae and other plants, where is also an convenient junction to other pavilions.There is a supermarket with two levels. Visitors arrive at a storage through a passage where mechanic system accepts instructions and prepares food that will be transported onto the second level. Food production process is completely displayed with proceeding of visitors. The Future Food District pavilions are highly interactive. Inside the supermarket it is possible to enjoy a shopping experience via flat screens, displays and interactive tables. In the kitchen pavilion it is possible to experiment with new ways of preparing food and the main square that connects the two pavilions is an ideal place for interacting and exchanging ideas with others.

foodie
veg & veg

THE RICE CLUSTER
大米集群区

Abundance and Security
富足和安全

大米集群区总面积达3 546 平方米，展示区1 000平方米，公用区2 420平方米，活动区738平方米。

进入大米集群区，游客将步入一个充满乡野氛围的一片片长着稻子的田间地头。因为里面设置了一面面的镜子，它们的反射，营造了一种万花筒似的效果。游客可以在活动区参与互动活动。等离子的屏幕就设置在水箱旁，它们在诉说着大米的神奇历史。这将会是一趟被赋予教育意义的游览经历。而在公共区域设置的亭子里，游客可以亲尝和比较各种大米。

孟加拉国、柬埔寨、老挝、缅甸和塞拉利昂属于大米集群区。

Total Area: 3,546 m²; Exhibition Area: 1,000 m²; Common Area: 2,420 m²; Events Area: 738 m²

In Rice Cluster, visitors will be immersed in a rural setting featuring different varieties of rice growing in paddy fields, thanks to a kaleidoscopic effect, created with mirrors. Visitors can also to engage in interactive games within this area. Plasma screens situated next to the water tanks will tell of legends and myths, as well as providing statistical information about rice and its cultivation: an authentic yet educational experience. The option to try actual rice products is available at the many kiosks situated throughout the public area.

Bangladesh, Cambodia, Lao People's Democratic Republic, Myanmar, Sierra Leone belong to this cluster.

THE COCOA AND CHOCOLATE CLUSTER
可可和巧克力集群区

The Food of the Gods
神赐之食

这个集群区的总面积达3 546平方米，展示区875 平方米，公用区2 541平方米，活动区696平方米。
一进入可可和巧克力集群区就像进入了一座热带和亚热带的丛林，里边长满了可可树。建筑外墙体采用轻型材料，给内部的树冠开辟了天窗。这样的设计能很好地保护里边香甜的果树。馆内温暖又湿润，室内环境布置得像一个真正的可可丛林，阳光穿过树冠投射下一道道光影。这个展馆的一大特色在于用了多个不同造型的支架来体现可可这种常绿植物的品种多样性。馆内各个国家的展厅用国旗和国名标牌在雷同的格局和颜色中加以区别。他们用丰富的图画，各种标志和栩栩如生的形象来讲述关于可可的传奇故事——有关于栽培的、加工的、运输的、以及分销到世界各地的故事。馆内的活动区有排成扇形的长凳供参观者休息，同时也可以欣赏到馆内的节目表演。馆外门口处也有草坪提供桌椅方便参观完的游客休憩或给行人作暂时的歇脚。
喀麦隆、科特迪瓦、古巴、加蓬、加纳和圣多美与普林希比共和国属于可可巧克力集群区。

Total Area: 3,546 m²; Exhibition Area: 875 m² ; Common Area: 2,541 m²; Events Area: 696 m²
Upon entering the Cocoa and Chocolate Cluster, visitors will feel as if they are walking into the jungle. The Cluster recreates the tropical and subtropical environment where cacao trees grow. The external parts of the buildings are made of very light materials, which open to reveal the internal canopy. This design symbolizes the need to protect such a valuable and aromatic fruit. The Cocoa and Chocolate Cluster features a large number of uprights of differing sizes. These represent the large number of species and types of tree under which the cacao-bearing evergreen grows. The atmosphere is warm and humid as in a real jungle, with sunlight penetrating the trees' crowns, casting its rays throughout the pavilions.The pavilions, all of a similar size and color, are identified by the exhibitor country's flag and name. Display panels featuring drawings, icons, and images tell the many stories of cacao: from cultivation, via processing and transport, to distribution worldwide.The events area features bench-seating in a fan-shape formation. In addition to being used by the audience during performances, these seats are also available for visitors' convenience throughout the day. Outside the pavilion is a green area with tables and benches where visitors leaving the Cacao Cluster, as well as passers-by, can take a quick break from exhibition-hopping.
Cameroon, Côte D'Ivoire, Cuba, Gabon, Ghana and Sao Tome and Principe belong to this cluster.

CHOCO
MATES

THE COFFEE CLUSTER
咖啡集群区

The Energy of Ideas
思想的能量

咖啡集群区的总面积达4 427平方米，展示区1 250平方米，公用区3 000平方米，活动区122平方米。

咖啡集群区的设计灵感来自于非洲和中美洲的热带咖啡种植园。集群区内的建筑让人自然联想到咖啡树的高大树冠，而区内的展馆则像一根根粗壮的树干支撑着这些参天大树。阳光穿透屋顶投射进咖啡展馆内，随着光线的变化，馆内呈现温暖的自然色彩，让参观者有一种置身于一座真实森林的感觉。进入咖啡展馆前，参观者将经过一片绿色地带，这里种植着咖啡树，而且参观者可以欣赏巴西著名摄影师塞巴斯蒂昂·萨尔加多的照片展。展馆入口处就能闻到咖啡香沁人心脾，在点心区，参观者可以品尝一杯馥郁浓香的咖啡；而在活动区会有一系列的研讨会和演讲活动。在点心区和活动区中间是一个咖啡市场，参观者可以在这里买到各个国家的咖啡产品。

布隆迪、萨尔瓦多、埃塞俄比亚、多米尼加共和国、危地马拉、肯尼亚、卢旺达、乌干达、也门和东帝汶属于咖啡集群区。

Total Area: 4,427 m²; Exhibition Area: 1,250 m²; Common Area: 3,000 m², Events Area: 122 m²

Taking its inspiration from the vast coffee plantations located at the edges of the tropical forests of Africa and Central America, this cluster's architecture evokes the highest branches of the trees in the shade which the coffee plants grow, with the pavilions serving as a metaphor for these tree trunks.The Coffee Cluster is characterized by warm and natural colors that change according to the changing light that filters through the roof, giving visitors the illusion of being in a real forest.A visit to the Coffee Cluster starts in the green area outside the pavilion. Ornamented with coffee plants, it provides the setting for Sebastião Salgado's splendid photographic exhibition.Once inside the refreshment area, visitors can sample a cup of aromatic, delicious coffee. In the events area will take place a number of seminars, presentations, and other events. Between the bar and the events section, visitors will find the market area where they can buy coffee products from various countries. These will serve to remind them of the aromas and flavors they have experienced in this Cluster.

Burundi, El Salvador, Ethiopia, Dominican Republic, Guatemala, Kenya, Rwanda, Uganda, Yemen and Timor-Lest belong to this cluster.

BURUNDI
BURUNDI

illy
illy

THE FRUITS AND LEGUMES CLUSTER

水果和豆类集群区

Spirit and Substance, Myth and Subsistence

精神和物质，神话和生存

水果和豆类集群区的总面积达3 705平方米，展示区1 125平方米，公用区2 515平方米，活动区536平方米。

这个集群区种植了各种各样的果树和豆类灌木丛，在这个集群区的中央是一个中心广场，它有一个木质的屋顶作为天篷，参观者可以在这里观赏到各种水果和豆类植物，闻到各种果香并欣赏到各种水果的独特外形和颜色。这个集群区的出口端被设置成一个水果豆类市场，参观者可以在这里购买喜爱的水果和豆类。穿过这个市场，参观者就步入了香料集群区，轻松转移到下一个食物王国里。

贝宁、刚果民主共和国、赤道几内亚、冈比亚、几内亚、吉尔吉斯斯坦、乌兹别克斯坦、赞比亚属于水果与豆类集群区。

Total Area: 3,705 m²; Exhibition Area: 1,125 m²; Common Area: 2,515 m²; Events Area: 536 m²

The Fruits and Legumes Cluster features areas cultivated with different varieties of fruit trees and bushes. In the main central square of this Cluster, visitors can participate in, and enjoy the many events inspired by the shapes, scents and colors of the wide variety of fruits and legumes on offer. A wooden roof canopy covers the main square, around which the pavilions are grouped. At the end of their tour of the Cluster, visitors will have the chance to wander through the market, and perhaps purchase some of the tasty fruits and legumes on display. The market forms a natural link to the Spices Cluster, leading visitors seamlessly to their next experience.

Benin, Democratic Republic of the Congo, Equatorial Guinea, Gambia, Guinea, Kyrgyzstan, Uzbekistan and Zambia belong to this cluster.

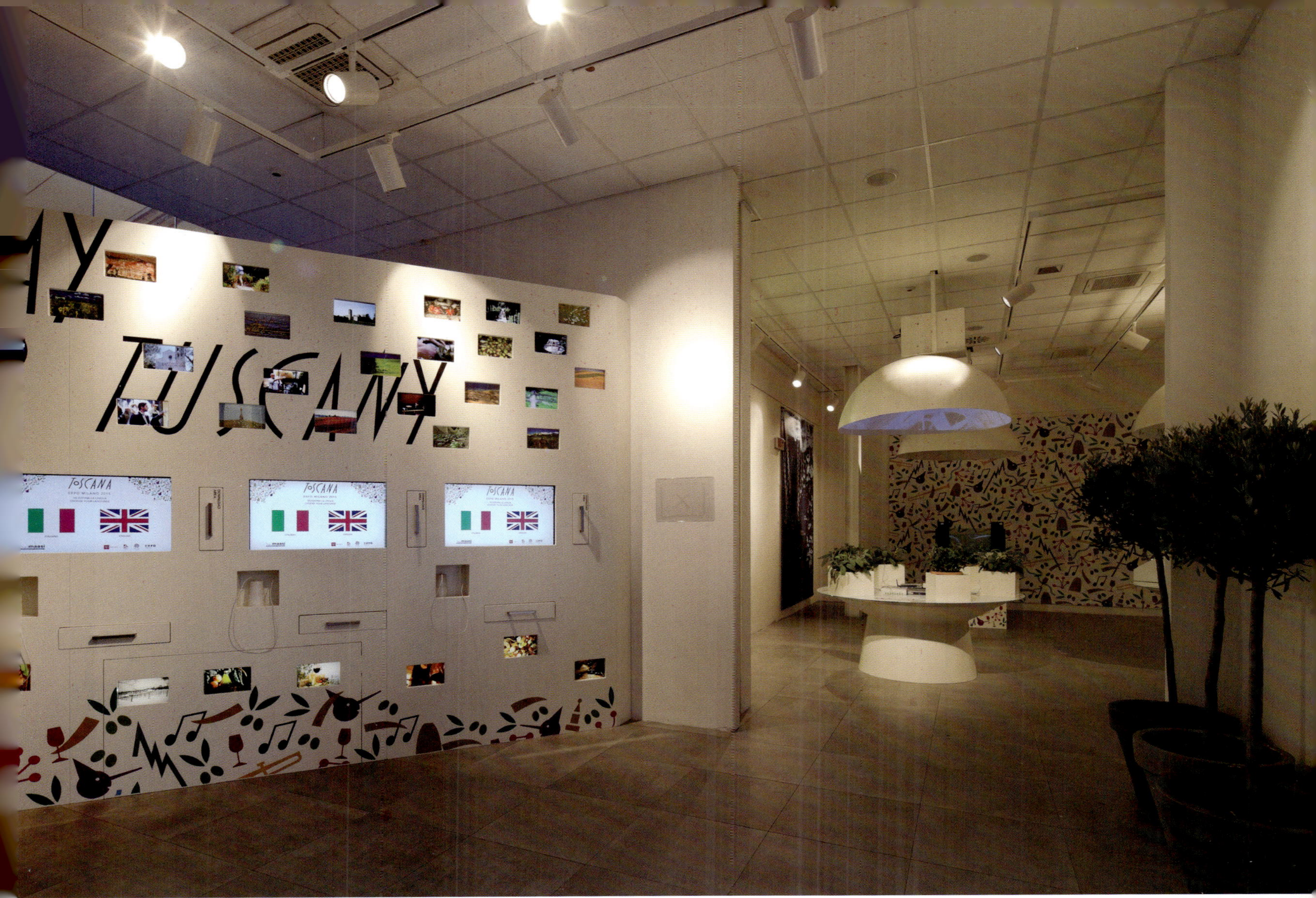
TUSCANY
TOSCANA

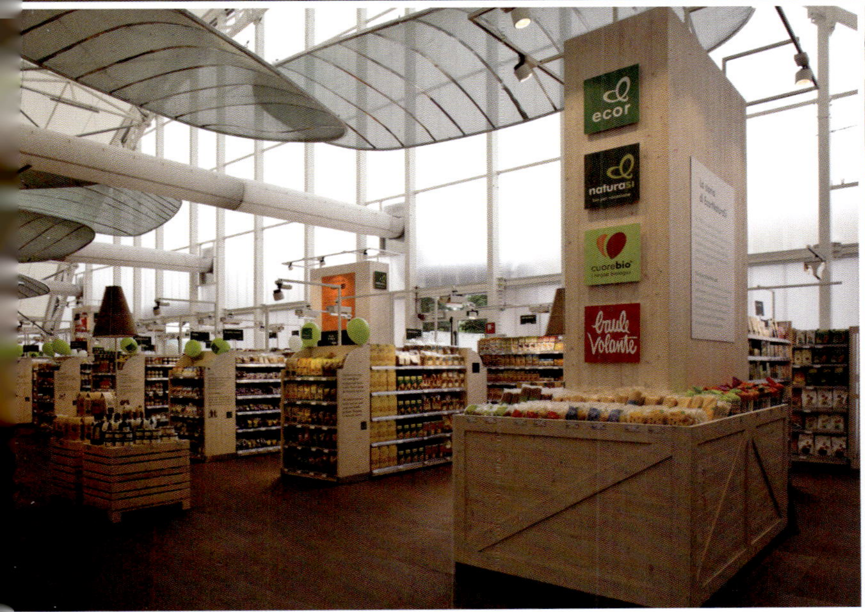

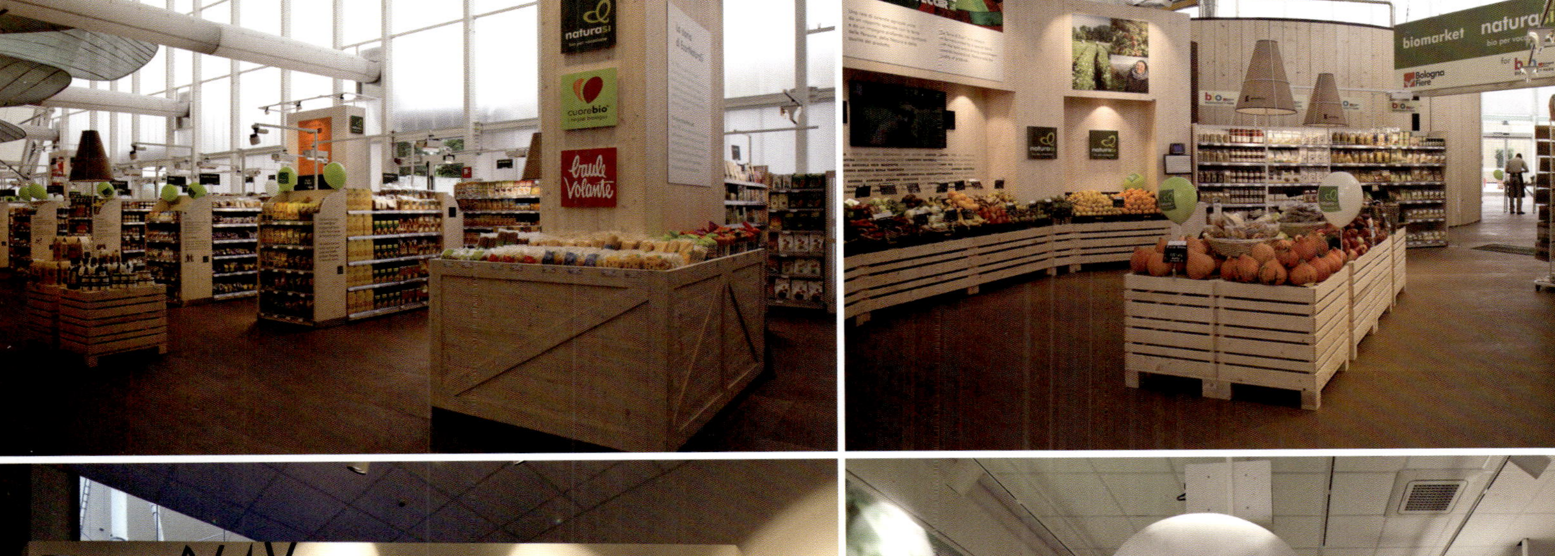

ecor
naturasì
cuorebio
baule volante

LE TERRE DI ECOR
biomarket
naturasì

PLAY
YOUR TUSCANY
TOSCANA

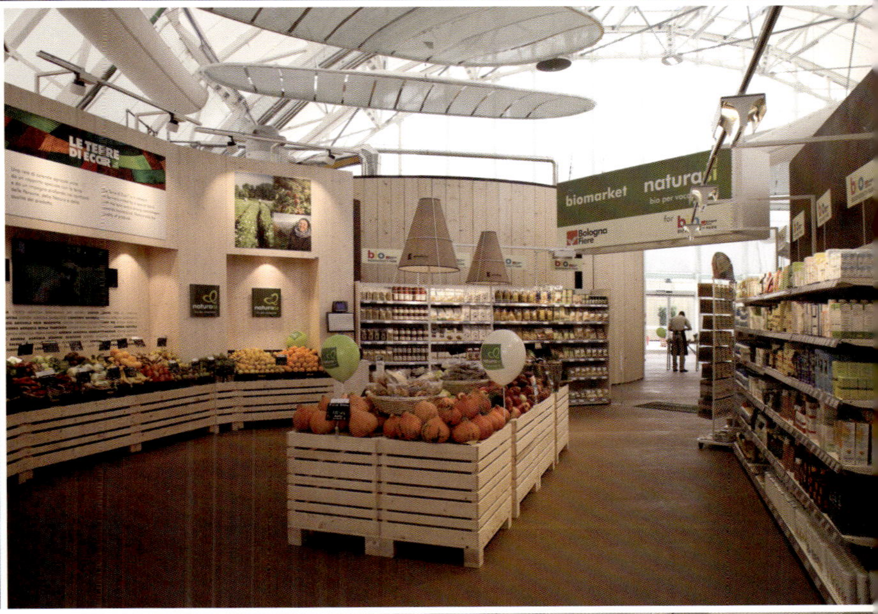

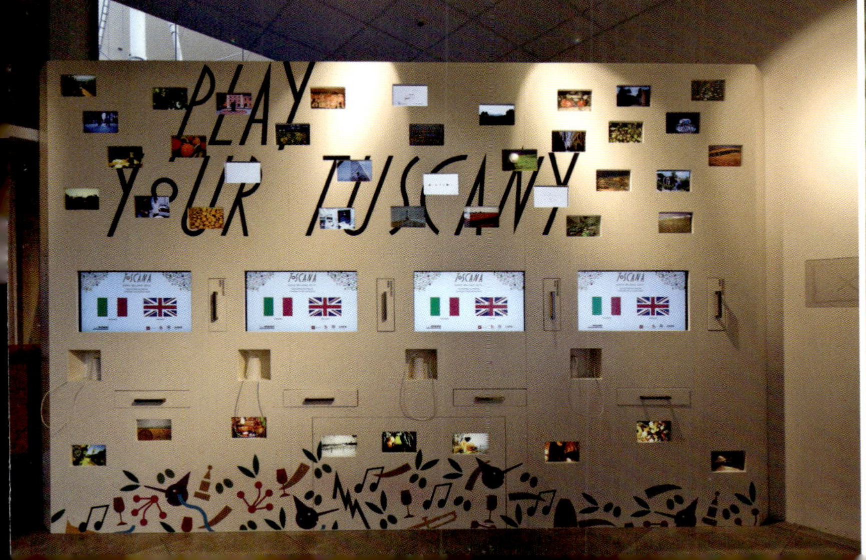

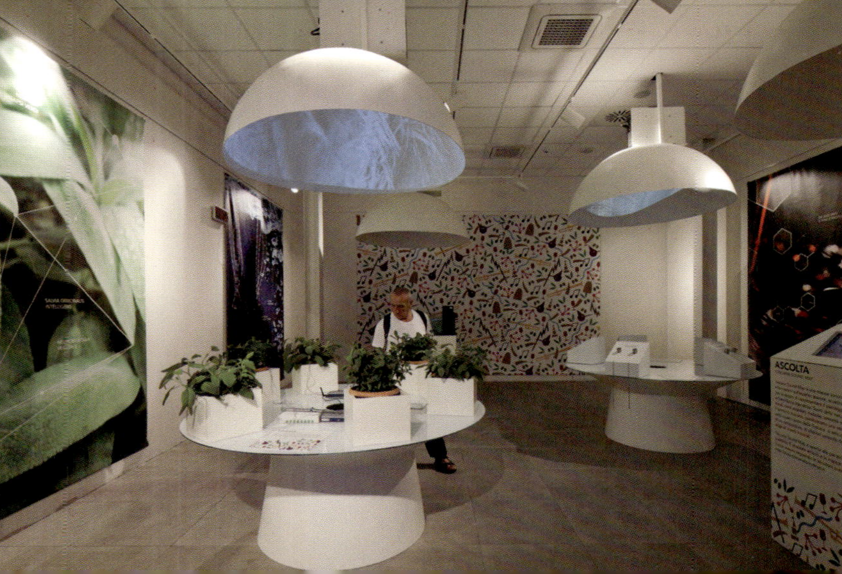

ASCOLTA

THE CEREALS AND TUBERS CLUSTER
谷物和块茎集群区

Old and New Crops
新旧作物

谷物和块茎集群区总面积达3 820平方米，展览区1 125平方米，公用区2 455平方米，活动区290平方米。

这个集群区的参观路线设计得像一条蜿蜒的小河，带领游客参观不同国家的展厅，在不同的展厅里，参观者将会看到不同的土地耕作方法。最终，“小河”会带游客到一处顶篷像烟囱的空间里，此处可供参观者参与馆内举行的活动，并可近距离观看各种特色烹饪。

玻利维亚、刚果、海地、莫桑比克、多哥和津巴布韦属于谷物和块茎集群区。

Total Area: 3,820 m², Exhibition Area: 1,125 m², Common Area: 2,455 m², Events Area: 290 m²

Like a river, this journey winds its way through the pavilions of the various member countries, finally flowing out into a great canopied space that hosts events and offers refreshments. Visitors can move in the space between the pavilions, letting themselves be gently drawn along by the different examples of land cultivation. The canopy of the building takes the shape of a chimney and hosts an area for events and the distribution of themed culinary specialties.

Bolivia, Congo, Haiti, Mozambique, Togo and Zimbabwe belong to this cluster.

Venezuela
Venezuela
RON DE VENEZUELA
فلينظر الإنسان إلى طعامه
متاعا لكم ولأنعامكم
GRAIN
E VI FACCIAMO GERMINARE CEREALI
RIHLA

THE BIO-MEDITERRANEAN CLUSTER
生态地中海集群区

Health, Beauty and Harmony
健康，美丽与和谐

生态地中海集群区总面积达7 304平方米，展示区2 625平方米，公用区4 350平方米，活动区486平方米。
“健康、美丽与和谐” 是生态地中海集群区的展示主题。参展方将重现食物的颜色、味道和芳香，突出地中海国家和地中海文化的特点。集群区的造型会让人联想起典型的地中海小镇，四个建筑物面对一个大的中心广场，游客可以试吃并购买到当地的食品和特产。中央广场铺砌了各种深浅不同的蓝色，会让人很容易联想到地中海的蓝。
阿尔巴尼亚、阿尔及利亚、埃及、希腊、黎巴嫩、马耳他、黑山共和国、圣马力诺、塞尔维亚和突尼斯属于生态地中海集群区。

Total Area: 7,304 m²; Exhibition Area: 2,625 m²; Common Area: 4,350 m²; Events Area: 486 m²
Evoking the image of typical Mediterranean towns, this Cluster features a large main central square, onto which faces four buildings where visitors can sample and purchase local foods and other products. The main square is paved in various shades of blue, reminiscent of the Mediterranean sea.
Albania, Algeria, Egypt, Greece, Lebanon, Malta, Montenegro, San Marino, Serbia and Tunisia belong to this cluster.

Everything Begins With Expo
WORLD EXPO MUSEUM
EXPO × EXPO
Comprensione
Comunicazione
Congregazione
Cooperazione
TUNISIA
ENVIRONNEMENT

ERIENCED AT EXPO MILANO 2015
TOUCH THE SCREEN, DISCOVER MALTA!
EGYPT

SALE OF DRINKS
SOUVENIRS
Il futuro dell' Esposizione Universale
The Future of World Expo
2016
small enough
abbastanza piccol

THE ARID ZONES CLUSTER
干旱作物集群区
The Food and Agriculture of the Arid Zones
旱地的食物和农业

干旱作物集群区总面积达4 030平方米，展示区1 250平方米，公用区2 715平方米，活动区253平方米。
有感于干旱区域的艰苦环境和生活在那片土地上的人们日常生活中要面对的种种困难，沙尘暴成了这个集群区的设计灵感。展示区里从天花板悬吊而下的半透明圆柱体让人联想到沙暴飓风，岩石造型的各国展厅喻示着荒凉的旱地景观。一进入此集群区，一口喷泉像镶嵌在旱地中的绿洲便跃入眼帘。在这个集群区，参观者将通过讲演和各种节目了解到干旱地区面临的挑战，它们特有的资源和典型的生态环境。在出口端，参观者将有机会品尝和购买到干旱地域中盛产的水果和其他特色产品。
吉布提、厄立特里亚国、约旦、毛里塔尼亚、马里、巴勒斯坦、塞内加尔、索马里属于干旱作物集群区。

Total Area: 4,030 m²; Exhibition Area: 1,250 m²; Common Area: 2,715 m²; Events Area: 253 m²
Desert sandstorms provide the inspiration for the design of this Cluster, symbolizing the harshness of life in so-called Arid Zones, and the daily challenges facing the people who live there. Despite the hostile environment, however, vital resources are to be found.The sandstorm is conjured by a multitude of slim, translucent cylinders suspended from the ceiling of the exhibition area, with the country pavilions having the appearance of rocks in this metaphorical wind-swept landscape.On entering this Cluster, visitors encounter a water fountain that conveys the image of a natural oasis in an arid landscape. In this area, visitors are also provided with information, via presentations and performances that highlight the challenges, and resources, typical of these arid environments. At the end of their tour of the Cluster, visitors will have the opportunity to sample and purchase some of the fruits and other products that thrive in these parts of the world.
Djibouti, Eritrea, Jordan, Mauritania, Mali, Palestine, Senegal and Somalia belong to this cluster.

SOMALIA
SOOMAALIYA
GIBUTI
DJIBOUTI
MAURITANIA
موريتانيا

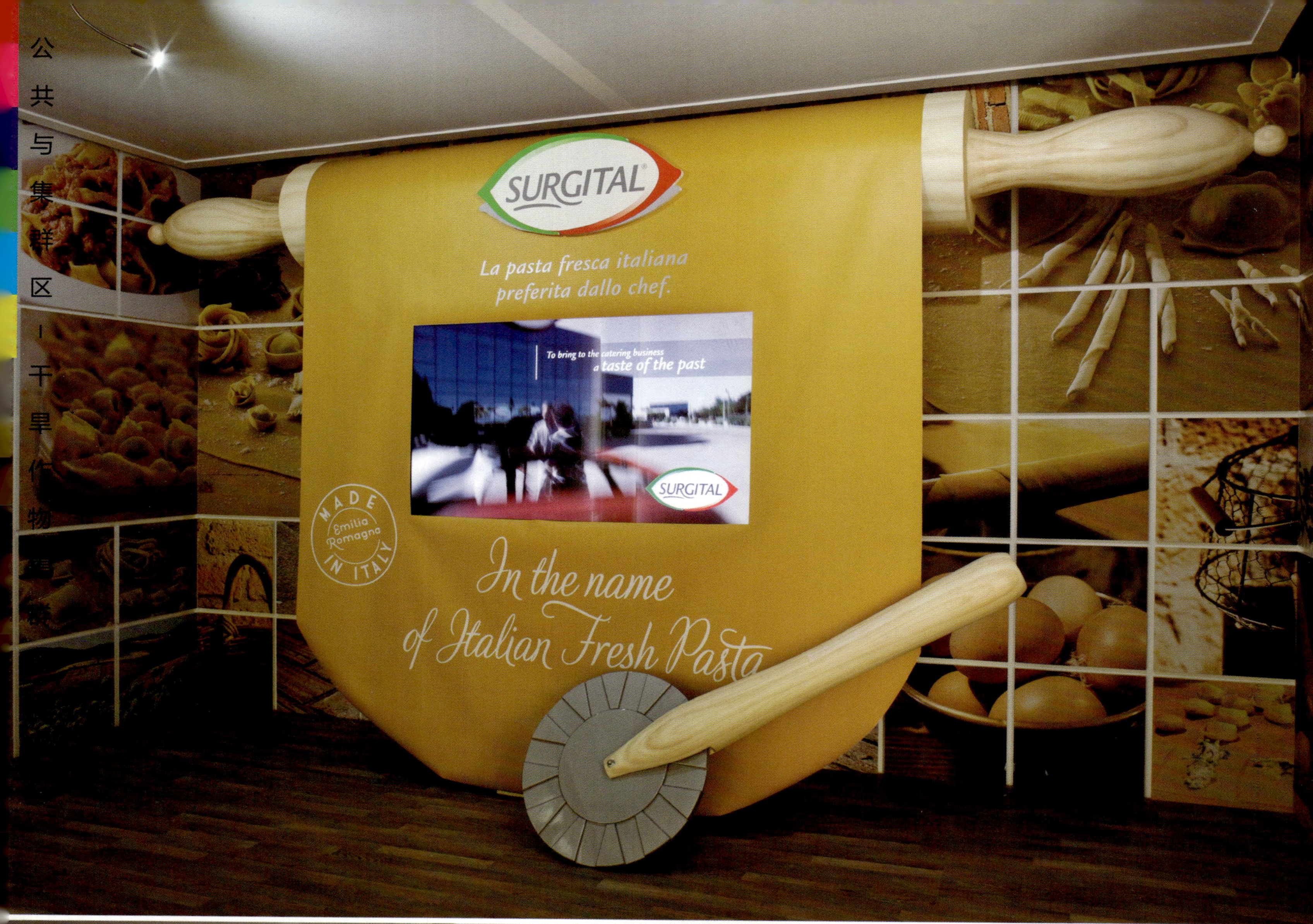

PDO CHEESES
ASIAGO
ASIAGO PDO

THE EVOLUTION OF ITALIAN TRADITI
FREEDOM WILL FEED THE PLANET.
Brazzale
since 1784
FORM
INNOVATION
SUSTAINABILITY
EFFICIENCY
TRADITION
OUR COMPANY IN THE WORLD

erations,
roots.
FARCHIONI

bio
BolognaFiere
BIODIVERSITY PARK

THE ISLAND, SEA AND FOOD CLUSTER
海产品集群区

No Man is an Island
世上无孤岛

海产品集群区总面积达2 535平方米，展示区750平方米，公用区1 720平方米，活动区315平方米。
参与这个集群区展览的各国展厅分布在由一个大型竹制顶篷相连的两个展馆里。这种装饰给这个集群区带来了独特的色彩和氛围。展馆的墙上引用了许多名家名言，包括：荷马（公元前9世纪前后的希腊盲诗人），约瑟夫·康拉德（英国小说家），克里斯多弗·哥伦布（意大利航海家），查尔斯·达尔文（英国生物学家）和赫尔曼·麦尔维尔（美国作家），这些名句唤起了人们对远洋海岛长途征讨的久远回忆。展厅出口部分是休息区和活动区，一个巨大的玻璃立方体架设在墙上，投影着海底的各种影像，让人仿佛置身海底，身临其境地感受神秘的海岛环境，同时也让游客们了解到瑰丽但脆弱的海洋生物的多样性。
佛得角、科摩罗、几内亚比索、马达加斯加、马尔代夫、加勒比共同体（巴巴多斯、伯利兹城、多米尼加、格林纳达、圭亚那、圣卢西亚、圣文森特、格林纳丁斯群岛和苏里南）属于海产品集群区。

Total Area: 2,535 m²; Exhibition Area: 750 m²; Common Area: 1,720 m²; Events Area: 315 m²
The nations exhibiting within this cluster are housed in two pavilions linked by a large bamboo canopy. This creates a unique environment of colors and atmosphere. The walls of the pavilions feature quotations from well-known writers, including Homer, Joseph Conrad, Christopher Columbus, Charles Darwin, and Herman Melville, these words evocative of long sea-journeys to remote desert islands.A visit to this Cluster ends at the refreshments and events area, a vast glass cube onto the walls of which are projected underwater images, conveying the feeling of actually being in the depths, enjoying these mysterious island seas, in close contact with their fascinating, yet fragile, biodiversity.
Cape Verde, Comoros, Guinea Bissau, Madagascar, Maldives and Caribbean Community (Barbados, Belize, Dominica, Grenada, Guyana, St. Lucia, St. Vincent and the Grenadines, Suriname) belong to this cluster.

THE SPICES CLUSTER
香料集群区

The World of Spices
香料世界

香料集群区的总面积达3 702平方米，展示区875平方米，公用区2 637平方米，活动区436平方米。

在这里，参观者将来到一个香料的世界。他们会沿着香料生长的足迹，跨越各大洲，越过陆地和海洋去领略香料的神奇魅力。香料在全世界范围内被用来烹煮食物，并被作为医用药材和化妆品原料。所以，这也将是一趟货真价实的"旅行"，随着香料在全球的盛行，它们促进了航海的发展以及对新大陆的探索。这个集群区的展览将以香料原产国为核心来展示各种香料。

阿富汗、文莱达鲁萨兰国、坦桑尼亚联合共和国、瓦努阿图属于香料集群区。

Total Area: 3,702 m², Exhibition Area: 875 m², Common Area: 2,637 m², Events Area: 436 m²

A truly sensorial experience awaits visitors as they step into the World of Spices Cluster. Here, they can follow the spice routes, across continents, via land and sea. enjoying their aromas, thinking about ways to use spices as cooking ingredients, medicinal remedies, or cosmetics. The experience becomes a veritable journey: according to some historians, demand for these highly-profitable commodities drove innovation in all areas of shipping, and exploration, leading to the discovery of new lands.This exhibition focuses on the spices that originate from the countries belonging to this Cluster.

Afganistan, Brunei Darussalam, United Republic of Tanzania and Vanuatu belong to this cluster.

PUBLIC FACILITIES AND LANDSCAPES

公共设施及景观

PUBLIC LANDSCAPES ANDFACILITIES

FERRERO

H2
chiccotosto

S.PELLEGRINO
IDENTITÀ EXPO
The Art of Fine Food

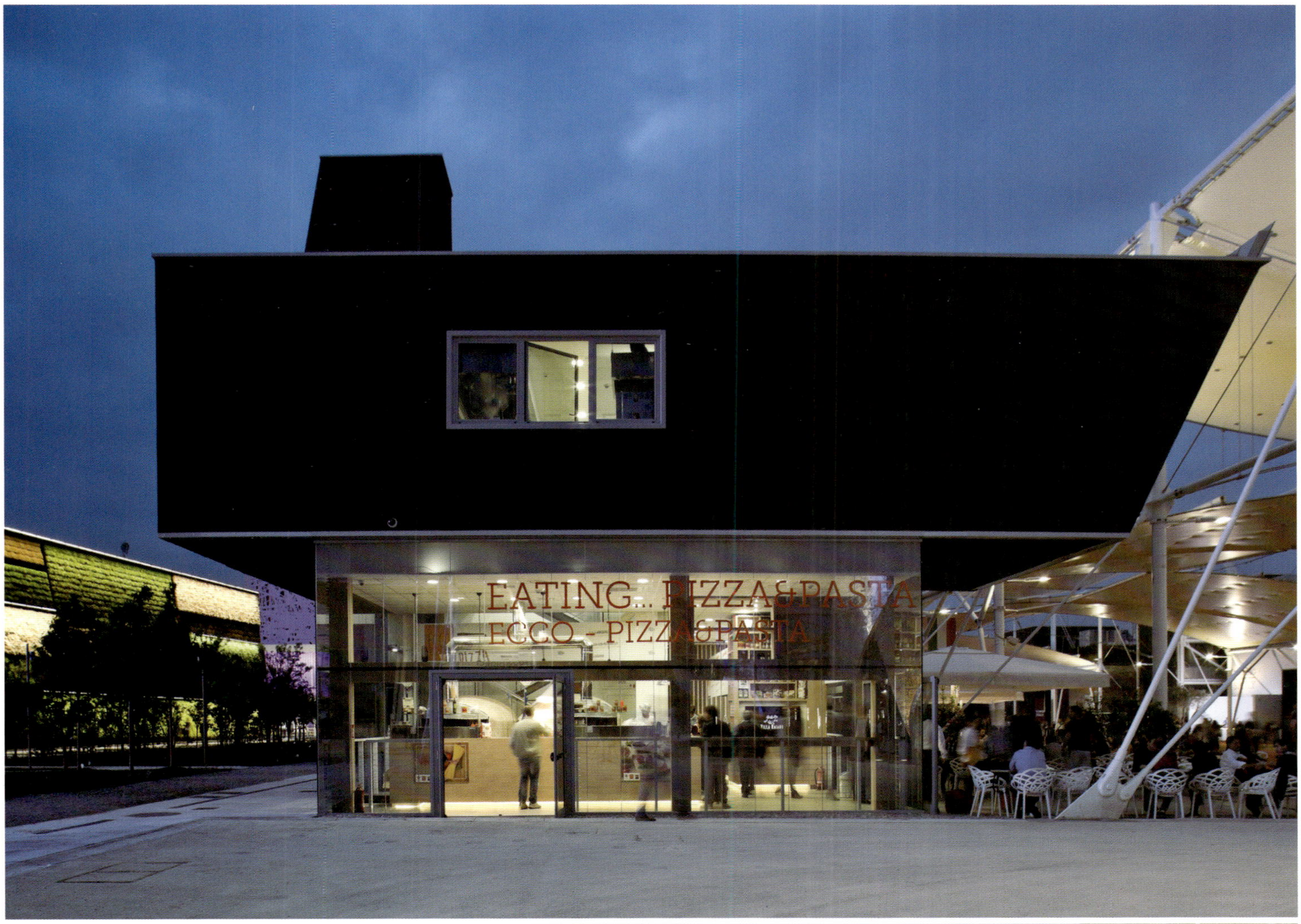
EATING... PIZZA&PASTA
ECCO - PIZZA&PASTA

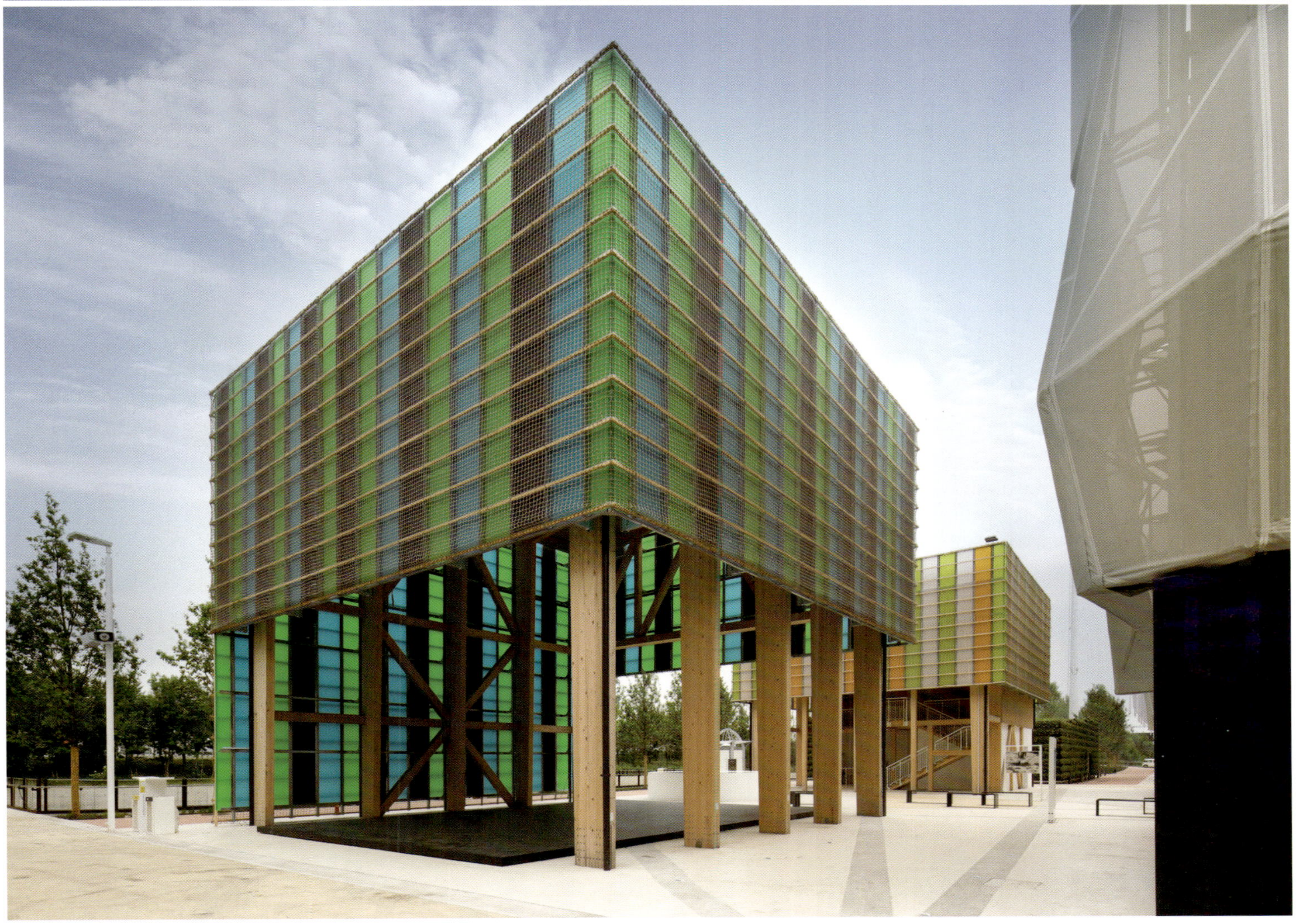

ITALY'S FAVOURITE COFFEE
LAVAZZA
COFFEE
EXPERTISE
HERITAGE
ITALIANNESS
SUSTAINABILITY
RESPONSIBILITY
QUALITY
INNOVATION
RESEARCH
LAVAZZA

CIOCCOLATO

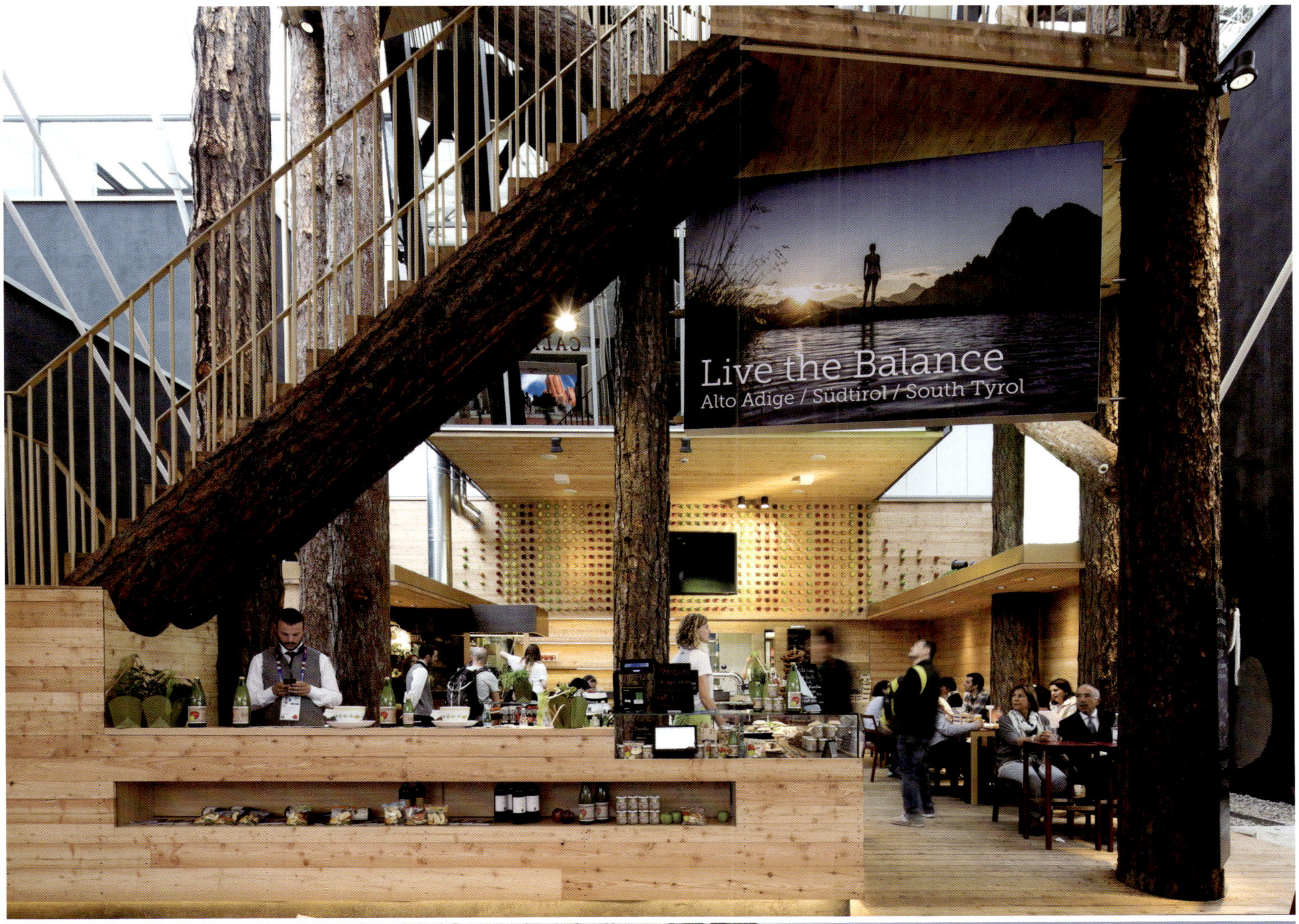
Live the Balance
Alto Adige / Südtirol / South Tyrol

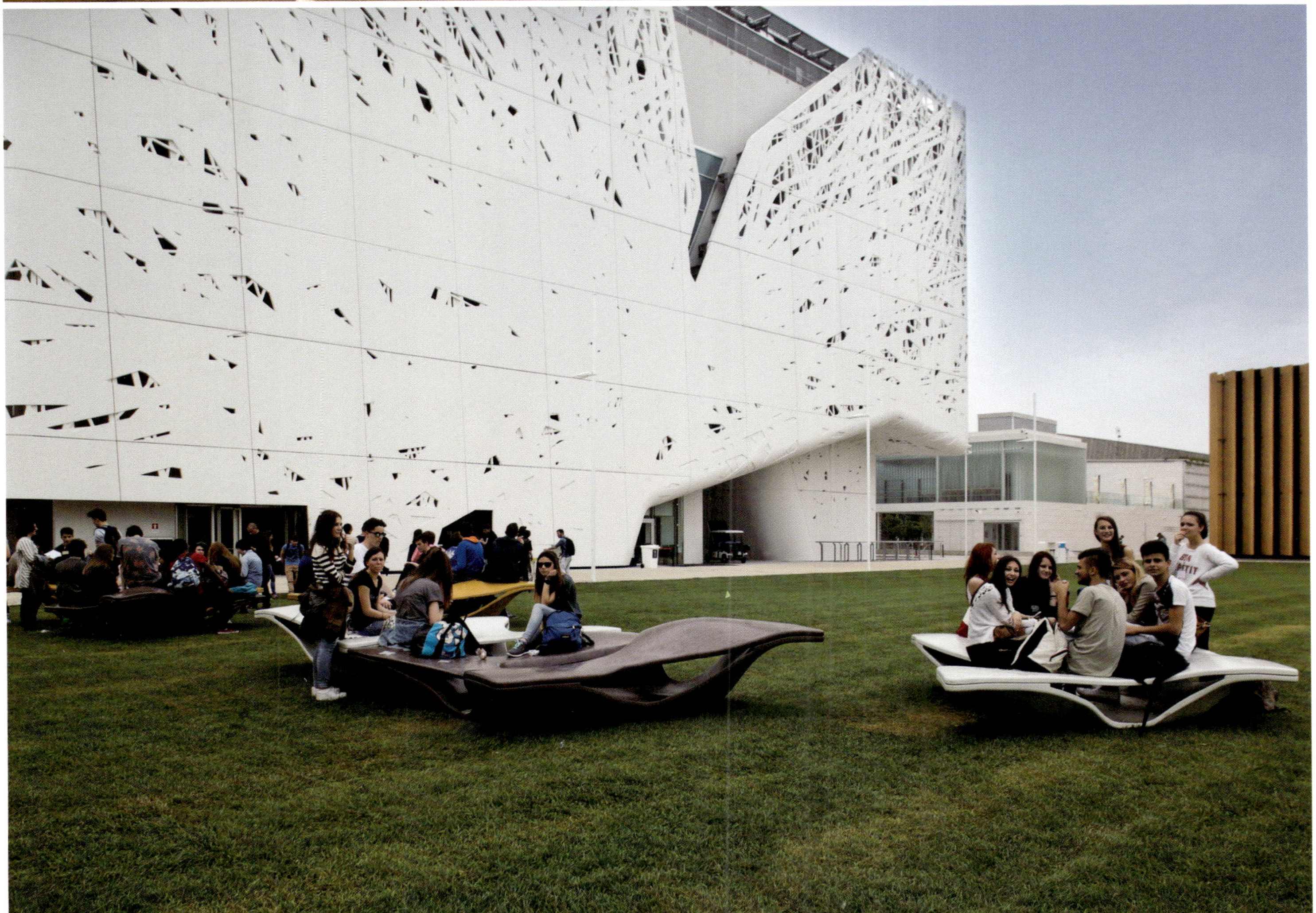

EATALY CHOOSES
Electrolux
Thinking of you
MANUEL RITZ
CERAMICHE
CÆSAR
LA CULTURA DELLA MATERIA
Rosenthal
sambonet
BOSCH
Tecnologia per la vita
CARAIBA
luxury
APP TEC
incold
OSCARTIELLE
RUBELLI
PADERNO
WORLD CUISINE
RICOH
imagine. change.
Novamont
WINCOR
NIXDORF
CAMPARI

SARDEGNA
SICILIA
THE BEST OF EATALY
DELIVERED WORLDWIDE